THE
PAINTINGS AND SKETCHES
OF LOUIS I. KAHN

THE PAINTINGS AND SKETCHES OF
LOUIS I. KAHN

Jan Hochstim

Introduction by Vincent Scully

RIZZOLI
NEW YORK

First published in the United States of America in 1991 by
RIZZOLI INTERNATIONAL PUBLICATIONS, INC.
300 Park Avenue South, New York, NY 10010

Copyright ©1991 Rizzoli International Publications, Inc.

Library of Congress Cataloging-in-Publication Data
Hochstim, Jan.
    The paintings and sketches of Louis I. Kahn/Jan Hochstim:
  introduction by Vincent Scully.
       p. cm.
    Includes bibliographical references.
    ISBN 0-8478-1381-9
    1. Kahn, Louis I., 1901–1974--Catalogues raisonnés. I. Kahn,
  Louis I., 1901–1974. II. Title
  N6537.K228A4 1991
  759.3--dc20   91-2032
                                                        CIP

Designed by Charles Davey and Betty Lew
Printed and bound in Japan

Cover: *Piazza del Campo, No. 1*, Siena, Italy, 1951
Back cover: *Bay Houses*, Amalfi Coast, Italy, 1928-1929

To my wife Ruth and son Richard and the
rest of my family, I express my love and
gratitude for their many sacrifices and
constant encouragement.

CONTENTS

ACKNOWLEDGMENTS

The materialization of this book was made possible through the efforts of countless individuals who supported me in various ways. My initial gratitude must be directed to my original team of advisors at the University of Miami: Dr. Andrew W. Morgan, former Chairman of the Art Department, for suggesting this book's area of investigation; Professor William E. Betsch, for his constructive assistance and continual encouragement; and Professors Arlene R. Olson and Thorne Shipley, for their time and effort in reviewing my original work.

I reserve my deepest appreciation for the late Louis I. Kahn, who in December of 1972, despite his very busy schedule, devoted almost two full days and evenings to me, with an opportunity to photograph his artwork and record our conversations. His enthusiastic encouragement was critical. Special thanks are reserved for Esther I. Kahn, who made me feel like one of the family. Without her gracious hospitality, her untiring search for long-forgotten sketches and paintings, and her recollections of past events, this book would not have been possible. It is difficult to do justice in this limited space to my feelings of gratitude toward Sue Ann Kahn, for her relentless efforts in helping to get this book published, her countless hours of assistance in gathering the original artwork for photography, for the many productive discussions and, of course, for the permission to reproduce her father's sketches and paintings in this book. In addition, other members of Louis I. Kahn's family, his friends, associates, and a host of museum officials were most kind in helping me to obtain photographs of Kahn's artwork in their possession and to publish them. My expressions of gratitude go to the following: Olivia and Milton Abelson, Edward Abelson, Sandra A. Zagarell, Regina Sooper, Samuel M. Sooper, Marshall Alan Kahn, Anne Griswold Tyng, Alexandra Tyng Kantor, Harriet Pattison, Robert Sherman, Paul Alpers, David Alpers, William S. Huff, M. Louis Goodman, Richard Saul Wurman, Janice Gubelman, Robert Venturi, Der Scutt, Kazi Khaleed Ashraf, Romaldo Giurgola, Wojceich Lesnikowski, Julia Moore Converse, Director of the Architectural Archives at the University of Pennsylvania; Heinrich Klotz, Director of the Zentrum für Kunst und Medien Technologie in Karlsruhe, Germany; John Zukowsky, Curator of Architecture at The Art Institute of Chicago; Vivian Paterson, Curator of the Williams College Museum of Art; Richard Tooke, Director of Rights and Reproductions, The Museum of Modern Art, New York; Theodore Newbold, Director of the Philadelphia Maritime Museum; and Gail Rawson, Registrar of the Pennsylvania Academy of the Fine Arts. Special thanks also go to Rizzoli's David Morton, Charles Davey, Daniel Waterman, and Betty Lew.

I am especially indebted to Professors Kenneth Frampton and Vincent Scully, who, after reading my embryonic attempts at this book, offered the positive encouragement and support necessary for me to obtain grants and a publisher. Professor Scully's offer to write an introduction and his numerous discussions with me concerning Kahn were of seminal importance in making this book a reality. Special thanks are due Professor Peter McCleary for his encouragement and for his assistance in reestablishing my contact with Esther I. Kahn. I also wish to thank William H. Sippel for supplying me with valuable personal glimpses of Kahn's travels in Italy, Greece, and Egypt.

I will be forever indebted to Professor Paul Buisson, whose untimely death in June 1990 left me without his expert counsel and help in identifying the historical sites in Kahn's sketches. Among the many associates and assistants whose able and enthusiastic support made my task much easier, I would like to thank Rick Echelmeyer, responsible for most of the reproductions in this book, for his keen photographic skills and patience; John Medina for letting me convert his New York flat into a photographic studio; Timothy Slawson for his assistance in reproducing and organizing the illustrations; Nancy Finlason for transcribing the static-loaded tape recordings of my conversations with Louis Kahn; Maria Romeu for transcribing my original writing onto computer; and Adam Krantz for relieving me, during the crucial period of finishing this book, of the burden of running my architectural office. I would also like to commend and thank the staff of the Richter Library at the University of Miami and especially Mildred Merrick, Reference Librarian, for all her assistance in securing much-needed material. My appreciation is also extended to the University of Miami Research Council for a financial grant to defray part of my photographic and travel expenses.

PREFACE

With the passing away of Frank Lloyd Wright, Le Corbusier, Gropius, and Mies—the great architectural form-givers of the twentieth century—a considerable void and confusion became evident. The singular bright spot in this dismal scene was the appearance of Louis I. Kahn. His short, cometlike entry and departure generated an awakening which provided a much-needed source of philosophical energy for countless younger architects disenchanted with the dogmatism of the established leaders of the first half of this century.

As an architect, Kahn occupied an unusual, almost anachronistic position. In spite of prevailing post-World War II trends toward anonymity on the one hand and formal exhibitionism on the other, he produced works of extraordinary clarity and power which bore his unmistakable signature. He managed to provide the vital ingredients missing in modern architecture: a sense of continuity with the past, without reliance on historical styles; concern for context; and the restoration of architecture's role as an urban art. There can be no argument about what effect Kahn has had on architecture of the past two decades. His theories and projects continue to influence the work of new generations of architects and his unique view of the building arts will remain in the forefront of architectural debate for a long time.

Considering Kahn's architectural prominence, it is not surprising that most of the available literature about him deals with his projects and his magnificent gift of poeticizing theoretical issues of design. Less known is his extraordinary artistic talent, which he directed toward sketching and painting. It is this facet of Kahn's creativity which this book attempts to reveal and analyze.

A glimpse of Kahn's nonarchitectural sketching and painting first became available in two articles he wrote long before he became known professionally.[1] In the early 1960s, at the beginning of Kahn's ascendence into architectural prominence, Vincent Scully wrote the first book devoted to Kahn's architectural career.[2] In it, Scully included several reproductions of Kahn's travel sketches which displayed his artistic prowess and hinted at a possible connection between his drawings, philosophy, and architectural designs. The same year, a beautiful publication by Richard Saul Wurman and Eugene Feldman devoted exclusively to Kahn's architectural and nonarchitectural sketches and theoretical statements provided a much-needed overview of Kahn's artistic talent. [3] However, the seventeen black-and-white artworks in that volume left the reader without the benefit of exposure to a broader representation of the immense body of work, much of it in magnificent color, that Kahn produced over his lifetime. From 1973 on, various architectural journals, especially *Architecture and Urbanism*[4] in Japan, began to devote space to selected travel sketches in black-and-white and in color in the context of describing Kahn's architectural projects.

My interest in Kahn, especially the relationship between his artwork and his architectural career, was stirred during a slide lecture he delivered at the Lowe Art Museum at the University of Miami in the fall of 1968. The slides of his architectural projects and completed buildings appeared to me then to be rigid, formalistic, and tediously geometric. In contrast, slides of his crayon, ink, and pastel sketches, made during his European travels, were beautifully lyrical and free. They represented to me at that time the greatest possible contrast between the two areas of his creativity. When confronted by me at the end of the lecture with my surprise at the dichotomy between his architecture and artwork, Kahn managed to devastate my ego by stating that if there was a dichotomy it existed only in my mind, and that I evidently lacked any understanding of his architecture and his philosophy. From that time on I began a systematic search for an understanding Kahn's "double personality." In subsequent meetings with him I was somewhat better prepared through a more careful study of his work and philosophy. However, while access to his architectural and philosophical output presented no problem, the availability of originals and reproductions of his sketches at that time was quite problematic. The galleries which held exhibitions of Kahn's work had either no photographic record whatsoever or only a limited documentation of his architectural design sketches along with presentation drawings and photographs of completed buildings.[5] In a last ditch effort I gathered enough courage to contact Mr. Kahn with the request for help in locating his artwork. To my utter surprise he invited me to Philadelphia for a few days in order to make available to me a great number of his sketches and paintings which he kept at his house and his office, and he broke away from his

busy schedule in order to have a discussion with me about this aspect of his work.

My meeting with Kahn and his wife Esther in December 1972 resulted in my taking slides of over two hundred sketches and paintings,[6] as well as recording on tape my conversations with him regarding his artwork. The product of this research became a thesis which I submitted for my Master of Art History degree at the University of Miami in 1976. It had been my wish to complete the thesis immediately following my visit with Kahn and to have him review the final draft, as he indicated he hoped to do. However, due to various circumstances the completion of the thesis was delayed and then additionally set back by Kahn's unexpected death in 1974. His untimely passing left me with a great sense of loss, both of a truly great architect and a wonderful human being. But I will always remain grateful for the privilege of having known him, for the patience and kindness he showed me, and for the lasting source of inspiration he provided through his works and words.

Since the publication of my thesis in 1976 there have been a number of books and periodicals in which reproductions of Kahn's artwork were given a modest exposure. Several exhibitions of Kahn's sketches and paintings were also organized. The most notable was the 1978–79 traveling exhibition by the Pennsylvania Academy of the Fine Arts, with an excellent accompanying catalogue prepared by William G. Holman and a very revealing introduction by Vincent Scully. It contained ninety-one pieces of artwork, most of them works I had included in my thesis.

In the early part of 1987, Peter McCleary of the University of Pennsylvania urged me to pursue further my original research and was instrumental in my contacting Esther and Sue Ann Kahn. They were most encouraging and eager for me to publish a comprehensive collection of Kahn's artistic work, which as yet had not been assembled in its totality and made available to the public. To my surprise I discovered that there were at least twice the number of sketches and paintings that I had originally photographed in 1972. Thus, following an almost four-year effort at obtaining reproductions of all available artwork and relying on the most helpful cooperation of Kahn's family members, friends, and many institutions, I have been able to gather the 480 reproductions contained in this book.

Since the greatest effort on my part was expended in gathering, transcribing, reproducing, identifying, cataloguing, and analyzing the material, the Catalogue Raisonné constitutes the principle creative portion of this book, with the preceding chapters serving as both introductory and analytical resources. This is a slight variation and change in scope from my original intention. When I started this project I was hoping to answer the nagging question of how Kahn's artwork affected his architecture. But the more involved I became, the more Kahn's own pronouncement that a good question is better than the best answer became evident to me. Of course, there are hints at answers, and they are very tempting, especially when images of travel sketches and paintings bear a marked resemblance to his architectural designs. However, the fact that, with a few exceptions, the entire artistic oeuvre of Louis I. Kahn is assembled in this book is perhaps tantamount to asking a good question rather than coming up with the best answer. I hope that the pursuit of the proper questions will not stop here, but gain momentum so that the makeup of Kahn's creative genius can be better understood by allowing the reader to see the world through his beautiful and humanistic vision.

NOTES

1. Louis I. Kahn. "Pencil Drawings," *Architecture* 43 (January 1931): 15, 17; and "The Value and Aim in Sketching," *T-Square Club Journal* (May 1931): 18-21.

2. Vincent Scully, Jr. *Louis I. Kahn* (New York: George Braziller, 1962).

3. Richard Saul Wurman and Eugene Feldman. *The Notebooks and Drawings of Louis I. Kahn* (Philadelphia: The Falcon Press, 1962).

4. "Louis I. Kahn—Silence and Light," *Architecture and Urbanism* 3 (January 1973).

5. My investigation revealed that the Pennsylvania Academy of the Fine Arts in Philadelphia, which exhibited Kahn's drawings and paintings in 1929, 1930, 1931, and 1932, was able to find only two cards with listings of twelve titles and no other records. The Museum of Modern Art in New York, which in 1966 held an exhibition titled "The Architecture of Louis I. Kahn," had some originals as well as a few reproductions, but only of architectural projects.

6. At that time it was my erroneous impression that I had discovered almost the entire oeuvre of Kahn's artwork, with the exceptions of several pieces which were being processed for publication in Japan.

INTRODUCTION

It has clearly been a labor of love for Mr. Hochstim to search out every known example of Kahn's paintings, drawings, and sketches and to present them for publication in this systematic and deeply respectful way. There have of course been earlier publications of them, to which Mr. Hochstim refers, but they were all partial and fragmentary compared to this. The catalogue of the traveling exhibition organized by the Pennsylvania Academy of the Fine Arts in 1978–79 was the most authoritative of them, and it established the fundamental relationships between Kahn's architecture and his paintings and drawings—all primarily travel sketches after all—in a way that still seems generally satisfactory today. There were, however, only ninety-one items in that exhibition as against the hundreds Mr. Hochstim has gathered together here. In comparison, the wealth of Mr. Hochstim's collection is staggering, and the beauty of some of the sketches never seen before quite takes one's breath away. Here again it is Kahn's liberating return to the Mediterranean in 1950–51 that provides some of the most powerful new examples.

Mr. Hochstim's No. 339, a pastel of the Campo in Siena, seems extraordinarily fresh and vital as a complement to No. 338, published so often before. The Campidoglio (No. 337) recalls Matisse in its brick-red, black, and lavender shadows, out of which burst the two white blossoms of the Dioskouroi. The classical figure on a plinth in the empty spaces of No. 333 now looks like a companion study for the great urban theater of No. 336, which is in fact nine-tenths Mussolini's Forum—the Foro Italico—(stairs, figures, truncated obelisk, oblong building in the background, and so on).[1] On the right, however, a facade remotely suggesting St. Peter's intrudes. It is pushed in to close the space on that side and to set up the haunting perspective in the mode of De Chirico that Kahn and the Fascists before him, and Rossi after him, have all loved so well. The title *Rome* is fair enough for this pastel. It evokes the Rome of Pope and Duce, and it was primarily Mussolini's Rome, with its modern, stripped classicism, that seems to have moved Kahn to its composition, whose whole tone was to become so important to him and to other architects later. The *tendenza* at least is all right there.

It is disappointing that more drawings by Kahn of the ruins of Roman brick and concrete architecture have not come to

15

light. No. 335 is an excellent example of what could well have been hundreds of the kinds of brick and concrete Roman architecture that Kahn saw in his excursions around Rome and Ostia with the late Professor Frank E. Brown of the American Academy in Rome, and upon which it is not too much to say that the core of Kahn's later work came to based. Perhaps such ruins seemed simply too common to be recorded. Yet, knowing Kahn, who—caught up in modernism's romantic need to invent—tended to conceal his sources from everyone other than those before whom it would have been ridiculous to try, the relative absence of such drawings is perhaps not so surprising. Nevertheless, the relationship between Kahn's designs and his travel sketches is often very direct indeed. It is also extremely touching and important, because Kahn was a passionately convinced modern architect who eventually discovered that he could not "invent" except through history— which was made up for him of the forms he had seen, drawn, and made his own "forms in the mind." So Rossi was later to say, "I do not invent; I remember."

I have tried to trace the path of some of those forms through the drawings into Kahn's buildings in other publications, as in the catalogue noted above, to be reprinted in *Lotus International* in 1991, and in my introduction to the Garland edition[2] of Kahn's drawings, and it would seem unnecessarily repetitive to rehash the argument here. This collection will surely serve as a primary source for research into such questions in the future. At the moment it seems more reasonable to enjoy the drawings for themselves as Mr. Hochstim so admirably presents them to us. If we think of them for a while not primarily in relation to Kahn's buildings, but in context with the drawings of other major modern architects, some of their uniqueness may become more apparent.

Frank Lloyd Wright, surely one of the greatest architectural draftsmen of all time, normally drew only his own work. So all his drawings are traditionally architectural, well inside the canon of architectural rendering as it had come to the full flower of plan, section, elevation, and perspective during the nineteenth century. With Mies, though enormously simplified, even minimalized, it is essentially the same. Mies draws his own buildings, most of all his own places. He lays out dreamy perspectives, barely defined by a few lines and planes. They are wish-fulfilling environments of endless expansion, inhabited by one or two classical figures derived from Lehmbruck or Maillol. These figures and those architectural environments distinguish Mies' drawings, and his architecture as well, from the main line of pictorial influence on architecture as it developed from the early twentieth century onward. This was the influence of abstract painting, especially as it was interpreted and turned into the model for a new kind of architecture by Rietveld and Van Doesburg, wherein the architect can be as free as the painter and the building can be as abstract as a painting because it has no material weight, no up or down, roof or water table, or urban context, and avoids perspective to enshrine isometric—precisely because real buildings can never be seen in that way. A whole style of architecture, the International Style, grew up along those lines and is still being practiced today— why not, it is entirely self-referential and so ideal for teaching in schools. But the point should be made that Kahn's architecture, for all his painting, was never that. It was most of all a built architecture: solid, weighing on the ground, assembled of weighty materials with beautiful joints expressive of compression. That is the major reason why Kahn broke the hold of the International Style on modern architecture and opened the way for that revival of the vernacular and classical traditions of architecture which has been going on during the past generation and was initiated by Robert Venturi, along with Charles Moore and Aldo Rossi, each indebted to Kahn in fundamental ways.

But, as always, there is Le Corbusier to be considered, and Le Corbusier was deeply involved in the pictorialism of his time. He tells us that he painted every morning after 1919, and it might be argued that the forms in his paintings came to dominate those in his architecture even more strongly as time went on. Yet that is surely not the whole story. Le Corbusier differed profoundly from the pure abstractionists, especially in the central role played in his work by sketches made during journeys. Mr. Hochstim rightly stresses the kind of awe in which Kahn, like so many of his generation, held Le Corbusier, as well as the love of classical architecture that filled them both. For Kahn, Le Corbusier was a man recording what he saw in order to put it to use, something Wright and Mies either did not do or did only in secret. Le Corbusier's line drawings made around the Mediterranean, visually available to Kahn at least from 1923 onward—and thus through the years at the University of Pennsylvania and his apprenticeship under Cret—do not seem to have affected Kahn's drawings stylistically until the 1930s, when he was also experimenting with American Scene techniques of landscape and figure painting as well. Moved, one might say driven, by Le Corbusier's vision, Kahn moved to thin linear and planar perspectives in the 1940s, in which his architecture was clearly being drawn back and forth between poles of geometric discipline and physical attenuation. It had lost the mass and weight with which it had begun.

What a passionate struggle it must have been for Kahn, surely a frustrating one until, in 1950, he refound the classical world for himself at last. There too, beneath his joy in the urban spaces and the structural masses, Le Corbusier's thin, pitiless, analytical line still helped direct Kahn's hand until an outward vision of the world and an inward vision of geometric order came together in his studies of the pyramids at Gizeh, some in pastel in the light of Ra, some in line and plane tracing patterns in the mind (Nos. 421, 425, and 427). These are perhaps the greatest of all Kahn's drawings, and in a sense the last, because from them he moved directly into the tetrahedral forms of the ceiling slab of the Yale University Art Gallery of 1951–53, and the true pyramids of Trenton of 1955. After that he was building and drawing his buildings and, with the exception of one trip in 1950, which produced a series of travel sketches on the whole much more offhand than the earlier ones, he seems to have needed this class of work no more.

Now, gathered together as they are, Kahn's paintings and drawings of buildings and places can be seen to represent an extraordinary achievement. There is a curious humility about them, suggested in part by the fact that they are not representing Kahn's own buildings but those of other architects, mostly long dead, and not buildings only but landscapes too, appreciated for themselves. Nor are they all in one uniform style, as Wright's and Mies' and even Le Corbusier's (though these with a good deal of development) are from a very early period. They are done instead in several different modes, growing only slowly toward a powerful pictorial style of their own. The earliest examples, especially the watercolors made during the first trip to Europe in 1928, are more art deco than anything else, thus modestly reflecting the dominant style of their time. In the 1930s they explore, as we have noted, styles running from Grant Wood to Le Corbusier. It is only in the fateful trip of 1950–51 that they become wholly distinct as a completely realized pictorial mode. Pastel was clearly the medium that answered Kahn's need at that moment, easier to use than the watercolors of the 1920s; denser and more architectural itself, it could not only join his carpenter's pencil in broad crayon strokes but could also be made to burn with light, to smolder with the heat of the matter it was trying to record under the classical sun. Here again it was Egypt, I think, that most called up Kahn's fire, even beyond that inspired by Italy's squares and the white landscapes of Greece. Especially in those landscapes is Kahn's inner vision felt. He makes them hotter than they are, more orange under a fiercer African sky. All this he finds at last in Egypt, in the pyramids and in ancient Thebes as well (Nos. 401–406). There the great shapes truly burn, hypostyle columns and pylons alike, columns of heat, gates of fire. But Kahn doesn't need pastel for some of his greatest effects. Sketch No. 403, with its papyrus columns, is drawn with a carpenter's pencil and seems the ultimate of all the drawings in physical power. Kahn revives the column's vegetable nature, causes it to swell up, growing into the sublime. That is what he was dealing with, after all: the concept of the sublime. Like an eighteenth-century visionary, much like Piranesi himself, whom he loved and from whom he also derived some essential forms, Kahn was a true romantic classicist, seeing antiquity anew through a fresh modern passion and through its ruins, not its finished buildings. This is why, like the architects of the beginning of the modern age, Kahn was able to begin architecture anew in his own time, or to revive it, because he took the ruin and remade it, not as it had been once but as his own.

Vincent Scully
1991

NOTES

1. As in A. Munoz, *Roma di Mussolini*, Milan, 1934, p. 355.

2. Vincent Scully, *Louis I. Kahn Archive Set*, New York, 1987.

1

2

3

4

5

6

7

8

9

10

BIOGRAPHICAL SKETCH

1. *Yale University Art Gallery, New Haven, Connecticut, 1951–1953*

2. *Alfred Newton Richards Medical Research Building, University of Pennsylvania, Philadelphia, Pennsylvania, 1957–1965*

3. *Salk Institute for Biological Studies, La Jolla, California, 1959–1965*

4. *First Unitarian Church and School, Rochester, New York, 1959–1969*

5. *Eleanor Donnelley Erdman Hall, Bryn Mawr College, Bryn Mawr, Pennsylvania, 1960–1965*

6. *Indian Institute of Management, Ahmedabad, India, 1962–1974*

7. *Capital of Bangladesh, Dhaka, Bangladesh, 1962–1983*

8. *Library Phillips Exeter Academy, Exeter, New Hampshire, 1965–1972*

9. *Kimbell Art Museum, Fort Worth, Texas, 1966–1972*

10. *Yale Center for British Art, New Haven, Connecticut, 1969–1974*

Photo Nos.1, 2, 4, 5, 8, & 10 by Wojciech Lesnikowski
Photo No. 3 by Jan Hochstim
Photo Nos. 6, & 7 by Kazi Khaleed Ashraf
Photo No. 9, courtesy Kimbell Art Museum, Fort Worth, Texas

This brief biographical sketch in no way pretends to provide the reader with the wealth of information regarding Louis Kahn's life which is to be found in Vincent Scully's *Louis I. Kahn*,[1] and a number of books and articles which have been written since.[2] It is my intent to present only a very brief biographical outline with the emphasis on Kahn's artistic development, leading up to his world-wide recognition as an architect.

Louis Isadore Kahn was born February 20, 1901, on the Island of Osel in Estonia. Both his parents were involved in the arts: his father as a stained-glass craftsman, his mother as a harpist. Like so many Jewish families living under czarist Russia's persecutions, the Kahns fled Europe and in 1905 settled in Philadelphia.

Kahn's childhood years were marked by the emergence of his notable talents in drawing and music. His family's impoverished condition made it impossible to give Kahn private instruction.[3] However, he received art lessons in public school and at the Graphic Sketch Club, which was part of Philadelphia's Public Industrial Art School. His artistic abilities were recognized quite early. At the age of thirteen he won the first prize for drawing and painting in the John Wanamaker Children's Drawings Art Contest, and at the ages of eighteen and nineteen he was awarded first prize for best drawings in Philadelphia high schools by the Pennsylvania Academy of the Fine Arts. Thanks to William F. Gray, a sympathetic high school art teacher, Kahn was introduced to the world of architecture,[4] and the practice of architecture became his professional goal while sketching and painting became his favorite pastime.

In 1920, Kahn entered the prestigious School of Fine Arts of the University of Pennsylvania in pursuit of a four-year Bachelor of Architecture degree. At the time, the Department of Architecture was second only to the Ecole des Beaux Arts in Paris.[5] The curriculum, an adaptation of the French Beaux-Arts system,[6] provided Kahn not only with the finest traditional architectural education under Ecole-trained academicians—among them the renowned Paul P. Cret—but also with an excellent opportunity to further his drawing and painting skills. As an architecture student, Kahn was required to complete a total of sixty-one hours of studio freehand drawing and painting. In comparison, the Fine Arts students' requirements were limited to twenty-two hours.[7] This intense training paid off when, in his last year at the University of Pennsylvania, Kahn was honored for his abilities with an appointment as a teaching assistant.[8]

While still a student at the University of Pennsylvania, Kahn worked as a draftsman and designer for various Philadelphia architectural firms. Following his graduation in 1924 he became senior draftsman in the office of John Molitor, City Architect for Philadelphia. The following year he was promoted to chief of design with responsibilities for overseeing design and drafting for all exposition buildings at the Sesquicentennial Philadelphia Exposition. Staying with Molitor until the spring of 1927, Kahn also gained experience working on municipal buildings and city planning studies. Between April 1927 and April 1928, he worked as a draftsman for Philadelphia architect William H. Lee.[9]

In April 1928, with the money he had managed to save, Kahn embarked on a year-long trip through Europe. Traveling mostly on foot and by train he worked his way from England through the north countries, managing to visit his ancestral home in Estonia. He then proceeded to central Europe, traveling through Switzerland on his way to Italy.[10] The impressions of his explorations of the Old World were recorded in a great number of graphite stick and watercolor sketches, most of them from Italy. It was in Italy that Kahn's artistic urges found their necessary inspiration. Upon his return he was able to exhibit some of his travel sketches at the Pennsylvania Academy of the Fine Arts in 1929. In 1931 several of his European drawings and an article entitled "Value and Aim in Sketching" were published in the architectural magazine *T-Square Club Journal*,[11] and another article, "Pencil Drawings," was printed in *Architecture* the same year.[12]

Armed with his vivid European experience and his Beaux-Arts training, Kahn entered the office of his former teacher Paul P. Cret. However, a lack of work forced Kahn to move to the office of Zantzinger, Borie and Medary, where he served as a designer from December 1930 to February 1932. Immediately after leaving that firm, Kahn became the organizer and director of a large group of unemployed Philadelphia architects who, because of the country's poor economic situation, were obliged to get involved with public works projects such as city planning, housing studies, slum clearance, and investigations into new construction methods. Kahn's involvement with city planning and housing studies in Philadelphia continued under various agencies and in association with other architects all the way into 1962.

In August 1930, Kahn married Esther Virginia Israeli. He and his young bride spent their short summer vacations in New England and Canada, where Kahn sketched and painted with great vigor. These were the years of the Great Depression and there was hardly any work for architects. To supplement his meager income from sporadic architectural jobs, Kahn attempted to sell his artwork, but was totally unsuccessful in finding any buyers.[13] His work, however, was exhibited several times at the Pennsylvania Academy of the Fine Arts from 1930 to 1938. The Depression was hardly the time to make a living in the fine arts. However, government efforts to fight the depression through federal funding encouraged Kahn to open his own architectural practice in 1934. He began to sustain himself on a few government-sponsored commissions in planning and public housing.

During World War II, his architectural practice put Kahn in association with George Howe and Oscar Stonorov. Howe, who was educated at Harvard and the Ecole des Beaux Arts, was the first prominent American architect to make a complete transition to the International Style by designing, in collaboration with William Lescaze, the famous Philadelphia Saving Fund Society (PSFS) skyscraper in Philadelphia. Both Howe and Stonorov played an important role in clarifying modern architectural theory to Louis Kahn, whose ignorance and mistrust of the European architectural avant-garde was due to his Beaux-Arts indoctrination.[14] Of particular interest to him was the work of Le Corbusier, to whom he owed his inspirational allegiance for the rest of his life.[15] Le Corbusier, while condemning eclecticism, did poeticize the link between the classical and the modern,[16] something which was missing in the polemics of many International Style leaders. In addition, Le Corbusier was also a serious artist, who claimed to arrive at his architecture through his painting.[17]

In 1947, thanks to George Howe, who three years later became chairman of the Department of Architecture at Yale, Kahn was appointed Chief Critic of

Architectural Design and Professor of Architecture at Yale University, a position he held for ten years. After a semester of teaching at M.I.T. in 1957, Kahn was put in charge of the postgraduate studio in architecture and urban design at his alma mater in Philadelphia, while maintaining an increasingly busy architectural practice. In 1966 he was appointed to the prestigious Paul Philippe Cret Chair in Architecture which he held until his death in 1974. Teaching combined with practice helped Kahn to formulate a very personal and unique architectural philosophy and allowed him to reconcile the dichotomy between his Beaux-Arts training and the design theories of the modern masters.

Up until 1950, Kahn's architectural practice, while significantly broad, brought him little recognition. As if to compensate for his difficulties in achieving success in architecture, he continued to sketch and paint, activities which he always loved and continued almost to the end of his life. The birth of his daughter, Sue Ann, in 1940[18] added significant joy to his life but did not help to ease mounting financial difficulties. His customary summer vacation trips to New England and Canada had to be abandoned. Thus, during the war years most of Kahn's artistic production was executed in Philadelphia, with sketches from his previous travels serving as models for a remarkable group of pen-and-ink drawings and watercolor paintings.

In the fall of 1950, Kahn was appointed Resident Architect at the American Academy in Rome. While in Europe, he had an opportunity to revisit some of the Italian sites he had sketched on his first overseas journey in 1928 and 1929, and he also traveled to Egypt and Greece. With an expanded and mature visual judgment, he sketched in charcoal and pastels a variety of landscapes, paying particular attention to architectural subjects. This small but powerful series of sketches overshadowed Kahn's marvelous drawings and paintings of the previous thirty-seven years.

The years following Kahn's return from Europe in 1951 were marked by his emergence as one of the most important architects and theoreticians of his generation. He dared to question the well-entrenched orthodoxy of the International Style and particularly the structural exhibitionism and formalistic expressionism so popular in America. His

designs and philosophy provided at that time a much-needed missing link between the Beaux-Arts tradition and the nearsighted iconoclasm of the Bauhaus-inspired modern movement. Starting with such projects as the Yale University Art Gallery in New Haven and the Bath House for the Jewish Community Center in Trenton, Kahn's visibility at the national level was assured. But it was the Richards Medical Research Building at the University of Pennsylvania (1957–1964) that established Louis Kahn as one of the nation's foremost architects. So, at the age of fifty-six, Kahn emerged from virtual obscurity into international prominence. In 1963 he was honored for the Richards Medical Research Building with a "Single Building Exhibition" at the Museum of Modern Art in New York. Through his theoretical writings and his successive projects—from the First Unitarian Church in Rochester, the Yale Center for British Art in New Haven, the Salk Institute in La Jolla, the Indian Institute of Management in Ahmedabad, the National Capital in Dacca, and his undisputed masterpiece, the Kimbell Art Museum in Fort Worth—Kahn ascended to the leadership of architecture world-wide. His office on Walnut Street in Philadelphia became a place of pilgrimage for many young and aspiring architects from around the world. While Kahn was central to all design decisions, his office assistants—Anne Tyng, William Huff, David Wisdom, Jack MacAllister, Tim Vreeland, Marshall Meyers, and many others—devotedly maintained Kahn's passionate goal of serving architecture.[19]

In 1959, on the occasion of being invited to deliver the closing remarks at the Tenth C.I.A.M Congress in Otterlo, Holland, Kahn took advantage of the trip and managed to visit France. His sketchbook accompanied him again as it did on previous European trips. He filled it with very quick pencil and pen-and-ink gesture drawings of architectural monuments ranging from the medieval fortifications of Carcassonne and the towers of Albi Cathedral to the light-imbued interior of Le Corbusier's Ronchamp Chapel. During the last fifteen years of his life, architectural practice and his continued commitment to teaching left almost no time for sketching and painting, a fact he regretted very much.[20] Thus, the 1959 European trip ended Kahn's creation of nonarchitectural artwork.

During the height of his career, Kahn's contributions were well recognized through a great number of accolades and honors, including the Gold Medal of the American Institute of Architects in 1971, membership in the American Academy of Arts and Letters in 1973, numerous medals and fellowships, and nine honorary doctorates from prestigious universities in the United States and Europe—Yale, Columbia, the Polytechnic Institute of Milan, the University of Pennsylvania, and Bard College, among others.

On March 17, 1974, upon his return from Ahmedabad, India, Kahn suffered a heart attack and died at New York's Pennsylvania Station.

NOTES

1. Vincent Scully, Jr., *Louis I. Kahn* (New York: George Braziller, 1962).

2. Of special interest are Alexandra Tyng, *Beginnings: Louis I. Kahn's Philosophy of Architecture* (New York: John Wiley & Sons, 1984); Alessandra Latour, *Louis I. Kahn: l'uomo, il maestro* (Rome: Edizioni Kappa, 1986); Richard Saul Wurman, *What Will Be Has Always Been: The Words of Louis I. Kahn* (New York: Access Press Ltd. and Rizzoli International Publications, Inc., 1986); and Heinz Ronner and Sharad Jhaveri, *Louis I. Kahn: Complete Work 1935–1974* (Basel and Boston: Birkhauser, 1987).

3. Jan Hochstim, "Conversations with Louis I. Kahn." Transcription of tape recordings, Philadelphia, December 1972.

4. Patricia McLaughlin, "'How'm I Doing, Corbusier?' An Interview with Louis Kahn," *The Pennsylvania Gazette* 71 (December 1972), 19.

5. Carl A. Ziegler, "The Sesqui-Centennial Exposition in Philadelphia," *American Architect* 121 (1922), 382.

6. *Bulletin: School of Fine Arts—Courses in Architecture, Music and Fine Arts,* Announcement, 1922–1923 (Philadelphia: The Press of the University of Pennsylvania, 1922), 16.

7. Ibid., 22–23, 42–46.

8. *Bulletin: School of Fine Arts—Courses in Architecture, Music and Fine Arts,* Announcement, 1923–1924 (Philadelphia: The Press of the University of Pennsylvania, 1923), 22.

9. Scully, *Louis I. Kahn,* 45.

10. Hochstim, "Conversations."

11. Louis I. Kahn, "The Value and Aim in Sketching," *T-Square Club Journal* 1 (May 1931), 4, 18–21.

12. Louis I. Kahn, "Pencil Drawings," *Architecture* 43 (January 1931), 15–17.

13. Hochstim, "Conversations."

14. Ibid.

15. McLaughlin, "'How'm I Doing, Corbusier?'" 22.

16. Le Corbusier, *Toward a New Architecture,* trans. Frederick Etchells (London: Architectural Press, 1927; reprint ed., New York: Praeger Publishers, 1960).

17. Norman Rice in Latour, *Louis I. Kahn, l'uomo, il maestro,* 181.

18. Kahn subsequently became father to daughter Alexandra Tyng and son Nathaniel Pattison Kahn.

19. Marshall D. Meyers in Latour, *Louis I. Kahn, l'uomo, il maestro,* 77.

20. Hochstim, "Conversations."

ANALYSIS OF ARTWORK

Since the Catalogue Raisonné, which comprises the main part of this book, contains commentaries for practically every plate, this chapter is of a summary nature. The analysis which follows is based primarily on my own observations and research, as well as comments supplied by Louis I. Kahn during tape-recorded conversations while reviewing his artwork with me in 1972.[1] The introduction by Professor Vincent Scully and catalogue entries written by Mr. William G. Holman for the 1978–1979 traveling exhibition of "The Travel Sketches of Louis I. Kahn," organized by the Pennsylvania Academy of the Fine Arts, were consulted and their thoughtful insights significantly added to my understanding of Kahn's artwork. Of special significance was information supplied by Mrs. Esther Kahn, Sue Ann Kahn, and the many individuals mentioned in the acknowledgments.

General Characteristics

An examination of Kahn's paintings and sketches permits us to look into the very soul of his creativity. They are the most private expressions of his artistic nature. A great number of the sketches were not meant to be viewed by the public. They were notations which marked impressions and the discovery of situations that moved him. In many cases, on the other hand, they served as preparatory sketches for paintings which Kahn proceeded to complete in his studio.[2]

No matter how attractive his sketches and paintings appear, it should be noted that Louis Kahn, apart from his architectural prominence, was not considered nor recognized as a significant painter during his lifetime. While they are not accorded an important place in the world of art, his sketches and paintings nevertheless possess great charm and are executed with the talented and skillful hand of a person who loves what he sees and is eager to capture the essence of the moment for future reflection.[3] However, from the standpoint of the development of his architecture, Kahn's sketches provide an important insight into his creative mind.

When viewing the scope of his sketches and paintings over a period of some forty-six years, from his youth to his maturity, a definite trend is discernible in Kahn's treatment of details and modeling. His early work shows a preoccupation with representing forms by modeling them with shades and shadows—a very architectonic approach derived from a thorough Beaux-Arts training of making washes from casts.[4] By the 1930s, linearity comes into play and forms acquire more abstract characteristics; his dependence on modeling surfaces occasionally, but mainly when Kahn picks up a paint brush. The decade of the 1940s shows a furthering of this trend, during which even his sketches with paint become more abstract. Lines and patches of color replace the careful modeling of the early period. Lines are surer and sparser, acquiring the characteristics of an artistic shorthand. During Kahn's overseas trip of 1950–1951, modeling is almost completely abandoned and forms are delineated by crisp, daring lines and contrasting areas of black and white or complementary colors. The drawings he made on his 1959 European trip and which he elaborated upon his return are almost pure gesture drawings capturing the very soul, rather than the physical appearance, of subjects sketched. The progression from the early works to his mature drawings reflects his attitude toward subject matter. He started by reacting to the outer appearance of form in light and proceeded through an ever-deeper penetration of the subjects to an understanding of their nature and their essential character. His last works are almost devoid of concern for exterior appearance and reflect Kahn's feelings about the spirit of the subjects he sketched. This attitude clearly parallels his emerging perception of architecture and is evident in his philosophical statements, writings, and, of course, in the legacy of his buildings.

Influences

Louis Kahn's exposure to the world of art must have occurred very early, since his father was a stained-glass craftsman. When his natural ability to draw became evident, several school teachers played important roles in his artistic development. Of special importance was William F. Gray,[5] who recognized Kahn's artistic ability but perceived his greater potentials and steered him toward architecture. Not much is known about the kind of art instruction Kahn received before his college years. However, his talent was recognized as early as 1913 when he won the First Prize in the Children's Drawings Art Contest for the Philadelphia region, sponsored by John Wanamaker. Lessons which Kahn obtained as a student of the Graphic Sketch Club, the Fleischer Memorial Art School, the Public Industrial Art School, and especially the Pennsylvania Academy of the Fine Arts between 1912 and 1920, led him to receive the prestigious first prize for best drawings in Philadelphia high schools, sponsored by the Pennsylvania Academy in 1920. His artistic training at the University of Pennsylvania thereafter was thoroughly influenced by the Ecole des Beaux Arts in Paris, deeply immersed in the classical academic tradition.

The United States during Kahn's high school and college years was becoming exposed to the avant-garde art movements from Europe and to the work of American artists carving their own path away from traditionalism. Kahn was intuitively attracted to this wave of modernism in art and began to collect illustrations from magazines and art catalogues. The reproductions, which he stored in a thick folder, represented the work of leading figures from the mid-nineteenth century on. By far, the greatest number of clippings were from the work of Impressionists, Post-Impressionists, Cubists, and Expressionists. The work of Americans was sparsely represented; however, Kahn was quite familiar with the work of artists who, like himself, had a close association with the Pennsylvania Academy of the Fine Arts in Philadelphia.

Of particular interest is the relationship of Kahn's work to that of John Marin, an affinity which becomes especially evident in the 1930s. Kahn as a youth attended drawing classes at the Pennsylvania Academy of the Fine Arts, participated in drawing competitions sponsored by the Academy, and exhibited his travel sketches and paintings there.[6] John Marin, who started as an architect, quit the profession and for two years (1899–1901) studied at the Academy when William Merritt Chase, "the best known, influential teacher in the country"[7] taught there part-time.[8] Chase, who must have influenced the teachings at the Academy for some time, wanted artists to reveal the process of creation rather than conceal it. He felt that this could be accomplished through the joyful act of making a quick sketch which should be transmitted later into a finished picture.[9] Kahn's sketches exhibit just these qualities and might very well owe the same debt to the Academy as does the work of John Marin.

The art education Louis Kahn acquired at the University of Pennsylvania tempered his creative spirit. The Beaux-Arts system was strongly oriented toward the classical approach and did not tolerate any deviations. Kahn admitted that he had complete trust in his instructors,[10] who vilified the modern trends which began to appear in America after the Armory Show of 1913. The teachings of Kenyon Cox, who was honored by a medal from the Architectural League at that time, reinforced the academic stand.[11] Yet, the ever-increasing exposure of modern artists' work in art periodicals such as *Arts*, which published reproductions of paintings by Cézanne, Matisse, and Marin in articles and in announcements of exhibitions in various galleries, did not escape Kahn's notice.[12] Especially significant to him must have been the famous exhibition of modern art at the Pennsylvania Academy of the Fine Arts in the spring of 1921.[13] It is particularly interesting to note that John Marin's watercolors were being exhibited in Philadelphia over a period of many years: at the Pennsylvania Academy of the Fine Arts in 1901, 1911, 1913, 1914, 1918, 1919, 1922, 1945, 1955, 1958, and 1967; at the Little Gallery of Contemporary Art in 1929; at the Pennsylvania Museum of Art in 1931; and in other Philadelphia galleries all the way through 1969.[14]

While it is possible to perceive similarities in Kahn's work of the 1930s to paintings of Cézanne and Marin, due partially to his early exposures to those artists' work, his 1928–1929 sketches have a coincidental affinity to their paintings resulting from similar attitudes toward form. Kahn's architectural training steered him toward perceiving forms as crisp geometries with clearly defined planes, a style of representation that Cézanne mastered in his work and which Marin, with his own architectural training,[15] conveyed in his paintings.

The technique of using all the edges of a graphite stick might also be partially responsible for Kahn's expression of forms in a fragmented, faceted way. But the most likely source of inspiration was the appearance in the United States of the industrial arts movement known as Art Deco. From its origins in Art Nouveau, Cubism, and Futurism, and as the springboard of the International Exposition of Modern Industrial and Decorative Art in Paris of 1925,[16] the mode of zig-zag repetitive lines with gradations in shading, stylized figures, and lettering "immediately obtained credence in New York and in less than three years spread with the rapidity of conflagration in a high wind throughout the United States."[17] Popular magazines such as *The New Yorker*, *Vogue*, and *Vanity Fair* were influenced by Art Deco in their graphic design; *The New Yorker* of January 23, 1926, carried the first "modern" advertisement by Saks & Co.[18] Architectural magazines, the most likely source of inspiration for Louis Kahn, began to publish architectural designs with strong Art Deco-influenced decorations beginning in January 1928. *Architectural Record* published photographs of projects showing the substantial integration of stylized relief ornaments with structural elements.[19] A stylized watercolor by J. Franklin Whitman, Jr., a study for a fresco decoration for the new Telephone Building in Newark, which appeared in an *Architectural Forum* article in January 1928,[20] carried in it elements which are quite recognizable in Kahn's work from the 1928–1929 period (see Nos. 45 and 53). And, of course, the architectural and decorative work of Ely Jacques Kahn (no relation) which was appearing in architectural and art magazines of this period[21] must have had a significant impact on Kahn's attitude toward the representation of natural and architectural subjects.

While a considerable number of Kahn's sketches from the 1920s and 1930s show the influences of Art Deco, many of them demonstrate that he was not afraid to experiment with artistic modes derived from sources as diverse as Camille, Corot, Charles Sheeler, and both the French and American schools of Impressionism (see Nos. 16, 66, 115, and 261). During the 1930s, these influences reached a new intensity and were blended with many new and divergent sources. His watercolors of this period achieve a new power and self-assurance, with strong echoes of Cézanne and Marin (see Nos. 136–143).

The new Bauhaus-inspired architectural style which was emerging from Europe and was slowly entrenching itself on American soil during 1930s was poeticized by Kahn in his watercolor entitled *Child's Room* (No. 272). It was a tribute to the new spirit of simplicity, cleanliness, openness, transparency, and functionalism. And although it appears at first glance to be a rather clumsy and insignificant painting, it symbolized a great many things to Kahn: "I would say this really comes out of my fascination with the early-modern Bauhaus work, with the kind of bareness and the new lighting fixtures and the unstructured entrance—the openness." Kahn made the sketch around 1929, "when I was probably more conscious of the emergence of modern architecture in this country, after I was in Europe."[22]

Answering a question about other symbolisms, especially the meaning of the blackboard in the sketch, Kahn said:

"It's the child's room symbolism. At that time I didn't have any children. It was probably leafing through books and being acquainted with the human scale as it relates to everyday life—houses, schools, things that we didn't bother with at the Beaux-Arts. . . . I really saw it quite differently then. I really saw [modern architecture] as a great emergence. It gave me a tremendous feeling, but before I was always full of references and here the references were lost. I didn't know references. I started from zero. I hold this drawing very dear because it represents a hint of search. It's like an athlete who wants to excel, though he may be short where he has to be tall in order to accomplish something. And in this drawing I try to sum up all the freedom I had. In a way this drawing is sort of a beginning in which I try to take pieces and parts out of what were images not understood very well, but very much believed in. And this drawing is really quite a key drawing. Everything in a way that I do now is not very far from this, even providing for things on window sills and the things of that nature."[23]

During the 1940s the influence of Le Corbusier's drawings emerges in Kahn's work. The linear mannerism of this great master of modern architecture becomes the model for Kahn's pen-and-ink sketches (Nos. 185, 196, and 232). Kahn admitted that his late exposure to Le Corbusier's books[24] had a profound influence not only on his architectural philosophy[25] but also on his manner of drawing: "At first I started to draw trees like [Le Corbusier] drew them, but soon I became much freer."[26] His pen-and-ink sketches also explore the nervous moods reminiscent of the Expressionists and the calculated linearity of Picasso (Nos. 147, 297, and 299).

By 1950, all of Kahn's various influences had settled into a singular style and he was able to maneuver quite comfortably within the course he established for himself, even though he occasionally showed preferential leanings toward expressionistic semiabstractions and stylizations derived from popular artistic trends (Nos. 337–340, 353, and 354). The results of Kahn's short European trip

in 1959, for instance, were highly personal and unmistakable, the outcome of his own impatience with pen-and-ink sketching, but derived to some extent from the influence of Le Corbusier. This phase is also the last one in which Kahn produced drawings which were not intended for architectural projects.

TECHNIQUES

Kahn worked primarily with quick, simple media, preferring the immediacy and spontaneity of recording what he saw and felt at the spur of a moment. Only occasionally did he attempt to work with more permanent media such as oils, lithographs, and woodcuts (Nos. 117, 307, and 316). In many instances he made notations on his pencil or crayon sketches designating colors with the intent of translating them into permanent paintings (Nos. 136 and 149). This was particularly true during the Depression years when he unsuccessfully attempted to sell his work. Notations on his sketches which appear after World War II were meant more for his personal reflection and without serious consideration for future work of a more permanent nature.

Kahn was extremely sensitive to the characteristics of the medium he was handling and the nature of his sketches directly relate to it. His pencil sketches, for instance, have a crisp linear quality with a few halftones acting as transitions between accented areas and the white of the paper. This is perhaps best demonstrated by an exquisite drawing, *Harbor* (No.14), which succeeds because Kahn exploits to the fullest the potential of pencil as a medium.

By far Kahn's favorite media before World War II were graphite stick, charcoal, crayon, and watercolors. This is particularly true of the 1928–29 period where graphite stick dominated. He used it in a way which benefited from its square configuration. Using the flat edges as well as corners, and by varying his application pressure, he was able to achieve a quick method of gradation and shading.[27] Fragmentation of planes by means of broad strokes of graphite, as seen in *Hill Road* (No.45) and *Hilly Street* (No. 58), is characteristic of Kahn's sensitivity to form which he demonstrates through this technique. The same method, when used in the *Self-Portrait With a Pipe* (No.90), produces soft, velvet-like textures. This technique, of course, is not the unique domain of

Kahn. Quite a number of artists employed it, as seen in reproductions of works by many artists appearing in *Arts* magazine at that time.[28]

The linearity in Kahn's work, which began to emerge with consistent frequency in the mid-1930s, was due to a great extent to his abandonment of the graphite stick and development of his considerable skills with charcoal pencil, pen, and ink. Kahn elaborated on his ability to express himself with a line while discussing the 1951 sketch *The Oracle* (No. 364):

"It's really a line of a hill, which to me is the line of the ending, the ending line, which constituted a serious meaning. That line couldn't be any other line because nature makes whatever it does by the interplay of circumstances—by a succession of equilibriums—and that line is an absolute end line of conscious being, an absolutely different form of the laws that govern nature. And it does it without any purpose, and that's why that line is absolutely the manifestation of evidence of being. So in drawing this line you draw your reverence for that which is also devised as the maker of all things. If you have something you wanted to do and you call on nature, nature will make that particular line. . . . So when I was drawing Delphi and the hills surrounding it, I couldn't draw them verbally, like any drawing. I could only draw them as though they were endings, a manifestation of natural ending. I was trying to make the whole picture to see the mountains and the line. It was a great privilege to draw this line."[29]

Watercolors, as used by Kahn during his 1928–1929 European trip, are handled by filling in large areas with color and modeling through a crisp separation of planes (Nos. 60 and 63). This results in a visual character that is very close to the one he achieved through the use of graphite stick. There are only a few exceptions to this, such as the San Gimignano watercolor *Towers* (No. 95) where a more fluid application of color is evident. The freeing of Kahn's watercolor technique occurs during the 1930s, when his sketches acquire characteristics reminiscent of Cézanne and Marin. There is a striking similarity between certain sketches (Nos. 139–143) and John Marin's watercolors of the late 1930s.[30] Keen awareness of the power of color as a delight in itself makes it possible for Kahn to dissolve forms into patches of limber tones which result in an almost abstract pattern (No. 143).

Kahn painted the watercolor *Harbor with a Shelter, No. 3* (No. 180) following several studies: the first a charcoal sketch, and then a tempera (Nos. 178 and 179). Of the three, the first sketch is the most successful, since it represents an on-the-spot reaction to the subject. The sketch in tempera, a medium which does not lend itself to a quick manner of painting, pales tremendously in character when compared to the spontaneity and sureness of Kahn's charcoal sketch. The watercolor, even though painted from studies made in other media and not directly at the scene, is handled as if it were a spontaneous response to the subject. It is clear that Kahn was quite at home with watercolors; his early training gave him the necessary foundation for handling this medium with ease.

A similar situation exists with regards to Kahn's attempts at oil painting. If we compare the quaint *Tree-Lined Street, No. 3* (No. 118), which Kahn painted from studies made in charcoal and oil (Nos. 116 and 117), it becomes apparent that the discipline required to handle oils presented him with some difficulties. When asked if the oil technique was too slow for him and if it was hindering him, Kahn replied: "No, no, it didn't hinder me. I loved to do them [oils], but I had no teaching in them."[31] Nevertheless, it is obvious from an examination of his oil paintings that this medium was too slow and tedious for his customary needs for spontaneous expression. Employment of media such as lithograph, scratchboard, and woodcut occupied Kahn from time to time and he managed to acquire a remarkable competence in them, even though they were laborious means of achieving the results he desired (Nos. 51, 307, 291, and 317).

During his 1950–1951 European sojourn Kahn produced very remarkable sketches employing pastels. Again, a quick color medium, even less cumbersome than watercolors, allowed him to record his impressions with relative ease. The pastels also lent themselves to filling in large areas with color. In his images of Egypt, solid blues of the sky contrast sharply with strong areas of sunlit and shadowed architectural ruins (Nos. 405 and 406). The pastel sketches of Siena's Piazza del Campo (Nos. 338 and 339) may be compared with *The Plaza* of San Gimignano (No. 93) sketched by Kahn during his 1928–1929 trip using graphite stick. All these sketches are remarkably similar in terms of composition, form, and the handling of light and shade. However, the use of pastels allowed

Kahn to handle large masses as single color planes, focusing attention on the overall spatial character.

The numerous sketches which contain color notations, either for purposes of conversion into finished paintings or for personal reference, testify to the fact that Kahn was tremendously affected by color. His many watercolors of the 1930s, which break away from his careful handling of his palette in the previous period, lead toward the explosive employment of complementary hues in his pastels during the 1950–1951 period. His remarkable attitude toward colors was expressed by Kahn in this reply to the question of whether or not his use of blue shadows in *Piazza Campidoglio* (No. 337) was a conscious response to his perception:

"No, it's a consciousness of the fact that the yellow light would give you blue shadows, and that red light would give you green shadows. . . . It's something that I saw knowing about it. And at times it was absolutely evident. Of course, one time when I was in Paestum, knowing this is true, I was in a magenta sunset and the magenta sunset cast a green shadow that was as green as green could be. The green was so green that I had to feel that there wasn't paint; and on the shadow of my hands was also green. That's how green it was. This happened in Assisi once. Then I looked for it everywhere and when I was in Paestum the same magenta sunset gave you an inky green— it really wasn't just an ordinary green. It was ink green. And that cast a shadow on the stones which were a golden color and this green cast itself a purple shadow, because it had so much light in the green. So within iridescent stone there was a shadow caused by the green shadow on the stone itself, and that really set me off because I thought I could independently paint all of these things."[32]

In 1959, which marks the end of his non-architectural sketching career, Kahn depended almost exclusively on black-and-white linework techniques. Since pastels became too cumbersome to carry around on his trips, he employed pencil and pen and ink. Many of the pencil sketches which Kahn brought from his European trip in 1959 were translated by him into multiple sketches employing a very quick and scratchy pen-and-ink technique. (Nos. 439 and 440.)

It should be mentioned here that while Kahn, because of a lack of time, did not produce any drawings from nature during the last fifteen years of his life,[33] he was extremely prolific in making architectural design sketches employing pastels, crayon, charcoal, and pen-and-ink techniques in a manner very similar to his artistic work from the 1950s on.[34]

COMPOSITION

From his earliest sketches to his last, Kahn exhibited a complete mastery of composition. Natural ability coupled with excellent training allowed Kahn to handle this element of sketching with great ease. Since practically all of his work was representational, Kahn's love of plastic qualities manifested itself through the use of well-organized and balanced spatial compositions. By means of line and shading, his sketches from the early periods demonstrate well-thought-out arrangements of elements resulting in dynamic perspectives (Nos. 13, 40, 56, and 260). The use of color, especially in the watercolors of the 1930s, reduced the sense of depth and resulted in sketches exhibiting two-dimensional design qualities. This might not have been Kahn's conscious intention, but rather a reaction to the influence of Cézanne and Marin mentioned earlier, as well as his response to the feeling for the subject's "design and the lyrical rhythm and counterpoint of its mass."[35] In several watercolors from the 1930s and pastel sketches from Kahn's 1950–1951 overseas trip (Nos. 140, 166, 353, 354, 406, and 407), the purely two-dimensional quality of composition is offset only by drastic color contrasts. Lines and forms which establish strong design relationships to the plane of the paper, as well as colors, are used at certain times in the direct reversal of the rules of perspective. An example is the use of cool green in the foreground and warm orange in the background of the view of the *Piazza del Campo* in Siena (No. 339). By balancing forms and attracting attention to the center of interest, Kahn made his compositions comfortable without being boring. Rhythmic lines and forms and the use of value and color contrasts produced the ingredients necessary for successful compositions.

In choosing natural subjects and a vantage point from which to sketch, Kahn allowed himself the usual artistic license to reorganize what he saw so as to create a more pleasing arrangement.[36] However, his compositions were truer to the original settings in architectural landscapes, where his choice of the vantage point was determined by the most dramatic or unusual perspective (Nos. 339 and 377).

When reviewing some of the sketches he made as a young man, Kahn appeared generally happy to reminisce and expressed pride in his accomplishments; in one instance, however, he displayed strong self-criticism. Referring to his watercolor of *Ponte Scaligero, No.2* (No. 35), he expressed displeasure at the way the composition was split by a diagonal line of blue-green water at the bottom of the sketch:

"Now there is something here which is in a way very peculiar, which I would never do. This line you see here, that line is a very effective line and doesn't belong there. You can see where that line separates certain things. There is something about it that is immature."[37]

Predominantly, Kahn preferred compositions which were asymmetrical, dynamic, and baroque in character. His natural landscapes exploited the organic essence of hills, trees, and shorelines. His townscapes contained a quaint intimacy of scale which reflected his humanistic attitudes about architecture and urban planning.

SUBJECTS AND PHILOSOPHICAL ATTITUDES

Based on subject matter, the sketches and paintings of Louis Kahn may be grouped into the following categories: natural landscapes dominated by sketches of mountainous terrains or waterfronts; architectural landscapes exploring urban or rural spaces, buildings, architectural ruins, interiors, and building details; portraits and figures; graphic designs and still lifes. With the exception of the last decade of Kahn's artistic productivity, in which architectural landscapes dominate, there is a substantial amount of involvement with each genre in each period.

If one were to start with the analysis of Kahn's natural landscapes it would become evident that he preferred dramatic and sublime settings which offered him the least difficulty in making his subject interesting. Sketches from his first European travels (Nos. 17–24) are full of romantic renditions of spectacular scenery, where mountains, lakes, and the sky confront each other in a melodramatic ebullition. A less spectacular approach to natural landscapes appears in Kahn's work

during the 1929–1940 period, mainly due to his inability to travel to areas where the scenery could match the drama of the Swiss or Italian mountains. He discovers considerable beauty, however, in the humble settings of New England and Canada, from which he skillfully extracts the American mood and character (Nos. 120–175).

During the 1940–1950 period and his overseas stay in Europe of 1950–1951, the reemergence of the dramatic character in his landscapes takes on a slightly different appearance and Kahn shows strong expressionistic tendencies which border on semiabstractions (Nos. 143, 147, 356, 359, and 386).

Kahn explained his emotional attitude toward the subjects of his drawings, especially natural subjects, this way:

"I couldn't help but draw what I saw, but at the same time I was drawing a memory and I wasn't just drawing blindly. I was trying to get the essence of it all. . . . In a way I wanted to take the mountain home with me, to implant it in the memory of something that must remain as a lasting reverence. . . . Even when I was a kid, drawing trees, I wanted to take these trees home with me. I wanted to prove to others by reason that I loved the trees, that I was made of that which is constant."[38]

When asked about his perception of his subject matter, especially the relationships of parts to a whole, such as the relationship of rocks and trees to a mountain, Kahn replied:

"I think of it as a portrait. Because the mountain does more than that, and all that constitutes the mountain physically are manifestations of a natural ending and because they are not consciously made, you can, through your consciousness, neglect the outer manifestations of it. They are of no importance to the mountain. And it should be of no importance to you, except if you focus on one of the rocks and imagine that it is a mountain of its own. But if you were to imitate the edges and so forth, my tendency would be to reconstruct it as though it were a building. And I would definitely, if I would figure the faintest sense in its constructiveness only, I would construct it."[39]

Human subjects, including his many self-portraits, were convenient means for exercising his skill in the translation of form, rather than serious attempts at exploring inner meanings. An exception to this are Kahn's portraits of his wife, sketched during the early part of their marriage. Particularly sensitive and melancholy is a pencil sketch of Esther (No. 285), in which the eyes possess a hauntingly magnetic force. The two ink sketches of himself and his associate Anne G. Tyng (Nos. 270 and 271) are exercises in the reduction of complex forms to the barest linework. They do, however, convey a little more than form; there is a definite feeling of cockiness in Kahn's face and a shyness in the face of his friend. The most emotionally charged drawings in this category are three self-portraits most likely created as a set (Nos. 274–276). The transformation conveyed in these sketches from a contemplative mood to one charged with an inner turmoil is unusual in Kahn's portraits, even though that tendency emerges occasionally in his landscapes, where a commonplace scene in one rendition is transformed into an unsettling expressionism in others. (Nos. 251–253)

With the exception of a few graphic designs containing human figures Kahn dispensed with the human subject after 1949. This is due in large part to architectural interests which began to dominate his sketches during the last periods of his artistic activity.

Still lifes, various graphic designs, and graphic explorations (Nos. 306–329, 422–432), while not forming a very significant part of Kahn's artistic oeuvre, do offer an important glimpse at his attitude toward the natural and the manmade world at a particular time of his development as an architect. Of specific interest are the studies of transparency and the modern architectural vocabulary (Nos. 318–20, 327–29). They are important indicators of Kahn's emerging fascination with modernism. Equally significant are the mural studies (Nos. 422–432) reflecting the impact that Egyptian ruins, and in particular the pyramids, played on the consolidation of his theories of form.

Among Kahn's architectural landscapes, industrial subjects (Nos. 260 and 261) appear only during the first half of 1930s, most likely inspired by the work of artists like Fernand Léger and Charles Sheeler.[40] But architectural themes occur in many variations throughout his career. From romantic views of medieval monuments, ancient ruins, Italian hill towns, fishing villages, public squares, interiors, and architectural details to Le Corbusier's Ronchamp (Nos. 479 and 480), Kahn exhibits the profoundly passionate attitude of a man in love with architecture. But architecture to Kahn was obviously not something which, being manmade, differed greatly from the natural environment. In his sketches of architectural landscapes, nature and buildings seem totally integrated. When asked how he viewed the difference between the manmade and the natural environment, Kahn stated:

"Well, I never thought of this as being just manmade, but rather something that was all blended together. . . . One thing always occurred to me, that what nature can make, man cannot make. And what man can make, nature cannot make without a man. And thus, I thought, if I could draw, I can improve the constructiveness of what is being built by man that I could not the constructiveness of that built by nature."[41]

His architectural training and philosophy played a significant role in his attitude toward drawing buildings in his sketches. He made this comment viewing some of his urban landscapes: "I would never draw a very strong line coming to the ground. Why? Because the building is continuous below ground."[42]

Ancient ruins were among the architectural subjects which held a special fascination for Kahn. In them he sensed the timeless beauty derived from pure forms which had lost the need to perform their original function (Nos. 86–88, 331–335, 362–384, and 394–421). It seemed to him as if the very essence of the art of architecture was locked in those relics of past ages.[43] Kahn's sketches of these subjects, like those of public squares, served as lessons which needed to be diligently studied in order to derive the meaning of architecture.

The fact that Kahn's love for drawing and painting was strongly coupled with his deep involvement with architecture is quite evident in his prolific portrayals of architectural landscapes. But there also might have been a case of crossfertilization in which the subjects of his sketches became subliminal material for his architectural designs. We must accept as a basic truth the fact that sketching, and in particular drawing, "establishes a habit that is fundamental to expression in the visual arts, the habit of looking, seeing, and expressing one's perception in graphic, painterly, or plastic form."[44] The personal statement in drawing is the foundation and the beginning for all means of artistic expression, be they paintings, sculpture, or architecture.[45] Kahn's impulse to "file many hundreds of sketches stored haphazardly in portfolios revives unforgettable circumstances, places and attitudes of years past. The runes of these pages resemble seeds full of magic capable of germinating into future works."[46]

Kahn's sketches were not executed for the purpose of becoming sources of architectural designs. He stated, in fact, that many of them were meant as studies for paintings,[47] as Una Johnson indicated in the above quote. Yet, architectural educators have always advised their students to travel, to see the world, and to record settings which move them, so that their sensitivity to space, form, light, and texture will be sharpened and establish a storehouse of inspiration.

Paul Cret, Kahn's teacher at the University of Pennsylvania and later his associate, stated the need for a mastery of the art of drawing in relation to the study of architecture as follows:

"It is useful, also, to point out that almost all studies other than design are valuable only as a preparation for, or as a complement to it; some, like drawing and modeling, give to the designer the means of giving a concrete form to his ideas."[48]

Looking through Kahn's drawings and paintings, we can discern certain obvious formal similarities between some subjects of his sketches and his architectural works. In his book on Kahn,[49] Vincent Scully points out the formal and graphic similarities of Kahn's 1928–1929 sketch of an Italian street scene with a tower (No. 69)[50] to his 1960 perspective drawing for the design of the Alfred Newton Richards Medical Research Building at the University of Pennsylvania. The similarity, Scully noted, "shows that Kahn could now use what he had originally been trained to see and do. He had come into his inheritance."[51] As discussed in this volume's Catalogue Raisonné, a considerable number of architectural projects which followed Kahn's return from his 1950–51 travels in Italy, Egypt, and Greece began to exhibit formal relations to many of his travel sketches. Of special note is the exploration by Kahn of the pyramidal form. The sense of solidity and permanence in architectural

form that Kahn was able to return to the mainstream of architecture clearly relates to his exploration of ruins and of ancient monuments. In addition, his study of light on architectural forms supplied him with the foundation for his most poetic philosophical beliefs and the crystallization of his design theories.

One can dwell further upon the special fascination Kahn had for simple vertical, cylindrical, or prismatic forms such as silos, columns, and towers (Nos. 13, 39, 41–43, 53–54, 67–71, 88, 93–95, 244–254, 260, 339, 343–44, 352, 382–84, 402, 407, 436, 449, 467–78). The strong formal similarity of the Richards Medical Research Building and the watercolor sketch of the towers of San Gimignano (No. 95) may reinforce even further the theory that the subjects of his sketches found their way into his architectural designs, even though in this instance, Kahn categorically denied any conscious attempt to tap the formal character of the Italian towers.[52] The cylindrical and prismatic tower theme occurs again and again in Kahn's designs for the capital in Dacca, the Institute for Management in Ahmedabad, the Salk Medical Research Institute in La Jolla, and a project for an office building in Kansas City. However strong these similarities seem, it would be presumptuous to derive any one conclusion from them. An understanding of Kahn's seriousness and the sincerity with which he fought his way through the architectural design process makes the notion that he consciously applied or borrowed forms from his sketches incomprehensible. His denial of this proposition, mentioned above, is quite understandable, since there was likely an element of subconscious involvement with architectural symbolism. Le Corbusier, whom Kahn openly revered, was deeply fascinated by symbols which surfaced in his designs, ranging in scale from small details to entire city plans.[53] Le Corbusier also admitted that it was by "the channel of my painting that I came to architecture."[54] So, it is not inconceivable that Kahn's architectural forms surfaced subconsciously from his fascination with the natural and manmade forms which he admired and recorded in his sketches.[55]

What fascinated Kahn more than the outer manifestations of forms were the laws and the order at the heart of nature's processes and man's attempts at the modification of nature. Kahn's creative impulse drove him to record and interpret what he saw in order to better understand this order. Gyorgy Kepes noted in his *Education of Vision:*

"If, in the world, man sees around him the rhythm of nature's processes revealed; and if the colors, forms, and movements he sees are expressions of organic events, then his vision is nourished by the `primal sanities of nature' to use Walt Whitman's words. If the primal sanities of nature can be absorbed through his vision, if man is led to see them, he can reproduce them in the world he shapes for himself."[56]

Kahn himself stated that:

". . . nature records in everything it makes how it was made. This record is also in man and it is this within us that urges us to seek its story involving the laws of universe, the source of all material and means, and the psyche, the source of all expression, Art."[57]

Thus Kahn, in his search for the natural rule of order, sketched what looked congruous, that which contained the underlying law which makes unity out of diverse elements and, therefore, is perceived as beautiful.[58] His skillful eye and hand captured such lessons in many sketches of natural and manmade environments. They are loaded with the record of how he interpreted the order he saw in mountains, trees, and seacoasts. His early sketches of Italian towns, done in graphite, are constructed in a manner akin to real building blocks, layer upon layer. He remarked that he could not draw from the roof down because that was not the way buildings were made. He wanted to reconstruct the process of building by the use of graphite on paper.[59]

Such perception and insight into the nature of his artistic subjects obviously had a lasting effect. His mature architectural work reveals clearly the method of construction in the most direct way, be it in the joinery of wood, masonry, precast concrete, or formwork recorded in poured concrete. Kahn wanted to follow the natural order of growth. He stated that "I like my buildings to have knuckles, joints are the beginning of ornament."[60] It is this organicism with attention to minute details, rather than spectacular showmanship, that made Kahn such a refreshing change in the architectural arena of the late 1950s. As revealed in his designs, the intensely honest search for truth in each problem provided the lesson that "feeding on a pretentious and

dishonest manmade environment our vision can only rehash the false. It needs to be regenerated, re-educated to sharpen sensibility."[61]

The majority of Kahn's sketches reveal that the manmade subjects he sought contained lessons taught by anonymous builders responding in the most natural ways to circumstantial conditions. In his own architecture he wanted to recapture that same direct and natural character by cleansing himself of all extraneous contamination and approached his designs, like Paul Klee, "with maturity of experience, yet with a child's innocence."[62]

Kahn used a manner of architectural design similar to that described by Frank Lloyd Wright in the design of the Unity Temple.[63] To avoid a possibility of form contamination, Kahn began his designs from what he described as "Volume Zero."[64] He assigned a "symbolic configuration,"[65] a conceptual geometry, to the relationships of spaces for different activities. This usually took shape as a combination of squares and circles, a geometry of the simplest order, which he felt to be the beginning of all forms. He then attacked this conceptual arrangement with pragmatic arguments in order to test its initial validity. If the concept failed such a test, he would start from scratch by searching deeper for the true "Form."[66] If the concept withstood the attack, he would proceed through stages of materialization by molding the conceptual diagram into a shape that would reflect the demands of site, materials, structure, mechanical systems, and so on. He employed the same laborious method of concept testing in his choices of structural and enclosure systems. His famous saying, "I asked the brick what it liked, and the brick said, `I like an arch,'" is symbolic of his design methodology.[67] If the resulting building geometry bore some resemblance to the original conceptual sketch, then it was a proof of the validity of the initial "Form." His projects and completed buildings almost always contain this strong simple geometry which suggest that they do not adhere so much to Sullivan's principle of "Form follows function" as to his own statement that "Form evokes function,"[68] since the basic wish of the "Form" to encourage activities was satisfied. Kahn was totally dedicated to producing spaces which would be expressive of their use and which would have the potential of evoking a strong emotional response from those who experienced his architecture; or as he put it, that architecture is the ". . . creating of spaces that evoke a feeling of use."[69]

He envisaged serious architectural work as evolving through three stages of development:

"A great building, in my opinion, must begin with the unmeasurable, go through measurable means when it is being designed, and in the end must be unmeasurable."[70]

Yet the unmeasurable quality he preferred was not one of perfection, but one imbued with the potential for further development. Thus, he liked the temple at Paestum with all its semideveloped features more than the Parthenon, for which Paestum broke the ground. The Parthenon was the end of the line.[71] In this belief he comes very close to Horatio Greenough's definition of "beauty as the promise of function, action as the presence of function, character as the record of function."[72]

Kahn's philosophy was responsible for the unique characteristics of his work. His buildings, like the ruins he sketched, have a timeless quality about them which defies placing them in any category of stylistic development in the twentieth century. His preference for materials such as brick and precast concrete, materials which express the joinery, give his buildings the character of solidity. Spaces are thus clearly defined by structure and enclosure, a Beaux-Arts feature which was advocated by Guadet and which is in strong contrast to the spatial fluidity of the modern movement. His concern for sunlight as a vital element of design produced a system of bringing daylight into his buildings that utilized double enclosures perforated with simple geometric light apertures. "The sun never knew how great it was until it struck the side of a building," he said.[73] His architecture, like that of Le Corbusier's, was dedicated to sunlight in celebration of life.

Kahn's sketches and paintings have little meaning without being seen in the context of his total creativity. Besides his artwork and buildings, his deeply philosophical and poetic pronouncements as a teacher and author stand out among the best of the twentieth-century thinkers. Nothing explains his attitude toward creativity better than this quote from one of his last essays:

"I sense light as the giver of all presences, and material as spent light. What is made by light casts a shadow, and the shadow belongs to light. I sense a threshold: light to silence, silence to light—an ambience of inspiration, in which the desire to be, to express, crosses the possible. The rock, the stream, the wind inspires. We see what is beautiful in the material first in wonder, then in knowing, which in turn is transformed into the expression of beauty that lies in the desire to express. Light to silence, silence to light crosses in the sanctuary of art. Its treasury knows no favorite, knows no style. Truth and rule out of commonness, law out of order are the offerings within.

"Architecture has no presence but exists as the realization of a spirit. A work of architecture is made as an offering reflecting the nature of the spirit. One can also say that the realms of painting, sculpture, and literature exist in spirit, their natures revealed by works that are unfamiliar. In using the word `unfamiliar,' I recognize the singularity of every individual in attitude and talent. But the phenomena of individual realizations of a spirit are only new images of that same spirit. So it is in nature that the diversity of forms evolves from universal order."[74]

NOTES

1. Jan Hochstim, "Conversations with Louis I. Kahn." Transcription of tape recordings, Philadelphia, December 1972.

2. Ibid.

3. Louis I. Kahn, "The Value and Aim in Sketching," *T-Square Club Journal* (May 1931), 19–20.

4. Hochstim, "Conversations."

5. Patricia McLaughlin, "'How'm I Doing, Corbusier?' An Interview with Louis Kahn," *The Pennsylvania Gazette* 71 (December 1972), 19.

6. Vincent Scully, *Louis I. Kahn* (New York: George Braziller, 1962), 45.

7. Sheldon Reich, *John Marin—A Stylistic Analysis and Catalogue Raisonné*, two vols. (Tucson, Ariz.: The University of Arizona Press, 1970) 1:9.

8. Jerome Mellquist, *The Emergence of an American Art* (New York: Charles Scribner's Sons, 1942), 69.

9. Reich, *John Marin*, 1:9.

10. Hochstim, "Conversations."

11. Oliver W. Larkin, *Art and Life in America* (New York: Holt, Rinehart and Winston, 1960), 363.

12. "Current Art Exhibitions," *Arts* 1 (December 1920), 3–5, 25–48; Alan Burroughs, "Making History of Impressionism," *Arts* 1 (April 1921), 17–24; Hamilton Easter Field, "Comments on the Arts," *Arts* 1 (May 1921), 32–54; Virgil Barker, "The Water Colors of John Marin," *Arts* 5 (February 1924), 65–83.

13. Field, "Comments on the Arts," 32–34.

14. Reich, *John Marin*, 2:831–63

15. Ibid., 1:9.

16. W. Franklin Paris, "The International Exposition of Modern Industrial and Decorative Art in Paris, " *Architectural Record* 58 (October 1925), 370.

17. C. Adolph Glassgold, "The Modern Note in Decorative Arts," *Arts* 8 (April 1928), 225.

18. Ibid., 226.

19. *Architectural Record* 63 (January 1928), 67–76.

20. Ralph T. Walker, "A New Architecture," *Architectural Forum* 48 (January 1928), 42.

21. Leon V. Solon, "The Park Avenue Building, New York City," *Architectural Record* 63 (April 1928), 287–297; also in the same issue an article by Ely Jacques Kahn, "Economics of the Skyscraper," 298–301; and Ely Jacques Kahn, "The Province of Decoration in Modern Design" *Creative Art* 5 (December 1929), 885–86.

22. Hochstim, "Conversations."

23. Ibid.

24. Le Corbusier, *Toward A New Architecture*, trans. Frederick Etchells (London: Architectural Press, 1927; reprint ed., New York: Praeger Publishers, 1960); of special interest are illustrations on pp. 167–72, 178–80, 206, 212, 216–43.

25. McLaughlin, "How'm I doing, Corbusier?" 22.

26. Hochstim, "Conversations."

27. Ibid.

28. Dorothy Lefferts Moore, "Exhibitions in New York," *Arts* 15 (March 1929), 185.

29. Hochstim, "Conversations."

30. Reich, *John Marin*, 2:700–701.

31. Hochstim, "Conversations."

32. Ibid.

33. This observation is based on my last contact with Louis Kahn in December 1972, two years prior to his death.

34. See Kahn's architectural sketches in Heinz Ronner and Sharad Jhaveri, *Louis I. Kahn: Complete Work 1935–1974* (Basel and Boston: Birkhauser, 1987); and in *The Louis I. Kahn Archive: Personal Drawings* (Philadelphia: University of Pennsylvania and Pennsylvania Historical Commission; and New York: Garland Publishing, Inc., 1988).

35. Kahn, "The Value and Aim in Sketching," 21.

36. Ibid.

37. Hochstim, "Conversations."

38. Ibid.

39. Ibid.

40. *American Painting, 1760–1960* (Milwaukee: Milwaukee Art Center, 1960), 106.

41. Hochstim, "Conversations."

42. Ibid.

43. Ibid.

44. Daniel M. Mendelowitz, *Drawing* (New York: Holt, Rinehart and Winston, Inc., 1967), vi.

45. Una E. Johnson, *Golden Years of American Drawings: 1905–1956* (Brooklyn, N.Y.: The Brooklyn Museum Press, 1957), 5.

46. Ibid.

47. Hochstim, "Conversations."

48. Paul Cret, "The Training of the Designer," *American Architect* 155 (April 1909), 116.

49. Scully, *Louis I. Kahn*, 11.

50. This sketch, Scully's Plate No. 1, (page 49) is erroneously labeled *Siena*. The sketch is of the Duomo in Assisi.

51. Scully, *Louis I. Kahn*, 11.

52. Hochstim, "Conversations."

53. Stanislaus von Moos, *Le Corbusier: Elemente Einer Synthses* (Frauenfeld: Verlag Huber, 1968), 335–369; and Stephen Gardiner, *Le Corbusier* (New York: The Viking Press, 1975), 49, 98–106.

54. Gardiner, *Le Corbusier*, 49.

55. The reader is directed to an excellent article on this subject by Norman A. Crowe and Steven W. Hurtt, "Visual Notes and the Acquisition of Architectural Knowledge," *Journal of Architectural Education* (Spring 1986), 6–16. Also relevant is an article by Mark Hewitt, "Representational Forms and Modes of Conception: An Approach to the History of Architectural Drawing," *Journal of Architectural Education* (Winter 1985), 2–9.

56. Gyorgy Kepes, ed., *Education of Vision* (New York: George Braziller, 1965), i.

57. *Architecture and Urbanism* 3 (January 1973), 17.

58. Paul Weiss, "Organic Form: Scientific and Aesthetic Aspects," in Gyorgy Kepes, ed., *The Visual Arts Today* (Middletown, Conn.: Wesleyan University Press, 1960), 193.

59. Hochstim, "Conversations."

60. "Form Evokes Function," *Time* (6 June 1960), 76.

61. Kepes, *Education of Vision*, ii.

62. Paul Heyer, *Architects on Architecture: New Directions in America* (New York: Walker and Co., 1966), 392.

63. Frank Lloyd Wright, *An Autobiography* (New York: Duell, Sloan and Pearce, 1943), 153–160.

64. McLaughlin, "How'm I Doing, Corbusier?", 20.

65. Jan C. Rowan, "Wanting to Be: The Philadelphia School," *Progressive Architecture* 42 (April 1961), 131.

66. By "Form" Kahn meant the essence, the soul, or the psyche, the ideal state which all things "want to be."

67. "Louis Kahn's Death 'Diminishes the Century,'" *The Pennsylvania Gazette* 72 (May 1974), 7.

68. Frederick Gutheium, "Philadelphia's Redevelopment," *Architectural Forum* 150 (December 1956), 134.

69. Rowan, "Wanting to Be," 132.

70. Ibid., 133.

71. Hochstim, "Conversations."

72. Horatio Greenough, "Relative and Independent Beauty," in Don Gifford, ed., *The Literature of Architecture: The Evolution of Architectural Theory and Practice in Nineteenth-Century America* (New York: E.P. Dutton and Co., Inc., 1966), 163.

73. "The Mind of Louis Kahn," *Architectural Forum* 137 (July-August 1972), 55.

74. Louis I. Kahn, "Architecture: Silence and Light," in *On the Future of Art* (New York: The Viking Press, 1970), 21–25.

CATALOGUE RAISONNE

Reproductions contained in the Catalogue Raisonné represent virtually the entire oeuvre of Louis I. Kahn's sketches and paintings.[1] Omitted are several works which at the time of this publication are considered lost or their whereabouts unknown. The process of collecting the artwork began in December of 1972 with the assistance of Louis Kahn, Esther Kahn, and Kahn's office staff. Some 200 originals, which were then readily available, were examined and photographed in Kahn's private office on Walnut Street in Philadelphia over a period of two days. Of these, 193 were reproduced in my master's thesis "Sketches and Paintings of Louis I. Kahn, Analysis and Catalogue Raisonné," (University of Miami, 1976). Since the publication of that thesis it became very clear to me that my initial effort had uncovered only a very small, however significant, portion of Kahn's artwork.

With the intent of publishing a book containing the most comprehensive collection of Kahn's artwork ever assembled, the process of acquiring reproductions of every available sketch or painting resumed seriously in August 1987. I was able to obtain 404 photographic reproductions. Of the 480 plates contained in this book, seventy-eight are considered lost or their present whereabouts unknown. Ten of the missing sketches are reproduced here with the permission of other publications and the remaining sixty-eight are reproduced from my original slides taken in Kahn's office in 1972.

The Catalogue Raisonné is organized into five parts, each representing a significant period of Kahn's life as it affected his style or subject matter. Since only a few works bear any inscribed information, and because during our conversations Kahn was seldom able to supply accurate dates or locations, Mrs. Esther Kahn was invaluable in providing much of the missing data. Mr. William G. Holman's extensive research for the 1978–79 exhibition catalogue of "The Travel Sketches of Louis I. Kahn"[2] was also of great assistance in dating, titling, and analyzing the work. In many cases, where no information was available, I supplied dates, locations, and titles based on my own research and judgement. Dimensions of the artworks are provided in most cases, except for the pieces which were photographed in 1972 and, regretfully, were not measured because of the lack of time.

The organization of the sketches within each period is based predominantly on subject matter rather than on an exact chronological order. This was done to compare Kahn's attitude toward various subjects and his manner of sketching them over a certain period of time. In the absence of date and location information, the guiding principle for grouping the artwork within a specific period was an affinity in style as well as the geographic similarities of the subject matter.

The identification of each entry is organized in the following manner:

Plate number

Title (in quotation marks if inscribed on the work or titled by the artist), location of the subject or the place of execution, and date (a date after a slash represents the execution date of the work based on a previous sketch)

Medium and size

Additional information such as title, signature, date, or notations inscribed on the work

Record of major exhibitions of the work

Present location

Commentary (if applicable)

The commentaries accompanying almost every plate are subjective critical evaluations of the work based on personal observations and an analysis of Kahn's artistic interests, his architectural endeavors, and the works of other artists having a direct or indirect relation to his art.

NOTES

1. I photographed the original sketches and paintings with a 35mm camera and a 50mm, f/1.8 lens using Kodak High Speed Ektachrome 3200K color slide film. Illumination was supplied by two 500 watt, 3200K floods; however, in several instances daylight intrusion caused some color infidelity. Due to the imperfections of amateur photography and poor commercial processing the results do not always represent the true quality of the original artwork.

2. William G. Holman, *The Travel Sketches of Louis I. Kahn.* An Exhibition Organized by the Pennsylvania Academy of the Fine Arts, Philadelphia, 1978–79. (Washington, D.C.: Museum Press, 1978).

PERIOD I

Pre-1928

SCHOOLING AND TRAINING

The first group of Kahn's sketches and drawings in this series spans the period from 1913 to 1928. The earliest available sketch, *City of Para*, was made in 1913 while Kahn was still a youngster and was the springboard for a forty-six-year artistic career. This is followed by a seven-year gap with no known examples of his work. The next available sketches are ten studies of life models and plaster casts made between 1920 and 1924 as class exercises at the University of Pennsylvania (Nos. 2–11). After obtaining his architecture degree, and while training as a designer and drafts-man in Philadelphia architectural offices, Kahn continued his artistic avocation by producing very competent pencil and ink landscapes (Nos. 12–16). The artwork in this small group is organized in more or less chronological order with drawings of similar subjects kept together.

1
CITY OF PARA 1913
Pen and ink on paper, 8 x 10 in.
(20.3 x 25.5 cm)
Signed lower left (at a later date):
Louis I Kahn
Inscribed at lower center: *City of Para*
Shown at a traveling exhibition organized
by the Pennsylvania Academy of the Fine
Arts, 1978–1979, Catalogue No. 1
Collection of Sue Ann Kahn

This is the earliest available sketch made
by Kahn while he attended Central High
School in Philadelphia. The sketch,
most likely a copy of an engraving,
demonstrates the twelve-year-old Kahn's
talent and keen interest in the formal
relationships of buildings to each other
and to the natural setting. It was his great
skill in drawing that won the young Kahn
several John Wanamaker Children's
Drawing Prizes and in 1920 a full
scholarship to the Pennsylvania Academy
of the Fine Arts.

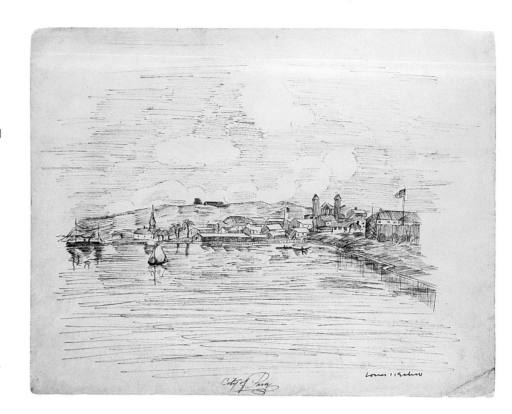

2
MALE NUDE, NO. 1 1920–24
Charcoal on paper, 23 1/2 x 19 in.
(60.3 x 48.3 cm)
Collection of Sue Ann Kahn

This is one of a series of figure studies
drawn by Kahn in an art class at the
School of Fine Arts, University of
Pennsylvania. It should be noted that
because of his ability and experience he
was made an assistant in charge of life
drawing classes. However, this sketch
and No. 3 are handled in a rather stiff
manner, exhibiting qualities more
commonly associated with the
representation of sculpture rather than
live models. This is no doubt due to the
fact that these sketches were made very
quickly, leaving little time for the
elaboration of details and modeling.

3
MALE NUDE, NO. 2   1920–24
Charcoal on paper, 23 1/2 x 18 4/5 in.
(60.3 x 48.3 cm)
Collection of Sue Ann Kahn

4
MALE NUDE, NO. 3   1920–24
Charcoal on paper, 23 1/2 x 18 4/5 in.
(60.3 x 48.3 cm)
Collection of Sue Ann Kahn

In this drawing the figure becomes more
human while still retaining some of the
stonelike characteristics of Nos. 2 and 3.
There is a much greater concern for the
realistic representation of form through
expertly handled shading.

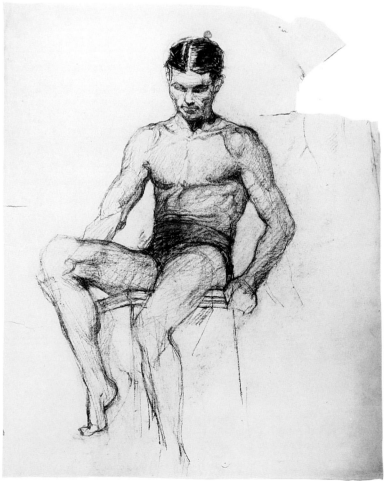

5
MALE NUDE, NO. 4 1920–24
Charcoal on paper, 24 x 18 4/5 in.
(61.6 X 48.3 cm)
Collection of Sue Ann Kahn

In these three drawings (Nos. 5–7),
Kahn's earlier sculptural tendencies
disappear. Kahn's assured handling of
charcoal allows the softness of the flesh
to come through more convincingly. The
rendition of proportions is very well
handled, considering the complexity of
the models' poses and the resulting
foreshortening of limbs.

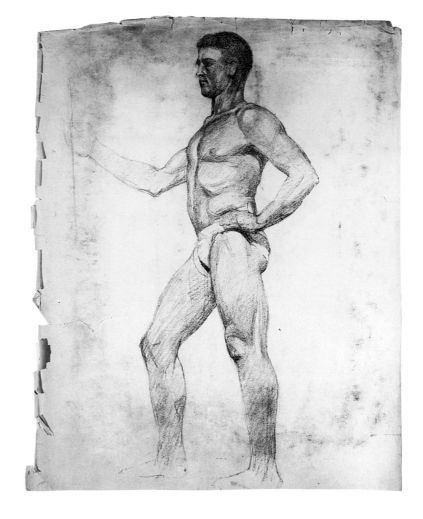

6
MALE NUDE, NO. 5 1920–24
Charcoal on paper, 23 1/5 x 18 4/5 in.
(59.4 x 48.3 cm)
Collection of Sue Ann Kahn

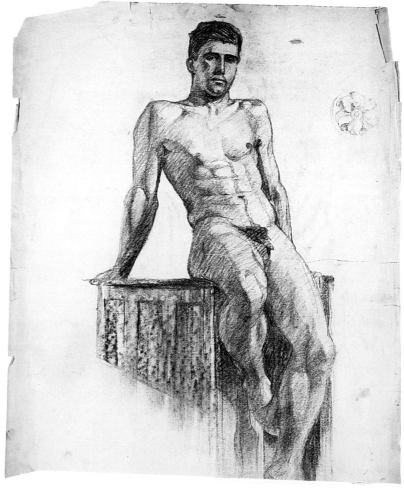

7
MALE NUDE, NO. 6   1920–24
Charcoal on paper, 23 x 18 3/5 in.
(59.0 x 47.6 cm)
Signed lower right: *L/I Kahn*
Collection of Sue Ann Kahn

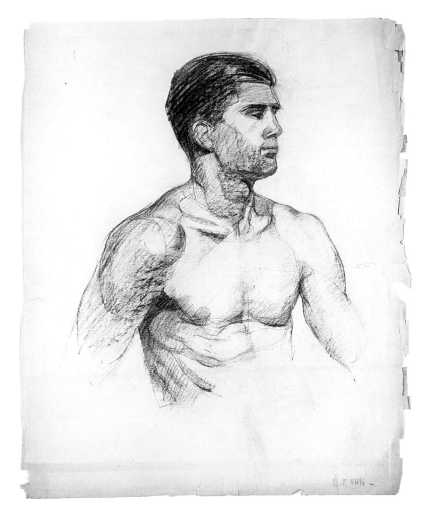

8
MALE NUDE DETAILS   1920–24
Charcoal on paper, 24 x 18 1/3 in.
(61.6 x 47.0 cm)
Verso of No. 7
Collection of Sue Ann Kahn

Kahn, as this drawing displays, had great
difficulty drawing hands. While the
rendition is very competent in general,
there are distortions which were
probably not intended.

9
SEATED WOMAN 1920–24
Sepia crayon on paper, size not available
Present whereabouts unknown

This poignant life-class exercise is
reminiscent of studies by Degas. There
is a strong emphasis placed on the
woman's head, whose face is darkened
dramatically by a shadow from her hair. .

10
VICTORY TYING HER SANDAL 1924
Charcoal on paper, 23 4/5 x 18 3/5 in.
(61.1 x 47.6 cm)
Signed lower right: *KAHN*
Shown at a traveling exhibition
organized by the Pennsylvania Academy
of the Fine Arts, 1978–1979,
Catalogue No. 3
Collection of Sue Ann Kahn

Like No. 9, this drawing from a cast
follows the standard learning procedure
at schools of architecture of the period.
Kahn's knowledge and understanding of
human anatomy is easily detected by his
competent rendition of the draped figure.

11
ARCHITECTURAL DETAIL   1924
Charcoal on paper, 23 x 18 3/5 in.
(59.1 x 47.6 cm)
Signed and inscribed lower right:
Louis I. Kahn '24, Architecture II
Shown at a traveling exhibition organized
by the Pennsylvania Academy of the Fine
Arts, 1978–1979, Catalogue No. 2
Collection of Sue Ann Kahn

This drawing made by Kahn in his last
year at the University of Pennsylvania
was sketched from a plaster cast. It is in
keeping with the doctrines of a Beaux-
Arts education, in which this school
excelled under the leadership of
professor Paul Cret. The small sketch of
an allegorical head at bottom left is also a
study of details for architectural
ornamentations.

12
OLD MILL   1920–28
Pencil on paper, size not available
Present whereabouts unknown

In an exhibition of pencil virtuosity, Kahn
reaches the peak of maturity with this
sensuous rendition of rustic Americana. It
is the quintessence of selectivity in line
work, shading, and detail. It is made in
the best tradition of pencil draftsmanship.

45

13
LIGHTHOUSE 1920–28
Pen and sepia ink on paper, 18 2/3 x
14 3/4 in. (47.9 x 37.8 cm)
Verso of No. 316
Collection of Sue Ann Kahn

This very competent work demonstrates
Kahn's extraordinary technical and
compositional skills. His fascination with
towers spanned his entire life and
manifested itself in numerous sketches

and paintings. The power of man-made
forms invading the domain of the sky
presented him with a great philosophical
challenge, which he addressed fully in
his architectural work.

14
HARBOR 1920–28
Pencil on paper, 13 9/10 x 11 9/10 in.
(35.6 x 30.5 cm)
Signed lower right: *Louis I. Kahn*
Collection of Sue Ann Kahn

Kahn's fascination with waterfront scenery stayed with him throughout his sketching and painting career. Starting with *City of Para* (No. 1), his childhood drawing, Kahn expanded his means of rendering this subject in almost every medium. In this delightful drawing the expertly handled light and dark pencil strokes create a sense of depth and the atmospheric diffusion of sunlight. The composition succeeds by balancing dark, contrasting, and detailed elements in the left foreground with a broad expanse of open, light, and vaguely suggested forms on the right.

15
COLONIAL CHURCH   1920–28
Pencil on paper, 20 1/3 x 13 4/5 in.
(52.1 x 35.5 cm)
Signed lower right: *Louis I. Kahn*
Collection of Sue Ann Kahn

Employing a technique similar to that
used in No. 14, Kahn establishes the
parklike foreground as a framing device
for the church. There is no question as to
the importance of the building, even
though the top of the steeple almost
disappears against the sky. With this
method Kahn manages to balance the
mass of the church behind heavily
delineated trees. The shadow cast by the
trees on the wall and roof of the building
acquires an importance equal to the
architectural details of the building.

16
ITALIAN LANDSCAPE   1920–28
Crayon on paper, size not available
Present whereabouts unknown

This study, which Kahn made before
he actually visited Italy, shows his
fascination with romantic Italian
landscapes. A distant view of buildings
cradled and framed by tree forms, along
with a solitary human figure leading the
eye to the center of the composition,
shows marked derivations from the work
of Camille Corot.

PERIOD II

1928–29

FIRST EUROPEAN TRIP

Following his graduation from the University of Pennsylvania in 1924, Louis Kahn worked in Philadelphia as a draftsman and designer for John Molitor, City Architect, and for William H. Lee. In April of 1928, he embarked on his first European journey. Arriving in England, Kahn proceeded to explore the European architectural treasures he studied in school. Traveling predominantly on foot, he made his way through France, Belgium, Holland, Germany, and Scandinavia and managed to work his way to his ancestral home in Estonia. From there he proceeded to Poland, Czechoslovakia, Hungary, Austria, and Switzerland, and by February of 1929 he had arrived in Italy. True to the tradition of architectural students making a grand tour of Europe, Kahn recorded his impressions in sketches made with graphite stick and watercolors. The record of his travels for almost the entire year before reaching Italy is very small. It was Italy which triggered an avalanche of artistic production. Here the architecture and the landscape provided him with an inexhaustible source of inspiration.

Kahn returned to Philadelphia in the fall of 1929, bringing with him a bountiful record of his travels. The sketches and paintings from this sojourn demonstrate the power that Europe exerted on his artistic sensitivity. It was the seed of a lesson that would grow to fruition many years later. That lesson was the power of an architecture of the humble and the heroic, the spirit of the architecture of the past, which Kahn finally harnessed in a burst of creativity after 1950.

The drawings and watercolors from Kahn's 1928–29 trip presented here are organized wherever possible by subject matter, rather than chronological order or geographic location. This arrangement allows a comparison of Kahn's attitudes toward various subjects. It also allows one to see the evolution of Kahn's stylistic expression with similar subjects. The main categories are:

Natural landscapes
Trees
Bridges
Landscapes, cityscapes, and
 architectural subjects
Figures and portraits

17
LANDSCAPES WITH HILLS,
Switzerland 1928
Graphite on paper, 10 2/5 x 8 1/2 in.
(26.7 x 21.9 cm); top and bottom images:
3 9/10 x 10 2/5 in. (10.0 x 26.7 cm)
Collection of Sue Ann Kahn

During the 1929 portion of Kahn's
European tour the most prevalent
medium he employed was a short,
square-shaped graphite stick. It allowed

him to achieve lines and shading by
utilizing the edges and sides of the
graphite. Varying pressure with the stick
produced shading reminiscent of airbrush
techniques popularized at that time in
Art Deco commercial art.

In these sketches Kahn explored the
relationship of hills against the flat
foreground of the lake. The bottom sketch
presents an intrusion on the middle

foreground in the form of a small island,
thus creating a spatial element that slides
in front of the hilly background and
becomes the focal point of the
composition. Kahn also investigated here
a means of perspective perception by
utilizing a progression from light to dark
in the upper sketch and its reverse in the
lower. In both sketches the overlapping
diagonals provide additional clues to
depth perception.

18
LANDSCAPES WITH WINDMILLS,
Holland   1928
Colored pencil on paper,
10 2/5 x 7 9/10 in. (26.7 x 20.3 cm)
Collection of Sue Ann Kahn

These sketches, drawn by Kahn from a train while crisscrossing Holland, stand out in bold contrast to most of his work. He had a great fascination with mountains and all kinds of natural and man-made vertical forms. The strong horizons of the Dutch landscape deprived him of the necessary drama which he usually sought. However, in these drawings Kahn managed to dramatize the contrast of sparse vertical elements, such as windmills and trees, against the vast monotony of the horizon and to capture vividly his view of the landscape from a fast-moving train.

19
MOUNTAIN LAKE WITH A BOAT,
NO. 1, Switzerland   1929
Graphite on tissue paper,
6 1/5 x 6 9/10 in. (15.9 x 17.7 cm)
Collection of Sue Ann Kahn

Fragmented and scalloped lines and
shades make natural forms appear to be
mere weightless puffs. Compositionally
there is an uncomfortable cleavage in the
tree forms at a point coincidental with
the highest mountain peak and the edge
of the rocky shore.

20
MOUNTAIN LAKE WITH A BOAT,
NO. 2, Switzerland   1929
Graphite on paper, 6 2/5 x 7 1/5 in.
(16.5 x 18.4 cm)
Collection of Dr. and Mrs. Paul Alpers

This sketch is very similar to No. 17.
Made from the same vantage point, but
executed with greater assurance and
contrast, its stylized Art Deco manner
does not detract from its sense of reality
and immediacy.

21
MOUNTAIN LAKE, Switzerland   1929
Graphite on bond paper, 8 1/2 x 11 in.
(21.9 x 28.3 cm)
Collection of Sue Ann Kahn

This drawing is by far one of the most
abstract of this series. It relies on a
graphite technique for its departure
from objective representation. For the
first time the sky becomes an important
compositional element, treated with
cloud patterns that both complement
the drama of the hills and provide a
reaffirmation of the mountain forms as a
counterthrust.

22
RIVER, Switzerland   1929
Graphite on paper, size not available
Present whereabouts unknown

23
CAPRI, Italy   1929
Graphite on paper, 11 x 8 2/5 in. (28.3 x
21.6 cm); image: 6 9/10 x 7 4/5 in
(17.8 x 20.0 cm)
Inscribed in lower right: *Capri 2/7/29*
Shown at a traveling exhibition
organized by the Pennsylvania Academy
of the Fine Arts, 1978–1979,
Catalogue No. 14
Collection of Sue Ann Kahn

This drawing, made with energetic surety
of hand, capitalizes on minimal yet
broad strokes to achieve a remarkable
portrayal of a mountain landscape. In
contrast to No. 17, the center of the
scene receives the darkest value without
sacrificing the illusion of depth.

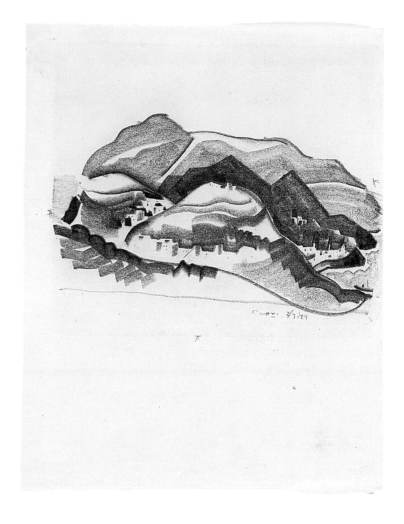

24
TREES AND HILL/WALL GATE,
Ravello, Italy   1929
Graphite on paper, 10 9/10 x 8 2/5 in.
(27.9 x 21.6 cm)
Collection of Sue Ann Kahn

25

GABLED MANOR, England 1928
Charcoal and white pastel on buff paper,
15 x 14 in. (38.7 x 53.3 cm); image:
15 x 20 4/5 in. (38.7 x 35.9 cm)
Collection of Sue Ann Kahn

In a series of seven sketches, beginning
with this one and ending with No. 31,
trees are the primary subjects. In this
drawing the trees are handled as a screen
through which Kahn suggests the facade
of a gabled building. Yet the trees
themselves become the dominant
element of interest. They act in unison
and it is difficult to distinguish individual
trees since the crowns merge into a
combined canopy.

The technique employed in this drawing
forms a bridge between Kahn's sketching
before the European trip and the assured
strokes of graphite he employed during
the second year of his travels, as seen in
sketches Nos. 24 and 28–30.

26

IN THE BORGHESE GARDENS,
Rome, Italy 1928–29
Watercolor on paper, 12 1/10 x 15 in.
(31.1 x 38.4 cm)
Collection of Sue Ann Kahn

This unfinished painting captures the
dignity of cedars as vertical forms which
frame and define the space in the near
and middle foreground. It has a strong
architectural quality and the trees may
as well be buildings around a public
piazza. It is interesting that Kahn worked
from the top down and abandoned the
painting once he had finished the trees.
Also remarkable is Kahn's avoidance
of color contrasts: it is an almost
monochromatic rendition, indicative
of Kahn's comfort in presenting forms
using only light and shade.

27
BORGHESE GARDENS, Rome,
Italy 1929
Watercolor on paper, 15 1/10 x
10 9/10 in. (36.2 x 27.9 cm)
Inscribed on back of original mat:
*Borghese Gardens Louis I. Kahn 5234
Chester Ave.*
Shown at a traveling exhibition

organized by the Pennsylvania Academy
of the Fine Arts, 1978–1979,
Catalogue No. 13
Collection of Sue Ann Kahn

In a translation of graphite technique into
watercolor, Kahn retains an Art Deco
touch but loses the clarity of the

repetitive stylized gradations of the
black-and-white medium. However, the
muted colors and his growing skill
allowed Kahn to overcome this
deficiency. The quick nature of
watercolors was perfectly suited to his
desire to capture the essence of a scene
with a minimum of effort.

28
TREES STUDY, NO. 1, Italy 1928–29
Graphite on paper 17 7/10 x 11 9/10 in.
(45.4 x 30.5 cm)
Collection of Sue Ann Kahn

In contrast to study No. 25, this sketch
suggests the nobility and grandeur of tall
cypresses with their well-shaped crowns.
There are three groupings in which
overlapping and a vertical reduction
in scale establish an interesting exercise
in perspective. Kahn eliminates the
foreground altogether and uses patches
of the sky as the clue to depth
perception.

29
TREES STUDY, NO. 2,
Borghese Gardens, Rome, Italy 1929
Graphite on paper,
17 3/5 x 11 3/5 in. (45.1 x 29.8 cm)
Shown at a traveling exhibition
organized by the Pennsylvania Academy
of the Fine Arts, 1978–1979,
Catalogue No. 11
Collection of Sue Ann Kahn

30
TREES STUDY, NO. 3,
Borghese Gardens, Rome, Italy   1929
Graphite on paper, 15 3/5 x 11 1/10 in.
(40.0 x 28.6 cm)
Exhibited at the 27th Annual
Philadelphia Watercolor Exhibition,
Pennsylvania Academy of the Fine Arts,
1929, Catalogue No. 223. Shown at a

traveling exhibition organized by the
Pennsylvania Academy of the Fine Arts,
1978–1979, Catalogue No. 12, titled:
*Study of a Tree, Borghese Gardens,
Rome, 1929*
Collection of Sue Ann Kahn

The twisted tree in this sketch and in

No. 29 show Kahn's fascination with
organic forms. He was exploring the
structures underlying the tree's gnarled
configurations. Compositionally, the trees
provided an opportunity to create
imagery that expressed his romantic and
analytic views of nature.

31
ITALIAN LANDSCAPE, Italy   1929
Watercolor on paper, 11 3/4 x 14 1.3 in.
(30.1 x 36.8 cm)
Signed lower right: *Louis I. Kahn '28*
Shown at a traveling exhibition
organized by the Pennsylvania Academy
of the Fine Arts, 1978–1979, Catalogue
No.6, titled: *Europe, 1928–29*
Collection of Dr. and Mrs. David Fleischer

In this watercolor Kahn repeats his
manner of representing the sky, trees,
and ground used in *Borghese Gardens*
(No. 27). Likewise, the colors are muted
and confined to a narrow range. There
are considerable hints of the influence of
Art Deco artists like William H. Bradley
and Maxfield Parrish, but it is more
deeply related to the work of Georgia
O'Keeffe and even Franz Marc, without
the daring colors. Although he did not
like to attend art shows, Kahn was aware
of the art scene on both sides of the
Atlantic through his collection of art
reproductions cut from magazines.

32
PERGOLA, Italy   1928–29
Watercolor on paper, 10 9/10 x 15 in.
(27.9 x 38.7 cm)
Collection of Sue Ann Kahn

This pleasant vignette captures the
contrast of twisting vines against the soft
forms of village architecture and the
rolling hills beyond. What appears to be
a human form is left unfinished and
stands in a strange, ghostlike relation to
the scene.

33
PONTE VECCHIO, Florence, Italy   1929
Graphite on paper, 15 3/5 x 22 9/10 in.
(40.0 x 58.7 cm)
Shown at a traveling exhibition
organized by the Pennsylvania Academy
of the Fine Arts, 1978–1979,
Catalogue No. 8
Collection of Sue Ann Kahn

This is one of four sketches dealing with
the subject of bridges (Nos. 33–36). An
opportunity to sketch strong architectural
forms in this famous setting gave Kahn
tremendous inspiration. This sketch
conveys the charm and complexity of the
ensemble through the deliberate graphic
integration of the bridge with the
buildings that it joins on the banks of the
Arno. Kahn concentrates his attention on
the bridge through the suggestive
dissolution of details in the background
and the subtle indication of water.

34
PONTE SCALIGERO, NO. 1,
Verona, Italy   1929
Graphite, charcoal, and white chalk
on paper, 11 1/10 x 15 1/3 in.
(28.6 x 39.4 cm)
Shown at a traveling exhibition
organized by the Pennsylvania Academy
of the Fine Arts, 1978–1979, Catalogue
No. 25, titled: *Italy, 1929*
Collection of Sue Ann Kahn

Kahn achieves a very dramatic and
moody handling of the bridge here
through the use of strong form contrasts
and a heavy, cloud-laden sky. The
lightness of the water beyond the arches
of the bridge and the light sky at the
horizon give added energy to the scene.
This view of the bridge is made from a
point which suggests some elevation
above the middle of the river, a rather
interesting choice of views that
eliminates the meeting of the bridge with
either shoreline. Kahn's mixed use of
black and white served him well in his
effort to portray the tension between
nature and the city.

35
PONTE SCALIGERO, NO. 2,
Verona, Italy   1929
Watercolor on paper, 12 1/3 x 12 1/3 in.
(31.7 x 31.7 cm)
Collection of Sue Ann Kahn

This watercolor appears overworked. It lacks the qualities associated with Kahn's use of this medium. While the sketch may convey the general character of the scene, as a composition it lacks refinement. Forms are truncated by the picture's edges at uncomfortable points and the work loses the potential for drama toward which Kahn was obviously striving. When reviewing this painting, Kahn himself called it immature.

36
VIEW WITH THE BRIDGE,
Verona, Italy   1929
Watercolor on paper, 4 7/10 x 8 1/3 in.
(12.1 x 21.3 cm)
Collection of Sue Ann Kahn

In contrast to No. 34, this color sketch presents a complete change of mood as well as choice of view. The scene, an impressionistic rendering in the manner of Cézanne, depicts Verona after a shower, where a low afternoon sun is washing facades of buildings on the river with a warm yellow light. The bridge is almost lost in the overall scene and it is relegated to a minor supporting role. The looseness with which Kahn handled this watercolor sketch, in contrast to No. 35, suggests a liberation in which he achieves a technical ease comparable to his use of graphite.

37
CONVENT OF ST. FRANCIS,
Assisi, Italy   1929
Colored pencils and pastel on brown
paper, 10 x 14 in. (25.7 x 35.9 cm)
Shown at a traveling exhibition
organized by the Pennsylvania Academy
of the Fine Arts, 1978–1979,
Catalogue No. 16
Collection of Sue Ann Kahn

With a rare application of colored
pencils and pastels, Kahn captures the
broad sweep of the monastery and the
surrounding countryside. This sketch may
have been left unfinished when Kahn
realized that elaboration on the
foreground would detract from the
overall effect. It is also interesting that, as
in No. 26, he apparently worked from
the top down, judiciously leaving certain
areas incomplete. The success of the
sketch is due not only to Kahn's extraordinary ability to draw but also to his
sound judgement of knowing what to
leave out.

38
BAY HOUSES, Amalfi Coast,
Italy   1928–29
Watercolor on paper, image: 14 3/5 x
10 3/5 in. (37.5 x 27.3 cm)
Collection of Mrs. Esther I. Kahn

In a mode similar to his graphite
sketches, Kahn produces here crisp
repetitive forms resulting in a moving,
dramatic composition. In this painting he
also manages to be more daring in his
use of color. With this spectacular scene
Kahn captured the close relationship of
the coast's vernacular architecture to its
natural setting. The houses appear to be
organically integrated into their natural
environment.

39
CAESAR'S TOWER, WARWICK CASTLE,
England   1928
Pencil on paper, 20 3/4 x 15 in.
(53.3 x 38.4 cm)
Shown at a traveling exhibition
organized by the Pennsylvania Academy
of the Fine Arts, 1978–1979,
Catalogue No. 4
Collection of Sue Ann Kahn

Kahn's lifelong fascination with the tower
form is demonstrated in this early sketch
in which he dramatizes the majesty of
the castle through exaggerated
perspective and by thrusting the tower
against a blank sky. The trees in the
foreground soften the stark forms of the
castle and establish a strong sense of
space that follows the moat away from

the picture plane. This drawing's style
and careful execution raise the possibility
that it might have been made by Kahn in
Philadelphia before his European trip.
He occasionally made drawings based
on postcards and photographs whenever
the subject attracted his interest.

64

40

VIADUCT, Amalfi Coast, Italy   1929
Pencil on paper, size not available
Present whereabouts unknown

It is revealing that the choice of the view in this sketch is characteristic of an artist with architectural training. The dramatic perspective, showing certain similarities to renderings by Frank Lloyd Wright, compresses the arches of the viaduct into mere vertical lines, thus echoing the distant tower. With only a few simple lines Kahn manages to hint at the deep drop of the ravine in the foreground and to produce a scene of sublime power.

41
GOTHIC COURTYARD, England   1928
Watercolor, pen, and ink on brown
paper, 17 9/10 x 11 3/4 in.
(45.8 x 30.2 cm)
Shown at a traveling exhibition
organized by the Pennsylvania Academy
of the Fine Arts, 1978–1979, Catalogue
No. 28, titled: *Europe, 1928*
Collection of Dr. Marshall Alan Kahn

This is one of the earliest attempts by
Kahn to use color. The Beaux-Arts
schooling which Kahn received did not
stress color as an essential mode of
artistic expression. That, of course, is
evident in this somewhat immature effort
to overlay with watercolor an otherwise
excellent pen-and-ink drawing. The
addition of white highlights further
diminishes the quality of this work.
Nevertheless, Kahn manages to create a
very lovely scene which has all the
characteristics of a fairy-tale illustration.
His knowledge and love of architecture
come through very clearly here,
especially in the manner in which the
forms are detailed and the way the space
comes alive.

42
TOWN WALLS,
Amalfi Coast, Italy   1929
Watercolor on paper, 12 x 9 in.
(30.8 x 23.2 cm)
Shown at a traveling exhibition
organized by the Pennsylvania Academy
of the Fine Arts, 1978–1979, Catalogue
No. 21, titled: *Amalfi Coast, Italy, 1929*
Collection of Sue Ann Kahn

The town in this view appears to be the
same as in No. 40, but viewed from a
slightly different angle. In abstracting
the scene through the dynamic repetition
of curved natural forms and contrasting
them against the angular shapes of
the town and its walls, Kahn produces
a highly charged dramatic effect. Again,
as in previous watercolors, the hues
are subdued, bordering on the
monochromatic.

43
TOWER, Positano, Italy   1929
Watercolor on paper, 14 1/3 x 10 3/5 in.
(36.8 x 27.3 cm)
Shown at a traveling exhibition
organized by the Pennsylvania Academy
of the Fine Arts, 1978–1979, Catalogue
No. 18, titled: *Positano, Italy, 1929*
Collection of Sue Ann Kahn

As in several of his sketches and
paintings from this trip, Kahn chooses to
leave portions of the picture unfinished.
He pays close attention to the details of
the tower and a palm in the left
foreground, and contrasts these with
abstract renditions of the cypresses and
distant hills. In his use of color, Kahn
employs a mix of yellow with
complementary purples, a color scheme
popular at that time. Here the colors are
especially effective in achieving a
distinctive sense of space.

44
CLIFF ROAD, Capri, Italy   1928–29
Graphite on paper, 11 x 8 2/5 in.
(28.3 x 21.6 cm)
Collection of Sue Ann Kahn

This sketch was published originally in
Kahn's article "The Value and Aim in
Sketching" in the *T-Square Club Journal*
(May 1931). The article also contained
reproductions of Nos. 56, 59, 69, and
307.

The weaving diagonal curve of the road,
appearing and disappearing among sheer
cliffs, results in a sense of rhythm which
Kahn utilized in a number of sketches
from his Italian travels. The soft
modeling of natural forms complements
the curves of the road and hills, thus
reinforcing the impression of movement.

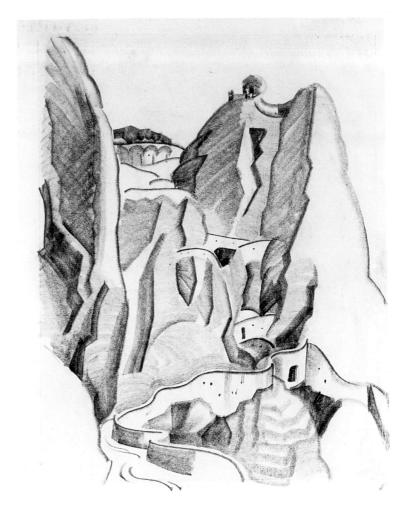

45
HILL ROAD, Capri, Italy   1928–29
Graphite on paper, size not available
Present whereabouts unknown

Though similar to No. 44, this sketch
dissolves into an abstraction in which
elements that suggested depth have
become flat and give the entire composition a two-dimensional character. Spiral
lines originating from the left are reinforced by rhythmic repetitions and
produce a swirling motion, even though
there is an attempt at balance through the
introduction of reverse curves. Kahn's
handling of repetitive zigzags and curves
with graduated shading suggests his
continuing fascination with that period's
popular Art Deco illustrations.

46
ROCKY COAST, Amalfi Coast,
Italy   1928–29
Graphite on paper 11 x 8 1/2 in.
(28.3 x 21.9 cm)
Collection of Sue Ann Kahn

This sketch resulted in an almost total

abstraction. The elements of the
composition are stylized, although they
combine to create a work of non-
objective expression. Only vague hints
designate the rocks and water, for
instance.

47
TOWN FORTIFICATIONS, Italy   1929
Watercolor on paper, 10 9/10 x
13 1/10 in. (27.9 x 33.6 cm)
Collection of Sue Ann Kahn

48
CLIFF FORTIFICATIONS,
Amalfi Coast, Italy   1929
Watercolor on paper, 7 9/10 x 9 9/10 in.
(20.3 X 25.3 cm)
Collection of Sue Ann Kahn

In this difficult composition a diagonal line extending from the upper left of the picture to the lower right divides the scene into neat halves. The left half is occupied by walls, cliffs, and the sea, and the right half by the sky. Kahn skillfully articulates the sky with clouds to achieve a comfortable balance. In representing the natural and man-made forms, he no longer contrasts them. In fact, they are treated in an identical manner, creating a perfect harmony between them.

49
COASTAL TOWN,
Amalfi Coast, Italy   1929
Watercolor on paper, image: 10 2/5 x
14 1/2 in. (26.7 x 37.1 cm)
Collection of Mrs. Esther I. Kahn

In a variation on the composition in
No. 48, Kahn here counteracts the strong
upper-left to bottom-right diagonal with
one rising from the bottom left. This
creates a triangle, a wedge, separating
the mountains from the sea. Deep
shadows delineating the town's towers
against the mountain backdrop provide
an added focal point at the end of the
wedge.

50
MOUNTAIN VILLAGE, NO. 1,
Amalfi Coast, Italy
Exact date unkown (c. 1930s)
Lithograph, 10 2/5 x 8 9/10 in. (26.7 x
22.9 cm); image: 9 x 7 in.
(23.2 x 18.1 cm)
Present whereabouts unknown

This lithograph and No. 51 constitute
Kahn's effort at creating from field
sketches or from memory compositions
with the qualities of fairy-tale illustrations.
While utilizing the medium of lithography,
which distinctly changed the character of
his graphite sketches, the composition
and the spectacular setting which
inspired these works closely resemble the
other sketches from Italy.

51
MOUNTAIN VILLAGE, NO. 2,
Amalfi Coast, Italy   1928–29
Lithograph, 11 1/4 x 9 3/5 in. (28.9 x
24.7 cm); image: 9 x 7 in.
(23.2 x 18.1 cm)
Signed lower right: *Louis I. Kahn*
Collection of Sue Ann Kahn

This lithograph, made with greater
freedom than No. 50, is almost a mirror
image of it. Also, the character of Kahn's
graphite sketches is better represented
here, even though most of the shading is
achieved with looped linework.

52
VIEW OF TOWN, NO. 1,
Positano, Italy   1929
Graphite on paper, size not available
Present whereabouts unknown

Kahn achieved this dramatic aerial view
of the town and the nestling mountains
through an efficient use of graphite stick.
The entire rendition is created by the use
of the flat sides of the graphite. The
resulting sharp definitions of forms give
them a three-dimensional reality very
difficult to attain with ordinary linework.

53
VIEW OF TOWN, NO. 2, Positano,
 Italy   1929
Watercolor on paper 10 2/5 x 8 3/4 in.
(26.7 x 22.5 cm)
Collection of Sue Ann Kahn

More than in others, this stylized
composition shows the influence of Art

Deco on Kahn. The crystalline rendition
of forms is also similar to those in the
paintings of André Derain and, as in No.
38, Kahn's brushwork retains chisel-like
clarity. The zigzag forms of the
mountains transform themselves into
curves which embrace the fragmented
building forms cascading from the hill.

The arrangement follows a reverse
figure-S which widens in its descent
toward the bottom of the picture where it
is rounded off and becomes contained.
The focal point of the picture, the church
tower, is contained in a dark, halo like
mountain form. The muted colors add to
the integrity of the abstraction.

54
TOWN HOUSES, Capri, Italy   1929
Watercolor on paper, size not available
Present whereabouts unknown

While retaining some of the crispness of the other sketches in this series, Kahn leaves the foreground and background in a state of fuzzy suggestion. This results in a picture in which forms are flattened and are of interest as abstract patterns.

55
FISHERMAN'S HUT, Amalfi Coast, Italy   1929
Graphite on paper, 11 x 8 in. (28.3 x 20.6 cm); image: 10 1/10 x 7 1/2 in. (26.0 x 19.4 cm)
Signed lower right: *Louis I. Kahn*
Exhibited at the 27th Annual Philadelphia Watercolor Exhibition, Pennsylvania Academy of the Fine Arts, 1929, Catalogue No. 251. Shown at a traveling exhibition organized by the Pennsylvania Academy of the Fine Arts, 1978–1979, Catalogue No. 22, titled: *Fishing Village, Amalfi Coast, Italy, 1929*
Collection of Sue Ann Kahn

In this quaint scene of a house almost appearing to be carved out of the sheer cliffs, Kahn reveals his greater interest in the building than in its setting. The rocky background is abstracted excessively in comparison with the rest of the picture.

56
STEPPED STREET, Positano,
Italy 1928–29
Graphite on bond paper, 10 9/10 x
8 1/2 in. (27.9 x 21.9 cm); image:
7 9/10 x 4 2/5 in. (20.3 x 11.4 cm)
Collection of Sue Ann Kahn

This is one of four drawings (Nos. 56–59)
in which Kahn explored scenes of
narrow, winding, and sloping streets.
The distant view of Positano in No. 53 is
replaced in this sketch with a close-up of
the inside of the town. It is remarkable
how skillfully Kahn managed to convey
the essence of this street scene by using
only a few broad strokes of his graphite
stick. The climber in the center of the
picture anchors the composition in
which the curves of the street and the
rooflines of the houses converge.

57
STEPPED STREET WITH A CHURCH,
Positano, Italy   1929
Graphite on paper, 10 3/4 x 7 2/5 in.
(27.6 x 19.0 cm); image: 8 3/4 x 5 in.
(22.5 x 13.0 cm)
Signed lower right: *Louis I. Kahn*
Inscribed lower right: *Positano*
Shown at a traveling exhibition
organized by the Pennsylvania Academy
of the Fine Arts, 1978–1979, Catalogue
No. 19, titled: *Positano, Italy, 1929*
Collection of Sue Ann Kahn

Again the tower form, which appears so
frequently in Kahn's work, assumes great
prominence. This is indicative of the
great fascination he had for their forms
and the compositional opportunities they
offered. In this sketch, as in No. 71,
Kahn captures the nature of the street
with a minimum of effort. The rooflines
of houses in the middle-ground provide a
sharp ending to the bottom half of the
picture. Above them rises the church
tower with a totally dissolved connection
to the street. This bright void, contrasted
against the dark edges of houses,
produces an excellent illusion of depth.
The human figure in the center was most
likely left unfinished once Kahn realized
its superfluousness to the composition.

58
HILLY STREET, Italy   1928–29
Graphite on paper, size not available
Present whereabouts unknown

In a slight variation on No. 57, and with
a judicious use of middle-ground
shadows, Kahn dramatically frames the
building in the background. Kahn's
sensitivity to forms and space, as well as
his awareness of the power of light,
reveals itself in this remarkably
expressive sketch.

59
HILL TOWN HOUSES, Italy   1928–29
Graphite on paper, size not available
Present whereabouts unknown

This powerful rendition of vernacular
forms predates Kahn's captivation with
industrial scenes during the 1930s (see
Nos. 260 and 261). There is a strong
foreshadowing of Kahn's interest and
enjoyment in modeling massive
cylindrical and prismatic forms and
placing them in dramatic light settings.

60
FISHERMAN'S HUTS, NO. 1,
Amalfi Coast, Italy   1929
Watercolor on paper, 6 1/2 x 9 9/10 in.
(16.8 x 25.4 cm)
Private collection

This picture is a more general view of
the fisherman's house in No. 55. With
sharp, precise, and broad brush strokes
Kahn dramatized the beautiful
relationship of the houses to their
shelflike existence between the cliffs
behind them and the beach and sea in
front. The sea is not visible and Kahn
supplies the clue to its presence by
placing beached boats in the foreground.
Strong, dark, and crisp shadows on the
cliffs contrast dramatically with the soft,
calm, and sun-drenched sand of the
beach.

61
FISHERMAN'S HUTS, NO. 2,
Amalfi Coast, Italy   1929–30
Oil on canvas, 23 3/4 x 29 7/10 in.
(60.9 x 76.2 cm)
Signed lower right: *Louis I. Kahn*
Inscribed on the back: *"Fisherman's
Huts" Amalfi #1027 PAFA oil, received
January 6, 1931*
Collection of Mrs. Esther I. Kahn

This oil painting, made by Kahn upon his
return from Europe, is based on graphite
sketches and watercolor No. 60. It was
most likely exhibited at the 29th Annual
Philadelphia Watercolor Exhibition of
1931, as Catalogue No. 1027. The low
catalogue number would suggest that this
painting was originally submitted for an
exhibition in 1929 and resubmitted with
the old PAFA number in 1931.

In using oil as his medium, Kahn lost the
spontaneity of both the graphite stick and
watercolors. The painting looks like a
stage set illuminated by spotlights. The
excessive contrasts of highlights, shades,
and shadows reveal Kahn's difficulty in
working in this medium.

62
HARBOR HOUSES, NO. 1,
Capri, Italy   1929
Watercolor on paper, size not available
Present whereabouts unknown

In a setting and a manner similar to that
shown in No. 60, Kahn wields his brush
as if it were a sculptor's chisel. Building
forms have the crystalline character of
tooled rock, softened only by the round
arches and curves of the background
hills. The blending of all compositional
elements is achieved again by an almost
monochromatic scheme, characteristic of
a number of watercolors in this series
from the coastal regions of Italy.

63
STREET, Positano, Italy   1928–29
Watercolor on paper, 15 x 10 9/10 in.
(38.4 x 27.9 cm)
Collection of Sue Ann Kahn

In Kahn's translation of graphite
techniques into watercolor, the great
sense of depth present in the black-and-
white sketches gives way to two-
dimensional abstract patterns. Working
with only a limited palette, Kahn's slight
variations of hues reinforce the sense of
abstraction. As in his graphite sketches,
Kahn employed in this painting the plain,
wide surfaces and simple geometries of
houses to contrast them with the sinuous
forms of clouds, the street, and the bare
tree in the foreground. In a manner
similar to Nos. 32 and 57, an unfinished
human figure makes an appearance and
helps to suggest scale.

64
RUSTIC HOUSE, Ravello, Italy   1929
Graphite on brown paper, 8 9/10 x
11 3/4 in. (22.9 x 30.2 cm)
Exhibited at the 27th Annual
Philadelphia Watercolor Exhibition,
Pennsylvania Academy of the Fine Arts,
1929, Catalogue No. 269
Collection of Sue Ann Kahn

In this work it is easy to note how closely
Kahn managed to bring his watercolor
brushwork to the level of his graphite
sketching technique. A comparison of
this drawing with watercolor No. 38
shows strong similarities in the isolation
of planes, shades, and shadows from
each other by white outlines. The
resulting crystalline purity is reminiscent
of Cézanne's fragmentations. In this
drawing, Kahn again abstracts the natural
forms of the mountains and trees in order
to extend more attention to the street and
distant houses.

65
TUDOR HOUSE, London,
England 1928
Pencil and black crayon on paper,
22 1/10 x 15 in. (56.8 x 38.7 cm)
Shown at a traveling exhibition
organized by the Pennsylvania Academy
of the Fine Arts, 1978–1979,
Catalogue No. 5
Collection of Sue Ann Kahn

In this exquisite drawing Kahn reveals
himself as a first-rate draftsman capable
of rendering forms through the
manipulation of light and shade
contrasts. With a subtle hand he
manages to reveal the most minute
details without sacrificing attention to the
overall composition. This drawing
relates closely to Kahn's pencil work
from his pre-European trip period. The
only connection of this new expressive
tendency to past techniques is his
handling of the sky with Art Deco-like
clouds.

66

STREET AT DUSK, Milan, Italy   1929
Watercolor, gouache, charcoal, and
crayon on blue paper, 13 9/10 x
10 1/10 in. (35.6 x 26.0 cm)
Shown at a traveling exhibition
organized by the Pennsylvania Academy
of the Fine Arts, 1978–1979, Catalogue
No. 29, titled: *Europe, 1929*
Collection of Sue Ann Kahn

In a marked departure from his usual
style, Kahn borrows heavily from
impressionist painters like Pissaro,
Renoir, and Childe Hassam to capture
the very essence of a busy street. Taking
an impressionist point of view high
above the street, he immerses the scene
in the soft glow of dusk with artificial
illumination competing with the pale

orange glow of the western sky. Flecks
of color and suggestive dark dashes
create the illusion of buildings, vehicles,
and people. The silhouetted towers of
Milan's cathedral form a transition
between the opposing rooflines of the
street.

67
SAN AMBROGIO, Milan, Italy   1929
Pencil on paper, 20 3/4 x 15 in.
(53.3 x 38.4 cm)
Shown at a traveling exhibition
organized by the Pennsylvania Academy
of the Fine Arts, 1978–1979,
Catalogue No. 7
Collection of Sue Ann Kahn

This and ten other sketches (Nos. 68–74

and 93–95) deal with the subject of
ecclesiastical and secular towers. As
previously mentioned, towers fascinated
Kahn and in this series of sketches he
explored the potential for drama inherent
in vertical masses reaching upwards from
their predominantly urban settings.

In this drawing Kahn presented this
famous site in the manner of an

eighteenth-century romantic engraving.
His preference for dramatic views suffers
in this rendition by making it too
contrived. Even the placement and
postures of human figures betray this
tendency. The pencil technique Kahn
employs here results in an overworked
drawing which suffers from the lack of
spontaneity present in his graphite
sketches.

68
STREET SCENE, Assisi, Italy   1928–29
Graphite on paper, size not available
Present whereabouts unknown

This is one of many streetscapes of Italian towns which Kahn captures in a dramatic light and shade orchestration. The light-to-dark-to-light sequence provides an exciting sense of depth and leads the eye toward the top of the distant tower. The confidence with which Kahn wields the graphite stick is in great contrast to the tentative handling of pencil in his San Ambrogio drawing (No. 67).

69
DUOMO, Assisi, Italy   1929
Graphite on ivory paper, 10 9/10 x
8 7/10 in. (27.9 x 22.2 cm)
Exhibited at the 27th Annual
Philadelphia Watercolor Exhibition,
Pennsylvania Academy of the Fine Arts,
1929, Catalogue No. 222. Shown at a
traveling exhibition organized by the

Pennsylvania Academy of the Fine Arts,
1978–1979, Catalogue No.17, titled:
Assisi, Italy, 1929
Collection of the Pennsylvania Academy
of the Fine Arts, Acc. No. 1978.2; Gift of
Mrs. Louis I. Kahn

Kahn concentrates in this sketch on the

juxtaposition of masses with only a hint
of details created by his expert handling
of graphite. In contrast to No. 67, the
viewer's participation is assured by the
elimination of all but the scene's most
essential elements.

70
CONVENT OF ST. FRANCIS, Assisi,
Italy   1929
Graphite on paper, 13 3/4 x 14 2/5 in.
(35.3 x 37.0 cm)
Signed lower right: *Louis I. Kahn*
Shown at a traveling exhibition
organized by the Pennsylvania Academy
of the Fine Arts, 1978–1979,
Catalogue No. 15
Collection of the Deutsches
Architekturmuseum, Frankfurt am Main,
Germany, Catalogue No. 276

Kahn obviously devoted more time to
this drawing than to some others in this
series. There is a much greater attention
to detail and the overall composition is
carefully constructed. However, the
modeling of forms is not as pronounced
as in No. 69, and the illusion of depth is
achieved mainly through convergent
perspective lines. The approaching

figure on the bicycle creates a reversal of
the direction of interest. The tower, its
peak truncated by the top edge of the
paper, is prominent in its location while
relegated to a lesser role than the church
and the arcade in the foreground.

71
STREET SCENE WITH A CHURCH
TOWER, Italy   1928–29
Graphite on paper, size not available
Present whereabouts unknown

This moody scene recalls some of the
works of Charles Burchfield. The sketch
has Gothic qualities which are present in
few other works (see No. 85). It is in great
contrast to the sunny treatment Kahn

imparted to most of his Italian landscapes
and street scenes. The faint image of the
church tower in the upper left appears to
symbolize purity and hope in opposition
to the gloomy foreground.

72
TOWN WITH A CASTLE, Italy
1928–29
Graphite on paper 10 9/10 x 8 3/5 in.
(27.9 x 22.2 cm)
Right bottom corner missing
Collection of Sue Ann Kahn

It was unusual for Kahn to treat skies as dark planes against which to silhouette illuminated building forms. However, in this drawing and in No. 65 he felt it necessary in order to dramatize the details and balance the composition.

The dark shadow at the bottom is thus made less obtrusive; it emphasizes the massive darkness of the sky and echoes in negative the lightness of the castle.

73
"CHIESA IN ROVINA," Rovina, Italy
1928–29
Graphite on brown paper,
8 9/10 x 11 3/4 in. (22.9 x 30.2 cm)
Inscribed on the back: *Chiesa in Rovina*
Collection of Sue Ann Kahn

Kahn's drawings of building parts and
ornamental details exhibit the same rapid
recording techniques he used with
subjects larger in scale. The graphite-
stick modeling technique served him
very well for imparting a three-
dimensional quality to complex
juxtapositions of forms. But by no
means was it an easy task. It took the
extraordinary skill that Kahn possessed to
impart shades and shadows in such a
way as to make forms spring to life. In
this sketch of the old church and the
adjoining vaulted roof forms, Kahn
captures the time- and weather-worn
softness of the masonry and the distant
mountain.

74
SAN TEODORO, Pavia, Italy   1928–29
Graphite on paper, 11 x 8 3/4 in.
(28.3 x 22.5 cm)
Inscribed bottom right: *St. Theodoric,*
Pavia

Collection of Sue Ann Kahn

Kahn retains the essence of this
Romanesque brick telescoping tower
through suggestive graphite strokes. He

judiciously dissolves the tower's
supporting base in order to focus
attention on the lantern.

75
PORTICO, SAN ZENO MAGGIORE,
Verona, Italy   1929
Graphite on bond paper, 10 1/2 x
7 3/5 in. (27.0 x 19.7 cm)
Signed lower right: *LIK*
Shown at a traveling exhibition
organized by the Pennsylvania Academy

of the Fine Arts, 1978–1979, Catalogue
No. 26, titled: *Portico Facade, Italy, 1929*
Collection of Sue Ann Kahn

Through the clever manipulation of his
graphite stick, Kahn managed in this
sketch to capture the intricacy of

architectural details without actually
analyzing them and representing
their true nature. The result is an
impressionistic rendition of a complex
subject that retains a strong textural
character.

76
DETAIL, SAN ZENO MAGGIORE,
Verona, Italy   1928–29
Graphite on paper, size not available
Inscribed lower right: *San. Zeno, Verona*
Present whereabouts unknown

In contrast to No. 75, Kahn treats
architectural details at a closer range
and, because of their scale, gives greater
attention to their forms. However, it is
still not an elaborate study but a
suggestive interpretation with concern for
textural rather than formal qualities.

77
COLUMN DETAIL, Milan, Italy
1928–29
Graphite on paper, 11 1/10 x 8 7/10 in.
(28.5 x 22.5 cm)
Inscribed lower right: *Milano*
Collection of the Architectural Archives,
University of Pennsylvania, Catalogue
No. 945.2, titled: *Travel Sketch, Column,
Milan, Italy*; Gift of Richard Saul Wurman

78
CHURCH INTERIOR, Italy   1928–29
Graphite on paper, size not available
Present whereabouts unknown ·

The chiseled strokes of graphite provide
an excellent means of catching all the
nuances of light as it plays in the
complex forms of this interior. Of special
note is the underlighting of the underside
of the arches and the trefoil opening
above the twisted column.

79

STATUES IN THE PIAZZA DELLA
SIGNORIA, Florence, Italy   1928–29
Graphite on bond paper, 10 9/10 x
8 3/5 in. (28.2 x 22.2 cm)
Inscribed lower right: *Firenze*
Collection of Sue Ann Kahn

This sketch is similar to No. 104 in that
the statue, as a center of attention, is
performing the admirable task of
providing a sense of space in the piazza.
Neither the statue nor the palace is given
enough detail to attract too much
attention. It is the void which Kahn
animates with wavy lines and ghostlike
figures.

80

THE BLUE HALL, STOCKHOLM'S CITY
HALL, Stockholm, Sweden   1928–30
Crayon on paper, size not available
Signed lower right: *Louis I. Kahn*
Present whereabouts unknown

Toward the end of his life, Kahn
paraphrased American poet Wallace
Stevens: "What slice of sun enters your
room. What range of mood does the light
offer from morning to night, from day to
day, from season to season and all
through the years."[1] This concept is
beautifully illustrated in this sketch. The
gentle streaks of sunlight make the reality
of the space come alive. The presence of
atmosphere is felt very clearly and it
dominates the details of the surrounding
surfaces. Kahn most probably made this
drawing from a photograph. Strangely,
the view is almost identical to a
photograph of this room in Steen Eiler
Rasmussens's *Experiencing Architecture*,
(Cambridge: MIT Press, 1959), page 195
in a chapter entitled "Daylight in
Architecture."

1. "Louis I. Kahn: Silence and Light,"
Architecture and Urbanism 3 (January
1973), 7.

81
INTERIOR OF PALAZZO BARGELLO,
Florence, Italy   1929
Graphite on paper, 12 1/3 x 8 3/5 in.
(31.7 x 22.2 cm.); image: 9 3/5 x
8 3/5 in. (24.8 x 22.2 cm.)
Shown at a traveling exhibition
organized by the Pennsylvania Academy
of the Fine Arts, 1978–1979, Catalogue
No. 9, titled: *Interior, Bargello,
Florence, 1929*
Collection of Sue Ann Kahn

In this drawing Kahn achieved so much
with so little. There is a complete sense
of the interior with all its textures, forms,
and details, and yet there are only broad
strokes of graphite with occasional
squiggles that produce this sensation.
Light, the revealer of form, became the
foundation not only of Kahn's artistic
prowess but of his architectural
philosophy.

82
COURTYARD WITH POTS, Italy
1928–29
Graphite on paper, 5 3/5 x 6 1/5 in.
(14.6 x 15.9 cm)
Collection of Sue Ann Kahn

When drawing interiors one encounters
problems considerably different than
those found outdoors. The source of
light is often multi-directional and the
effect of reflections and secondary
shadows makes the task of capturing
them very difficult. In a series of interior
sketches (Nos. 80–85), Kahn not only
displays no difficulties, but on the
contrary derives a source of strength from
the illumination's uniqueness. This
drawing demonstrates how skillfully he
handles a very difficult scene full of
scattered elements. It is a suggestive
rendition of lights and shadows, filling
the interior with mystery and charm.

83
ROMANESQUE FOYER, Italy   1928–29
Pencil, graphite, and ink on paper,
12 1/10 x 8 3/5 in. (31.1 x 22.2 cm)
Collection of Sue Ann Kahn

In comparison with No. 82, this drawing,
made in a mixture of black-and-white
media, achieves less with more. It loses
its clarity due to indecisive lines and
overworking. Yet in spite of these
shortcomings, it retains the drama
of light.

84
PASSAGE, Italy   1928–29
Graphite on paper, 11 9/10 x 8 7/10 in.
(30.5 x 22.5 cm)
Collection of Sue Ann Kahn

In this sketch, as in Nos. 78 and 85, Kahn
displays a mastery in portraying reflected
illumination. This skill came from his
Beaux-Arts training in which wash
drawings of classical details explored all
the nuances of light on architectural
forms, the shades and shadows it
produces, and the primary and secondary
highlights which light generates.

Atrio del Palazzo Rufolo.

85
"ATRIO DEL PALAZZO RUFOLO,"
Ravello, Italy   1929
Graphite on paper, 16 1/3 x 11 1/2 in.
(41.9 x 29.5 cm); image: 14 3/5 x
11 1/2 in. (37.5 x 29.5 cm)
Inscribed top center: *Atrio del Palazzo
Rufolo*

Shown at a traveling exhibition
organized by the Pennsylvania Academy
of the Fine Arts, 1978–1979,
Catalogue No. 20
Collection of Sue Ann Kahn

This sketch incorporates Kahn's virtuosity

in showing simultaneously the exterior
and interior of a building. With a few
well-placed strokes of his graphite stick,
Kahn also harnesses the dramatic lower
light, capturing both the downward- and
upward-directed illuminations.

86
TWO VIEWS OF THE FORUM, Pompeii,
Italy   1928–29
Graphite on paper, size not available
Present whereabouts unknown

These quick notation sketches capture
the spatial qualities of classical urban
spaces. Kahn also presents here two
aspects of a peristyle: as a transparent
plane in the top sketch, and as an
architectural facade in the bottom
drawing.

87
VIEW FROM THE PORTICO, Pompeii,
Italy   1928–29
Graphite and crayon on paper, 7 4/5 x
5 1/10 in. (20.0 x 13.3 cm)
Collection of Sue Ann Kahn

This is a very powerful and daring view
through the colonnade. Looking toward
the sunlight, Kahn captures thin
highlights on columns and sharp
perspectives of shadows coming at the
viewer. The background, with the
exception of suggested human figures, is
blurred and nondescriptive.

88
TEMPLE OF POSEIDON, Paestum, Italy
1928–29
Black, brown, and white crayon on
brown paper, size not available
Present whereabouts unknown

In this exciting sketch, Kahn managed to
convey the aging softness of this ancient
monument's stone ruins. Utilizing black,
brown, and white crayons on a buff
paper, he transformed the columns into a

cohesive group of elements which exist
in harmony with the scale of the
observer. Bathed in the warm glow of
sunlight, the columns, with their delicate
fluting, frame ruins in the background.

89
PORTRAIT OF AN ACQUAINTANCE,
London, England   1928
Graphite on notebook paper, 10 2/5 x
7 9/10 in. (26.7 x 20.3 cm.)
Signed and inscribed middle right:
Louis I. Kahn. June '28 London. Inscribed
lower right: *Indian on way to Calcutta.
Interesting head, but not a very deep*
*thinker. Spent 8 yrs in America but
thought A. Lincoln was the owner of
beautiful cars by that name.*
Collection of Sue Ann Kahn

Portraits and human figures appear
infrequently in sketches from Kahn's first
European trip. This and the next three
sketches are the only available examples
of his involvement with the subject from
this period. As in most of his black-and-
white sketches from this time, Kahn
employed graphite stick and used it to
draw portraits and figures in the same Art
Deco manner that he used for other
subjects.

90
SELF-PORTRAIT WITH A PIPE, Italy
1928–29
Graphite on bond paper, 9 9/10 x
7 9/10 in. (25.4 x 20.3 cm)
Collection of Sue Ann Kahn

In a rather cocky and self-flattering manner, Kahn demonstrates his prowess at wielding the graphite stick with the result resembling an illustration for a magazine advertisement. The Art Deco stylization also gives the impression of a sketch intended for materialization in stone by a sculptor. Kahn's sense of drama never escaped him and here he employed it in showing only one half of the face, leaving the rest to the imagination of the viewer, a tendency seen also in his landscapes (see No. 37).

91
SEATED MAN WITH A PIPE, Italy   1929
Graphite on paper, 11 1/10 x 8 2/5 in.
(28.6 x 21.6 cm); image: 10 1/5 x
6 2/3 in. (26.4 x 17.1 cm)
Shown at a traveling exhibition
organized by the Pennsylvania Academy
of the Fine Arts, 1978–1979, Catalogue
No. 24, titled: *Seated Figure, Italy, 1929*
Collection of Sue Ann Kahn

In sketching this man with a pipe, Kahn
demonstrated a greater concern for the
effect of light on human form than the
accurate portrayal of the subject's facial
features. He easily adapted his usual
graphite-stick technique here to forms
neither natural nor architectural. It was
suggested by Esther Kahn that the seated
man might have been John Richards, an
architect and friend who was also touring
Italy at that time.

92
SEATED MAN WITH A CANE,
Italy   1929
Graphite on paper, 11 1/10 x 8 2/5 in.
(28.6 x 21.6 cm); image: 10 2/5 x
6 1/5 in. (26.7 x 15.9 cm)
Shown at a traveling exhibition
organized by the Pennsylvania Academy
of the Fine Arts, 1978–1979, Catalogue
No. 23, titled: *Seated Figure, Italy, 1929*
Collection of Sue Ann Kahn

This sketch appears to have been a
companion to No. 91. It was made with
fewer graphite strokes without losing the
remarkably high quality present in the
other drawing. Of special interest is
Kahn's ability to draw the figure's face
with so few lines.

93
"THE PLAZA," San Gimignano, Italy
1928–29
Graphite on paper, size not available
Inscribed on the back: *The Plaza*
Present whereabouts unknown

Through a very decisive handling of
horizontal and vertical planes, Kahn
reveals his strong architectural interest in
urban spaces and their defining edges.
His expert handling of shadows reveals
the piazza's major forms and makes the
scene quite believable without the need
for elaborate details. The soaring
verticality of the tower anchors the
openness of the piazza and echoes the
vertical definitions of surrounding
buildings.

94
STREET WITH A TOWER,
San Gimignano, Italy   1928–29
Graphite on paper, 6 1/2 x 6 1/3 in.
(16.8 x 16.2 cm)
Collection of Sue Ann Kahn

As in his view of the Duomo in Assisi
(No. 69), Kahn concentrates on the
rendition of forms in light rather than the
portrayal of details of buildings. The
strong hatch marks capture the essence
of the building masses defining the street.
Especially unique is the manner in which

the tower comes to life with only a few
horizontal strokes of graphite stick.

95
TOWERS, San Gimignano, Italy   1929
Watercolor and red pencil on paper,
12 x 9 1/10 in. (30.8 x 23.5 cm)
Collection of Sue Ann Kahn

The famous towers of San Gimignano
allowed Kahn a chance to dramatize
simple prismatic forms using a variation
in watercolor technique. With a looser
application of color than he has used
before, Kahn manages to convey the
ancient character of this medieval setting.
This effect might have been lost had he
used his customary crisp, Art Deco–
inspired technique. By animating the
piazza with suggestions of children at
play and figures with a wagon, Kahn
brought life and a sense of place to this
scene.

96
DELIVERY, San Gimignano, Italy   1929
Watercolor on paper, 9 1/10 x 12 in.
(23.5 x 31.0 cm)
Shown at a traveling exhibition
organized by the Pennsylvania Academy
of the Fine Arts, 1978–1979, Catalogue
No. 10, titled: *San Gimignano, Tuscany,
Italy, 1929*
Collection of Dr. Marshall Alan Kahn

From the overall view of the square in
No. 95, Kahn zooms in on a detail of life
in the city. While the mule cart and the
delivery man are the primary subjects of
this composition, it is the ambiguity of
the space, the soft textures of walls, and
the vagueness of details, all painted with
rich and harmonious colors, that give the
scene its charm.

97
VIEW WITH BOATS, NO. 1,
Venice, Italy   1928–29
Crayon on paper, size not available
Present whereabouts unknown

Plate Nos. 97–103 depict scenes of
Venice. Interestingly, none of these
sketches and paintings concentrate on
the detailed depiction of architectural
monuments. Kahn appears to be
absorbed by the totality of experiencing
this fabulous city. Venice to him was not
just a collection of glorious architectural
gems but a rich and complete urban
entity, appreciated through a romantic
vision.

Kahn's delicate handling of crayon
captures the spatial qualities and the
misty atmosphere of the harbor. This
sketch recalls the *View of Venice* by
J. L. E. Meissonier, the nineteenth-century
French academician. Kahn, however,
manages to convey the atmosphere much
more successfully than the photographic
exactitude of Meissonier. Of interest is
No. 349, another rendition of this view
made by Kahn in 1950.

98
SAN GIORGIO MAGGIORE,
Venice, Italy   1928–29
Crayon on paper, 6 x 8 1/3 in.
(15.6 x 21.3 cm)
Present whereabouts unknown

The character of this sketch and No. 97,
executed in a manner more typical of
Kahn's work during the 1950–51 trip to
Europe, resulted to a great extent from
the use of crayon rather than the usual
graphite stick. Kahn's dependence on a
sharp separation of planes in light from
those in shade, utilized by him in the
bright sunlight of Positano, gives way
here to the subtle light transitions
characteristic of Venice. It is also
interesting to note that the size and the
expressionistic portrayal of Palladio's
masterpiece suggest that the sketch was
made very quickly from a moving boat.

99
VIEW WITH BOATS, NO. 2, Venice,
Italy   1928–29
Watercolor on paper, 11 1/10 x
17 1/2 in. (28.6 X 45.1 cm)
Collection of Mrs. Esther I. Kahn

Combining characteristics of romanticism
and impressionism, this watercolor and
No. 100 explore the waterfront
environment of Venice with fishing boats
forming the focus of the composition.
Again, as in Nos. 97 and 98, there is a
prevalence of softened forms bathed in a
gentle Venetian light.

100
VIEW WITH BOATS, NO. 3, Venice,
Italy   1928–29
Watercolor on paper, 10 9/10 x
15 9/10 in. (28.0 X 40.8 cm)
Collection of Dr. Sandra Zagarell

101
VIEW FROM PIAZZETTA and BASILICA
FROM PIAZZETTA, Venice, Italy
1928–29
Watercolor and graphite on tissue paper,
10 1/10 x 8 1/10 in. (26.0 x 20.9 cm); top
image: 1 9/10 x 3 1/3 in. (5.0 x 8.6 cm);
bottom image: 6 x 8 in. (15.6 x 20.6 cm)
Collection of Sue Ann Kahn

These two casual sketches speak of
Kahn's sensitivity toward urban spaces.
In the lower sketch, a few dark markings
against the light background of the base
of the Basilica di San Marco become
people, thus giving life to the Piazzetta.
The scale of the space, however, is
exaggerated. Compared to the scale of
people, the Basilica is larger than it
would appear from that vantage point,
thus creating an illusion of a huge urban
space. A lack of detail points to Kahn's
greater concern for the overall spatial
qualities as opposed to the particularities
of buildings. Of interest is No. 350,
Kahn's rendition of this scene more than
twenty years later.

102
CUPOLAS OF BASILICA DI SAN
MARCO, Venice, Italy   1928–29
Watercolor on paper, 8 9/10 x 10 in.
(22.9 x 27.6 cm)
Collection of Sue Ann Kahn

This unusual view of the roof structures
of the basilica and the distant San
Giorgio Maggiore was achieved by Kahn
by wetting the paper and allowing
pigments to spread, thus softening the
edges of forms and creating the illusion
of a hazy atmosphere.

103
CANAL HOUSES, Venice, Italy
1928–29
Watercolor on paper, 10 x 7 4/5 in.
(25.7 x 20.0 cm)
Collection of Sue Ann Kahn

In a much crisper manner than that
employed in No. 102, and relying on a
brighter color palette, Kahn used his
brush the way he handled a graphite
stick—broad strokes resulting in a good
sense of tonality.

104
"COMPOSITION FROM STEP OF
FOUNTAIN," Florence, Italy   1928–29
Pencil and watercolor on bond paper,
10 9/10 x 8 3/5 in. (27.9 x 22.2 cm)
Inscribed bottom right: *Composition from
step of fountain*
Collection of Sue Ann Kahn

With quick decisive strokes and
inattention to details, Kahn captures
the spatial quality of the fountain's
prominence in this urban setting. This is
an unusual combination of media in
which the watercolor wash fills in broad
areas of graphite-defined elements, thus
helping to define buildings and contrast
them against the sky.

105
ARCH, Italy
Exact date unknown (c.1930)
Watercolor on paper, 6 3/5 x 7 1/2 in.
(29.8 x 22.2 cm)
Private collection

Watercolors Nos. 105 and 106 were painted by Kahn with much more restraint than other works from this series. There is much more attention given to a correct representation of buildings, even though vegetation is still abstracted. The sky is treated as a single, deep blue plane, unlike the subdued or cloud-dominated skies of most other paintings.

106
ARCADE, Italy
Exact date unknown (c. 1930)
Watercolor on paper, 6 3/5 x 7 1/2 in.
(17.1 x 19.4 cm)
Private collection

Because of the stylistic departure from his
watercolor sketches of this period, Kahn
may have painted this scene in
Philadelphia from memory, or using a
now-lost sketch as a model.

PERIOD III

1929–50

DEPRESSION, WAR, AND POST-WAR YEARS

Upon his return from the European trip, Kahn continued his apprenticeship in architectural offices until he received his registration in 1935. From then on he formed several associations with prominent Philadelphia architects. During the Depression his architectural career left him a considerable amount of time to devote to sketching and painting. He managed to have his work exhibited at the Annual Philadelphia Watercolor Exhibitions sponsored by the Pennsylvania Academy of the Fine Arts from 1929 through 1938. The 1929 exhibition contained many of his European travel sketches. In May of 1931 his article "The Value and Aim in Sketching" appeared in the T-Square Club Journal. It contained seven reproductions of his sketches, five of which were from Europe.

Following Kahn's marriage to Esther Israeli in 1930, the couple, together with their friends Dr. and Mrs. Jacob Sherman, took frequent vacation trips to New England and Canada. During these travels Kahn sketched profusely, quite often from the rear window of the moving car. At times he would ask Jacob Sherman, who was the driver, to stop the car so that he could record a scene in his sketchbook. These sketches were meant to be converted into paintings upon return to Philadelphia. Many contained color notations and other information helpful in recalling the scene in the studio. Kahn was hoping to sell his art to earn enough to cover his periods of unemployment and to supplement very meager earnings whenever he did work. But art did not sell easily during the Depression, and Kahn never managed to get any money for his work. Most of the sketches and paintings he kept or gave away to friends and relatives.

Kahn's style of drawing and painting underwent a considerable change during that time. He almost totally abandoned his art-deco mannerism and the use of the graphite stick. His drawings acquired more linearity and his paintings became more abstract, approaching the looseness of John Marin's work. Kahn began to experiment in media which were more cumbersome than graphite stick and watercolors. There appeared translations of his sketches into tempera, oil, woodcut, lithograph, and scratchboard. However, the most prevalent techniques involved pencil, charcoal, pen and ink, and watercolors, media which allowed Kahn to record very quickly his impressions without a loss of spontaneity.

During this period Kahn sketched and painted landscapes, humble town and country scenes, fishing villages, portraits, animals, still lifes, and graphic designs. During World War II and shortly thereafter Kahn produced very little artwork. He experimented, however, with graphic exercises in transparency and lightness, features he was discovering in modern architecture.

The order in which Kahn's work from this period is presented here follows a formula similar to that used for the travel sketches from the European trip. There is little reliance on chronology, even though certain stylistic developments might have been explored through such an order. More important are Kahn's methods of handling certain subjects in similar settings and his attitudes toward those subjects. Stylistic differences resulting from his technical or philosophical evolution can thus be easily compared. Whenever possible, geographic locations formed the basis for the grouping of the artwork. The subjects are arranged in approximately the following order:

Tree studies
Landscapes
Waterfront, rural and small town scenes
Churches and towers
Industrial scenes
Interiors
Figures and portraits
Animals
Still life
Miscellaneous

107
"BOIS DES SABLES, P.Q.,"
Quebec, Canada 1936–37
Black crayon on paper, size not available
Inscribed and signed lower right: *Bois des Sables, P.Q., Louis I.Kahn*
Present whereabouts unknown

This sketch and the next eleven (Nos. 108–118) treat the subject of trees either as isolated studies or as scenes where trees play an important role in a picture. In a compositional manner similar to his European sketches, particularly No. 25, but with greater ease and skill, Kahn renders this view of a house behind a handsome stand of trees. The rough texture of the paper serves well to depict the impression of foliage and grass, especially since Kahn is beginning to rely more and more on the use of crayon and pencil, rather than his faithful graphite stick.

108
TREE-LINED ROAD, Gloucester, Cape Ann, Massachusetts
Exact date unknown (c. 1930s)
Black crayon on paper, size not available
Color notations
Present whereabouts unknown

As with his watercolors, Kahn exhibits in this crayon sketch the loosening of his style and a lesser dependence on the modeling of forms than in previous graphite sketches. The underlying structural character of the trees, translated into lines, takes precedence over Kahn's former interest in the solidity of their forms. Color notations at the bottom of the sketch are indications that Kahn intended to translate this study into a finished painting. However, there is no record of his fulfilling this intent.

109
FOREST ROAD, Gaspe Peninsula, Canada 1936
Charcoal on paper, 5 x 7 9/10 in.(12.7 x 20.3 cm); image: 3 1/2 x 4 7/10 in. (8.9 x 12.1 cm)
Collection of Sue Ann Kahn

This sketch is one of a series of four charcoals from Kahn's notebook that he made during his 1936 trip to Canada (see Nos. 152–154).

110
YOUNG FIR TREES, Adirondack
Mountains, New York
Exact date unknown (c. 1930s)
Pencil and watercolor on paper,
13 1/10 x 16 1/2 in. (33.6 x 42.5 cm)
Verso of No. 272
Collection of Sue Ann Kahn

111
WINDING STREAM, New England
Exact date unknown (c. 1930s)
Pencil on paper, 4 9/10 x 7 9/10 in.
(12.7 x 20.3 cm)
Collection of Sue Ann Kahn

112
TREES, Gloucester, Cape Ann,
Massachusetts
Exact date unknown (c. 1930s)
Watercolor on bond paper, 7 x 7 2/5 in.
(18.1 x 19.0 cm)
Collection of Sue Ann Kahn

115

113
"THE ROARING AMANUSACK, N.H.,"
White Mountains, New Hampshire
1934–35
Watercolor on paper, 13 1/10 x
15 3/5 in. (33.6 x 40.0 cm); image:
10 1/3 x 13 in. (26.5 x 33.3 cm)
Collection of Sue Ann Kahn

This watercolor of the Ammonoosuc
River differs greatly from another version
of the scene (No. 139). The sweeping
panorama of the other rendition is
replaced here with a twisted and abstract
close-up of the stream, which is almost
unrecognizable as a body of water.
Wavy tree trunks and branches,
supporting heavy tree canopies, establish
a middle-ground screen through which
small patches of sky provide a sense of
space.

114
GOLD IN THE TREES, Adirondack
Mountains, New York   1931–36
Watercolor on paper, 10 1/2 x
15 1/10 in. (27.0 x 38.7 cm)
Collection of Sue Ann Kahn

The impatient manner in which the trees
are presented in this picture results in a
scene of glowing transparency, of the
yellows, light greens, and oranges that
form the rich palette of autumn.

115
FAIRMONT PARK, Philadelphia,
Pennsylvania   1930–33
Colored pencils on paper, 9 1/2 x
7 9/10 in. (24.4 x 20.3 cm)
Collection of Mrs. Esther I. Kahn

This is a rare instance in which Kahn
used colored pencils to execute a
complete picture. Borrowing heavily
from French impressionists, Kahn
presents a "snapshot" of a scene in which
light, air, trees, and people are caught in
a moment in time. There is a convincing
sense of depth achieved through the use
of the curving path and the utilization of
color and value contrasts. According to
Esther Kahn, the scene depicts her and
her friends at a picnic in Fairmont Park.

116
STREET OF THE ELMS, NO. 1,
Gloucester, Cape Ann, Massachusetts
1934–35
Charcoal on paper, 8 2/3 x 11 3/5 in.
(22.2 x 29.8 cm)
Collection of Sue Ann Kahn

This is a charcoal study for two oil
paintings, Nos. 117 and 118. A small-
town street, canopied by tall trees, is a
subject of considerable contrast to the
heroic Italian townscapes Kahn sketched
only a few years before. Delightful in its
spatial and light qualities, this humble
scene was as charming and inspiring to
Kahn as any European site. It is precisely
this attitude which he advocated in his
article "The Value and Aim in Sketching"
(*T-Square Club Journal*, May 1931).

117
STREET OF THE ELMS, NO. 2,
Gloucester, Cape Ann, Massachusetts
1924–35
Oil on canvas, 9 9/10 x 13 9/10 in.
(25.4 x 35.6 cm)
Collection of Sue Ann Kahn

From charcoal sketch No. 116, Kahn
painted this oil as a preliminary study for
the finished painting (No. 118). Strictly
following both forms and shadows, he
translated the sketch by introducing the
dimension of color. The very dark
canopy of trees is at odds with the subtle
values of the remainder of the
composition, but color contrasts are well
handled, especially in the foreground
where the complementary orange and
blue hues give depth and interest to
shadows on the road.

118
TREE-LINED STREET, NO. 3, Gloucester,
Cape Ann, Massachusetts   1934–35
Oil on canvas, 15 4/5 x 21 4/5 in.
(40.6 x 55.9 cm)
Collection of Sue Ann Kahn

In this final development of two previous
studies (Nos. 116 and 117), Kahn
modifies the position of the dark values
in the composition in order to unify the
entire scene. The trees on the left side of
the road now form an L-shaped
arrangement which frames the street and
offers contrast to the sunlit houses in the
background. Kahn also eliminates in this
version the sharp contrasts of branches
against foliage and, when compared to
No. 117, subdues the palette, creating a
more serene picture. The sparse number
of oil paintings by Kahn is due largely to
his preference for more immediate means
of expression.

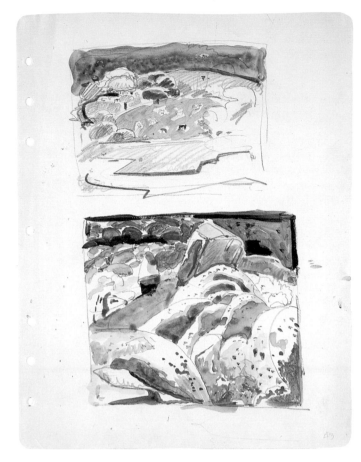

119 (*top left*)
FOLIAGE STUDIES
Exact date unknown (c. 1930s)
Watercolor and charcoal on bond paper,
10 9/10 x 8 2/5 in. (27.9 x 21.6 cm);
top image: 3 2/5 x 4 4/5 in. (6.7 x
10.8 cm); bottom image: 2 3/5 x 4 1/5 in
(8.9 x 12.4 cm)
Collection of Sue Ann Kahn

120 (*top right*)
TWO LANDSCAPES, Adirondack
Mountains, New York
Exact date unknown (c. 1930s)
Pencil and watercolor on notebook
paper, 10 9/10 x 8 2/5 in.

(27.9 x 21.6 cm); top image: 4 1/3 x
5 2/3 in. (11.0 x.14.5 cm); bottom image:
5 1/2 x 6 1/2 in. (14.0 x 16.6 cm)
Exhibited at Max Protetch Gallery,
New York City, June 1981, Catalogue
No. 18, titled: *1928 European Sketch*;
and at the Fine Arts Library, University
of Pennsylvania, Summer 1985.
Collection of the Architectural Archives,
University of Pennsylvania, Catalologue
No. 945.1; Gift of Richard Saul Wurman

121 (*bottom left*)
PURPLE HILL, Adirondack Mountains,
New York   1931–34
Pencil and watercolor on bond paper,
10 9/10 x 8 2/5 in. (27.9 x 21.6 cm); top
image: 6 9/10 x 8 1/2 in. (17.8 x 21.9
cm); bottom image: 4/5 x 9/10 in.
(2.2 x 2.5 cm)
Collection of Sue Ann Kahn

The daring mix of colors and the sharp
contrast of trees against the mountain
make this study worthy of a complete
painting. There is, however, no record of
Kahn having ever translated this sketch
into a finished version. The little pencil
sketch at the bottom is a study for
watercolor painting No. 268

122 (*bottom right*)
"WORCESTER," Worcester,
Massachusetts   1933–34
Pencil and watercolor on bond paper,
10 9/10 x 8 1/3 in. (27.9 x 21.5 cm);

image: 7 7/10 x 8 1/3 in. (19.0 x 21.5 cm)
Signed lower right: *Louis I. Kahn*;
inscribed lower left: *Worcester*
Collection of Sue Ann Kahn

Like No. 121, this is a watercolor study
for a projected painting. Kahn betrays
here his customary impatience with
representing details and manages to
create a mosaic of color patches which
suggest in an impressionistic manner the
forms of hills, fields, trees, houses, and a
pond. While there is an apparent attempt
at representing depth, the overall effect is
a flat, two-dimensional pattern of shapes
and colors.

123
SLEEPY TOWN, Isle Madame,
Nova Scotia, Canada   1935
Watercolor on paper, 7 9/10 x 10 in.
(20.3 X 25.7 cm)
Signed lower right: *Louis I. Kahn '35*
Collection of Sue Ann Kahn

The influence of Cézanne is clearly
visible in this watercolor. Kahn
constructed this painting using small
color surfaces, all related to their
surrounding color planes, built up to
form the entire scene. The composition
hangs together in a comfortable unity,
like an architectural monument
constructed of an immense number of
well-fitting elements. This tendency was
present even in Kahn's earliest period,
but it was during the Depression years
that this more mature style emerged.

124
COMING STORM, STUDIES,
Woodstock, New York   1931
Charcoal pencil on bond paper, 10 3/4 x
8 3/10 in. (27.6 x 21.3 cm); top image:
4 x 5 1/10 in. (10.2 x 13.3 cm); bottom
image: 5 1/2 x 6 2/5 in. (14.3 x 16.5 cm)
Collection of Sue Ann Kahn

The top sketch served as a study for three
watercolors: Nos. 125, 126, and 127.

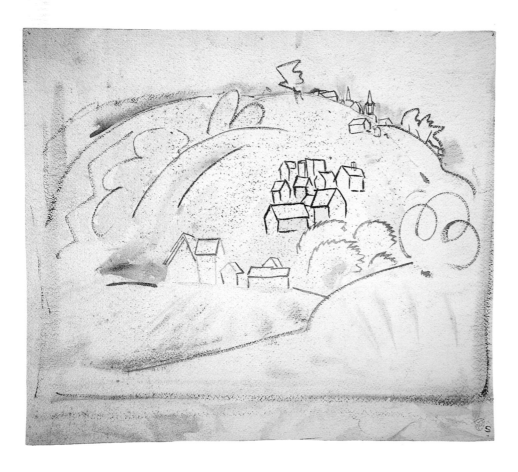

125
COMING STORM, NO. 1, Woodstock,
New York 1931
Watercolor on paper, 13 1/5 x 15 1/3 in.
(33.9 x 39.4 cm)
Collection of Sue Ann Kahn

This watercolor is a blockout for a
painting in which Kahn managed only to
lay down the very first washes of gray
and ocher. The outlines of the main
features of the composition were made
with a brush rather than a pencil. This
was Kahn's preferred way of making a
watercolor since such outlines can be
blended easily with adjoining washes.

126
COMING STORM, NO. 2, Woodstock,
New York 1931
Watercolor on paper, 13 1/5 x 15 1/3 in.
(33.9 x 39.4 cm)
Collection of Sue Ann Kahn

Recalling El Greco's *View of Toledo*, in
both versions of this scene, perhaps more
so in this one than in No. 127, the drama
of the approaching storm is played out by
contrasting the ominous clouds against
the little village bathed in the bright rays
of sunlight.

121

127
COMING STORM, NO. 3, Woodstock,
New York   1931
Watercolor on paper, 15 1/3 x 21 4/5 in.
(39.2 x 56.0 cm); image: 13 9/10 x
16 4/5 in. (35.6 x 43.2 cm)
Exhibited at the 29th Annual
Philadelphia Watercolor Exhibition,
Pennsylvania Academy of the Fine Arts,
1931; Catalogue No. 1789.
Shown at a traveling exhibition
organized by the Pennsylvania Academy
of the Fine Arts, 1978–1979, Catalogue
No. 34., titled: *Coming Storm, 1931*
Collection of Sue Ann Kahn

128
DANUBE COUNTRY   1930
Watercolor on paper, 15 1/5 x 21 4/5 in.
(39.0 x 55.9 cm)
Exhibited at the 28th Annual
Philadelphia Watercolor Exhibition,
Pennsylvania Academy of the Fine Arts,
1930; Catalogue No. 1881.
Shown at a traveling exhibition
organized by the Pennsylvania Academy
of the Fine Arts, 1978–1979, Catalogue
No. 33, titled: *Danube County, 1930*
Collection of Sue Ann Kahn

Kahn painted this watercolor in
Philadelphia as an ode to his European
travels of the year before. While there
are some technical differences between
this work and the watercolors painted in
Europe, Kahn's abstract manner of
treating mountains and adherence to a
limited chromatic range point to a rather
smooth transition into a new phase of
pictorial development.

129
HOUSES IN THE HILLS, Nova Scotia,
Canada   1936
Watercolor on paper, 7 2/5 x 10 2/5 in.
(19.0 x 26.7 cm)
Collection of Sue Ann Kahn

The velvety character of this watercolor
is derived from Kahn's experimentation
with applying pigments over a wet paper
surface and allowing the colors to run
into each other. Elements rendered in
this fashion may contrast with objects
delineated more precisely. This often
resulted in a good sense of depth and a
detailed composition. However, because
both the foreground and the background
here are painted in this manner, the
image appears blurred and out of focus.

130
ROLLING COUNTRYSIDE, NO. 1,
Cape Ann, Massachusetts   1936
Watercolor on paper, 6 4/5 x 9 in.
(17.5 x 23.2 cm)
Collection of Sue Ann Kahn

This is one of two renditions of the same
scene. This watercolor appears to be a
close-up view of No. 131. The fact that
Kahn signed the more panoramic picture
(No. 131) would indicate that he
considered it to be the better of the two.
Yet, both possess a sweeping sense of
space indicated by the barest of brush
strokes. Kahn's use of isolated planes of
color provides clues to the plasticity of
the landscape.

131
ROLLING COUNTRYSIDE, NO. 2,
Cape Ann, Massachusetts 1936
Watercolor on paper, 6 4/5 x 9 in.
(17.5 x 23.2 cm)
Signed lower right: *Louis I. Kahn*
Collection of Mrs. Esther I. Kahn

132
DISTANT MOUNTAINS, Adirondack
Mountains, New York   1931
Watercolor on paper, 7 x 10 1/4 in.
(18.0 x 26.3 cm)
Collection of Dr. David Alpers

This is a very subtle, well-controlled
painting in which the density of pigments
diminishes in direct relation to the
distance from the viewer. Kahn devotes
a very large portion of the image to the
sky and the distant, mist-shrouded
mountains. The pink clouds suggest an
early morning in the valley.

133
HAY WAGON, Adirondack Mountains,
New York   1931
Watercolor on paper, 8 9/10 x
11 9/10 in. (22.9 x 30.5 cm)
Collection of Sue Ann Kahn

134
SAND DUNES, Provincetown,
Massachusetts   1935
Watercolor on paper, 8 2/5 x 11 in.
(21.6 x 28.3 cm)
Collection of Sue Ann Kahn

Always sensitive to changes of terrain,
Kahn translated undulating sand dunes
into a dynamic landscape of sharp
contrasts between the rocks and the soft,
wavelike sand. This painting has
interesting formal similarities to Nos. 150
and 151, especially in the handling of
textural contrasts.

135
RIVER, Adirondack Mountains,
New York   1934–35
Tempera on paper, 8 x 10 3/5 in.
(20.6 x 27.3 cm)
Signed lower right: *LIK*
Collection of Mr. and Mrs. Milton
Abelson

During his summer travels in upstate
New York and New England, the humble
American landscape, without the
romantic bravura of Italy, stirred Kahn to
some very sensitive and delightful work.
In this painting, in which Kahn employed
tempera—a medium he did not use
frequently—Kahn achieved a looseness
and control found more often in his pure
watercolors.

136
MOUNTAIN ROAD NO. 1, Woodstock,
New York   1931
Watercolor on paper, 8 9/10 x 1/3 in.
(22.9 x 29.2 cm)
Collection of Mrs. Esther I. Kahn

This watercolor, one of three versions of
the scene, was made while on a four-day
trip to upper New York. The largest
rendition of the three, No. 138, was
made in Kahn's studio on Chester
Avenue. All of the works display the
loosening of style evident during this
period. In great contrast to his work from
the European tour, the brushwork is more
daring and the colors more varied. There
appears a greater tendency to flatten
forms in order to achieve a composition
dependent on the balance of color
masses.

137
MOUNTAIN ROAD NO. 2, Woodstock,
New York   1931
Watercolor on paper, 5 x 10 9/10 in.
(13.0 x 27.9 cm)
Collection of Sue Ann Kahn

138
MOUNTAIN ROAD NO. 3, Woodstock,
New York   1931
Watercolor on paper, 13 9/10 x 19 in.
(35.6 x 48.9 cm)
Collection of Mrs. Esther I. Kahn

This is the final version of the scene
based on watercolor sketches Nos. 136
and 137.

139
MOUNTAIN STREAM, White Mountains,
New Hampshire   1934–35
Watercolor on paper, 10 x 13 3/5 in.
(25.7 x 34.9 cm)
Collection of Sue Ann Kahn

This sketch and Nos. 140–43 represent
an important transition in Kahn's stylistic
development. The watercolors of this
phase of his career display the joint
influences of Cézanne and Marin. While
at first glance there might seem to be a
contradiction in this concept, it is
nevertheless a fact of Kahn's dual artistic
nature. His highly analytical attitude and
training led him in the direction of
Cézanne's style of constructive painting.
On the other hand, Kahn's impatience
with the technical aspects of sketching
and painting and his voracious appetite
to capture in a lyrical composition
all that moved him resulted in a Marin-
like expressionistic tendency. Both
influences can be detected in this
watercolor. The careful buildup of color
planes is complicated by the sketchy
handling of the overall masses. The
result is a pleasant amalgam of order and

impermanence (see No. 113 for another
rendition of the Ammonoosuc River).

140
FARMING VILLAGE, Adirondack
Mountains, New York 1931
Watercolor on paper, 7 2/5 x 6 3/5 in.
(19.0 x 17.1 cm)
Collection of Sue Ann Kahn

In this painting Kahn produced a
composition that relies on a patch-quilt
manner for its almost abstract character.
Small areas of color combine into larger
ones, then form even larger patterns, thus
forming a disciplined design which is of
far greater interest than the scene it
represents. The resulting two-
dimensional effect again suggests
Cézanne's influence.

141
HILLS, Woodstock, New York   1934–35
Watercolor on paper, 4 1/2 x 5 9/10 in.
(11.7 x 15.2 cm)
Collection of Sue Ann Kahn

This sketch and several other watercolors
in this group are quite distinct from
Kahn's previous work. They were
painted most probably in his studio using
field sketches made on location. This
watercolor transforms itself into an
almost total abstraction. Suggestions of
hills and trees are difficult to interpret
and Kahn leaves the completion of this
landscape to one's imagination.

142
ROCK FORMATION, Massachusetts
1934–35
Watercolor on paper, 8 9/10 x 8 1/2 in.
(18.1 x 21.9 cm)
Collection of Sue Ann Kahn

This splendid semiabstraction is based on
a now-lost sketch made during a tour of
the coast between Gloucester and
Rockport, Massachusetts, in 1934.

143
MOUNTAIN, NO. 1, Woodstock,
New York 1934–35
Watercolor on paper, 11 1/4 x 13 1/5 in.
(28.9 x 33.9 cm)
Collection of Sue Ann Kahn

This painting, based on field sketch
No. 145a, is the culmination of the
Cézanne-Marin influence on Kahn. Its
similarities to Cézanne's renditions of
Sainte Victoire are quite apparent, as is
the fiery expressionism of Marin's
paintings. Kahn succeeds in this work
beyond anything he had done before.

144
MOUNTAIN LAKES, White Mountains,
New England   1934–35
Watercolor on paper, 12 3/5 x 14 4/5 in.
(32.4 x 38.1 cm)
Collection of Mrs. Esther I. Kahn

In this watercolor rendition of charcoal
sketch No. 145c, Kahn remains true to
the overall character and composition of
the original without sacrificing its
spontaneity and vigor.

145 a-f
LANDSCAPE STUDIES, Adirondack and
White Mountains, New England
1934–35
Charcoal on paper: a, b, c, d, and e;
Pen and ink on paper: f; 7 9/10 x
4 9/10 in. (20.3 x 12.7 cm) each
Collection of Sue Ann Kahn

Kahn used the top left sketch (a) in this
composite of six field sketches to
produce one watercolor (No. 143) and
two ink drawings (Nos. 146 and 147).
The sketch below (c) served as a model
for another watercolor (No.144).
Notations, such as the ones appearing at
the bottom of the upper-right sketch (b),
describe either materials, proportions, or
colors, and allowed Kahn not to be too
concerned with a true representation of
reality. He was much more interested in
capturing the spirit of the scene which
later, with the help of his notations, could
be recaptured in the studio versions.

146
MOUNTAIN, NO. 2, Woodstock,
New York   1934–35/1937
Brushed ink on paper, size not available
Inscribed lower right: *Louis I. Kahn '37*
Present whereabouts unknown

This drawing, like watercolor No. 143,
was made from charcoal sketch No.
145a. Choosing the most important lines
to give substance to the scene, Kahn
succeeds in presenting the drama of the
mountain's convolutions and the
crannies in the terrain. A few carefully
chosen radiating lines hint at the position
of the sun. The rays blend with the lines
describing the hills and, without casting
shadows, suggest the brightness of the
sun in the upper-left corner of the
composition.

147
MOUNTAIN, NO. 3, Woodstock,
New York   1934–35/1946
Brushed ink on onionskin paper, 8 2/5 x
10 9/10 in. (21.6 x 27.9 cm)
Signed lower right: *Louis I. Kahn '46*
Shown at a traveling exhibition
organized by the Pennsylvania Academy
of the Fine Arts, 1978–1979, Catalogue
No. 41, titled: *Landscape, 1946*
Collection of Sue Ann Kahn

This is an interpretation of the scene
depicted in charcoal sketch No. 145a,
pen-and-ink drawing No. 146, and
watercolor No. 109. The jabbing,
aggressive application of ink is in drastic
contrast to the gentle handling of forms
in the 1930s. This technique bears a
striking resemblance to the proto-
expressionist work of Matisse and
Kandinsky. It displays nervous and
impatient penwork, expressive of Kahn's
feelings about natural forms rather
than their physical substance. The
composition is unified by the consistency
of Kahn's pen-and-ink technique, which,
while not as elegant as in his previous
ink sketches, is characteristic of his
emotional spontaneity

148
MOUNTAINS, Adirondack Mountains,
New York   1934–35
Charcoal on paper, 4 9/10 x 7 9/10 in.
(12.7 x 20.3 cm)
Verso of No.145e
Collection of Sue Ann Kahn

This is one of a series of on-site sketches
(see No. 145) which Kahn hoped to later
convert into ink or watercolor renditions.

149
COUNTRYSIDE, Adirondack Mountains,
New York   1931
Black crayon on paper, size not available
Color notations
Present whereabouts unknown

This loose and lively sketch is a study for
No. 136 and is one of many which Kahn
made as a source for future paintings.
Color notations define not only the main
forms but also their shades and shadows.

150

SNOW TRACKS

Exact date unknown (c. 1930s)

Graphite and black crayon on paper,
10 1/10 x 15 1/5 in. (26.0 x 39.0 cm)

Collection of Sue Ann Kahn

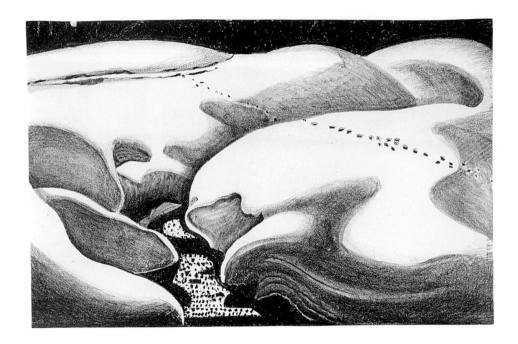

This drawing and No. 151 constitute a unique handling of ephemeral subjects when compared to Kahn's other work. *Snow Tracks* comes closest to Kahn's lithographs of Italy (Nos. 50 and 51) in the way he handles the soft shading of rounded forms. The mysterious tracks, while hardly prominent, are thrust into the limelight because of their peculiar intrusion on the scene and their odd scale. The picture is more of an exercise in fantasy, laden with unknown symbolisms, rather than an attempt at a portrayal of a winter scene.

151

FOG IN THE VALLEY

Exact date unknown (c. 1930s)

Black crayon on paper, size not available

Present whereabouts unknown

In an exquisite composition of light and shade contrasts, prismatic architectural forms, soft, pillowlike hills, and a blanket of fog across an inclined line at the bottom of the picture, Kahn skillfully captures an enchanting phenomenon of nature. He succeeded in balancing this distinctive composition by reserving a large portion of the upper part of the picture for an increasingly darkening sky. This in itself presents another contrast in which the calm of the sky is broken by the articulated forms at the bottom of the composition.

152
MOUNTAIN ROAD, New England
Exact date unknown (c. 1930s)
Pencil on paper, 4 9/10 x 7 9/10 in.
(12.7 x 20.3 cm)
Collection of Sue Ann Kahn

This is one of four quick sketches (see
also Nos. 111, 153, and 154) Kahn made
from a car during one of his 1930s trips.

153
MOUNTAIN LAKE, New England
Exact date unknown (c. 1930s)
Pencil on paper, 4 9/10 x 7 9/10 in.
(12.7 x 20.3 cm)
Color notations
Collection of Sue Ann Kahn

154
LAKE IN THE VALLEY, New England
Exact date unknown (c. 1930s)
Pencil on paper, 4 9/10 x 7 9/10 in.
(12.7 x 20.3 cm)
Color notations
Collection of Sue Ann Kahn

155
VIEWS FROM THE ROAD, Cape Breton,
Nova Scotia, Canada   1937
Pencil on paper, 13 7/10 x 10 in. (35.2 x
25.7 cm); top image: 2 9/10 x 4 2/5 in.
(7.6 x 11.4 cm); middle image: 13 1/3 x
5 4/5 in. (8.6 x 14.9 cm); bottom image:
3 9/10 x 6 1/3 in. (10.2 x 16.2 cm)
Color notations on top sketch
Verso of No. 156
Collection of Sue Ann Kahn

These three sketches are on the verso of
No. 156. All of them were drawn very
hastily from a car driven by Kahn's
friend, Jacob Sherman. Mr. and Mrs.
Sherman traveled with the Kahns to
Canada in 1936 and 1937. During these
short vacations Kahn unleashed his
pentup love of sketching directly from
nature. Nova Scotia and Gaspe Peninsula
provided him with countless opportunities
to explore waterfront landscapes, coastal
villages, and harbor activities. He
recorded them in a very hasty fashion in
pencil, pen, and ink. Watercolors and
renditions in other media were produced
back in Philadelphia. With a few
exceptions, Nos. 155–182 deal with
waterfront subjects. Nos. 178–182
specifically explore scenes of the
Massachusetts waterfront.

156
HARBOR SCENES, Indian Harbour, Cape
Breton, Nova Scotia, Canada   1937
Pencil on paper, 13 7/10 x 10 in. (35.2 x
25.7 cm); top image: 6 x 10 in. (15.6 x
25.7 cm); bottom image: 4 2/5 x
7 1/10 in. (11.4 x 18.4 cm)
Inscribed lower right: Indian Harbour
Verso of No. 155
Collection of Sue Ann Kahn

These sketches reveal Kahn's fascination
with the simple geometries of waterfront
structures disposed in apparent disorder.
Of special interest, however, is the
manner in which he managed to uncover
the intrinsic organizations of these
structures which he then transformed into
memorable images.

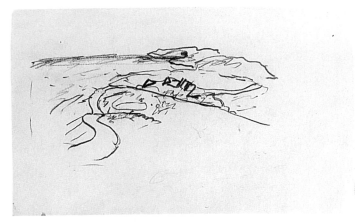

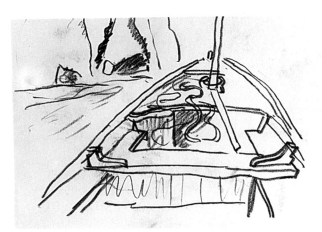
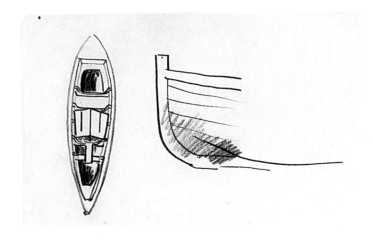

157
FIVE STUDIES OF A WATERFRONT
WITH BOATS, Cape Breton,
Nova Scotia, Canada   1937
Charcoal on bond paper, 4 9/10 x
7 9/10 in. (12.7 x 20.3 cm) each
Collection of Sue Ann Kahn

158
FISH NET STUDIES, Cape Breton Island,
Nova Scotia, Canada   1937
Charcoal on paper, 4 4/5 x 8 in.
(12.4 x 20.6 cm)
Color notations
Collection of Sue Ann Kahn

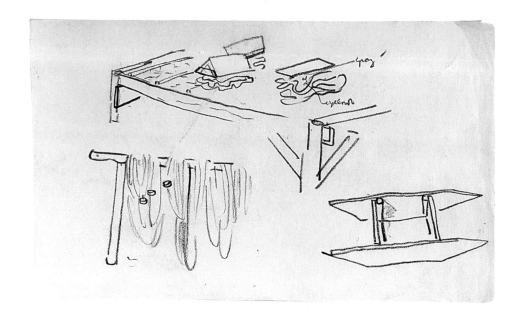

159
DRY DOCK, Nova Scotia,
Canada   1937
Pencil on bond paper, 8 1/3 x 10 3/5 in.
(21.3 x 27.6 cm)
Color notations
Collection of Sue Ann Kahn

160
STUDIES OF CATTLE AND DRYING
BEDS, Lunenburg, Nova Scotia,
Canada   1937
Pencil, brush, and ink on paper,
8 9/10 x 11 3/5 in. (22.9 x 29.8 cm)
Verso of No. 161
Collection of Sue Ann Kahn

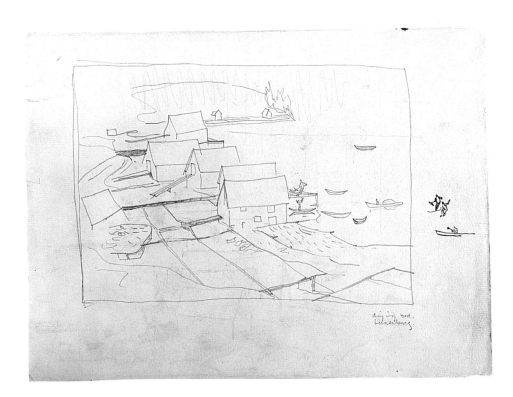

161
"DRYING BED. LUNENBURG,"
Lunenburg, Nova Scotia, Canada   1937
Pencil on paper, 8 9/10 x 11 3/5 in.
(22.9 x 29.8 cm); image: 5 9/10 x
8 2/5 in. (15.2 x 21.6 cm)
Pen-and-ink figure studies at middle right
Inscribed lower right: *drying bed.
Lunenburg*
Verso of No. 160
Collection of Sue Ann Kahn

The brush-and-ink sketch (No. 160) on
the back of this drawing served as the
first study for a planned painting. In
this sketch buildings are rearranged to
form a more interesting diagonal
formation. Kahn paid an unusual
amount of attention to the small, almost
insignificant figures of fishermen. He
studied them carefully in order to
animate them with a believable physical
presence.

162
HARBOR FROM THE DOCK,
Nova Scotia, Canada 1937
Pencil on paper, 5 9/10 x 8 7/10 in.
(15.2 x 22.5 cm)
Collection of Sue Ann Kahn

The lightly drawn docks in the
foreground of this sketch provide a
somewhat unusual framing device for the
distant view of a fishing village. The
modeled background demonstrates
Kahn's considerable interest in the formal
relation of the gabled structures to the
distant hills. The docks are clearly
necessary for the composition, but they
have an existence of their own because
of their complexity, and are competing
with the village for attention.

163
BOAT DOCK, Nova Scotia,
Canada 1937
Pencil on paper, 10 x 13 7/10 in.
(25.7 x 35.2 cm)
Collection of Sue Ann Kahn

In direct contrast to No. 162, this
drawing reverses the attention from the
distant village to the dock in the
foreground. Kahn creates a strong formal
relation between the gabled shack on the
dock and the distant structures across the
water, thus unifying the spatial separation
with a comfortable visual bridge.

164
HARBOR VILLAGE, Cape Breton Island,
Nova Scotia, Canada   1937
Pencil on paper, 9 9/10 x 13 3/5 in.
(25.4 x 34.9 cm)
Verso of No. 209
Collection of Sue Ann Kahn

In another exploration of the
compositional possibilities of No. 162,
Kahn accentuates the middle-ground in
this drawing while downplaying both the
foreground and the background.

165
HARBOR WITH BOATS, Cape Breton
Island, Nova Scotia, Canada   1937
Charcoal on paper, size not available
Present whereabouts unknown

This scene, more complex spatially than
No. 164, offered Kahn an opportunity to
juxtapose the boat-filled cove in the
foreground with house-studded hills
beyond the harbor.

166
MOORED BOATS, Cape Breton Island,
Nova Scotia, Canada   1936
Charcoal on brown paper, 4 1/5 x
6 2/5 in. (10.8 x 16.5 cm)
Collection of Sue Ann Kahn

This sketch translates the entirety of the
Cape Breton harbor scene into a few
linear symbols that transmit through their
simplicity the essence and nature of the
waterfront environment. A few vertical
lines below the boat hulls indicate the
presence of water, while darkly rendered
areas give the necessary clues of depth.
It was uncommon for Kahn to extol
featureless landscapes, but he skillfully
demonstrates here that he was moved by
the serenity of this place.

167
BAY VILLAGE, Cape Breton Island,
Nova Scotia, Canada   1936
Watercolor on paper, 10 3/5 x 10 in.
(27.3 x 25.7 cm); image: 3 2/5 x 10 in.
(8.9 x 25.7 cm)
Verso of No. 330
Collection of Sue Ann Kahn

This unfinished sketch may very well
have been a study for a watercolor
version of charcoal sketch No. 166.
There appear to be similarities in the
positioning of houses in relation to the
bay. However, the lack of details makes
this connection hard to ascertain.

168
MOORED BOATS, NO. 2,
Gaspe Peninsula, Quebec, Canada
Exact date unknown
Charcoal on paper, 8 x 9 1/2 in.
(20.6 x 24.4 cm)
Collection of Sue Ann Kahn

This abstracted version of No.175 was
probably sketched after Kahn's return to
Philadelphia since the style bears a
strong resemblance to abstractions
executed by Kahn during the 1940s.
Kahn abstracts trees, boats, and sky by
using squiggles, filled-in black areas, and
staccato dashes. The tree to the left of the
picture is a grotesque abstraction
reminiscent of contemporary
architectural renderings by Le Corbusier.

169
ROCKY COVE WITH BOATS, Gaspe
Peninsula, Quebec, Canada 1937
Graphite on paper, 9 1/2 x 14 in.
(24.5 x 34.0 cm)
Collection of Dr. Sandra A. Zagarell

The graphite stick technique in this
drawing would suggest that it was made
during Kahn's European journey.
However, the scene resembles a coastal
region of Quebec more than any site
Kahn sketched in Europe. In addition,
there is an absence of the Art Deco style
present in his 1928–29 work. Kahn may
have tried using the trusty old medium to
explore the formal nature of this subject
in contrast to his more prevalent linear
renditions.

170
GASPE PENINSULA, NO. 14,
Quebec, Canada   1937
Pen, brush, and ink on paper, 4 2/5 x
7 1/2 in. (11.4 x 19.4 cm)
Color notations
Shown at a traveling exhibition
organized by the Pennsylvania Academy
of the Fine Arts, 1978–1979, Catalogue
No. 38a–b., titled: *Sheets from a
Sketchbook of the Gaspe Peninsula, 1937*
Collection of Sue Ann Kahn

From this on-site sketch Kahn produced
three pen-and-ink sketches and one
watercolor rendition (Nos. 171–74). All
of them were most probably made upon
Kahn's return to Philadelphia.

171
FISHERMAN'S CAMP, NO. 1, Saguenay
River, Quebec, Canada   1937
Pen and ink on paper, 6 4/5 x 10 1/10 in.
(17.6 x 26.0 cm)
Signed lower right: *Louis I. Kahn '37*
Shown at a traveling exhibition
organized by the Pennsylvania Academy
of the Fine Arts, 1978–1979, Catalogue
No. 39., titled: *Gaspe Peninsula,
Nova Scotia, 1937*
Collection of Sue Ann Kahn

Using travel sketch No. 170 as a model,
Kahn recaptured the scene which
fascinated him so much on the boat ride
on the Saguenay River. This version
appears almost as fresh and spontaneous
as the original, even though the lines are
harsher and there is a greater
dependence on contours.

172

FISHERMAN'S CAMP, NO. 2, Saguenay
River, Quebec, Canada   1937
Brush and ink on paper,
7 2/5 x 9 9/10 in. (19.1 x 25.4 cm)
Signed lower right: *Louis I. Kahn '37*
Collection of Mr. and Mrs. Milton
Abelson

When employing brush and ink to sketch
this favorite scene again, Kahn allowed
forms to become more three-dimensional
by varying the pressure of the brush
against the paper. In this way the linear
character of the sketch is softened. This is
reminiscent of the varying line
thicknesses Kahn once obtained through
the application of the graphite stick.

173

FISHERMAN'S CAMP, NO. 3, Saguenay
River, Quebec, Canada   1937
Pen and ink on bond paper, 8 2/5 x
10 9/10 in. (21.6 x 27.9 cm)
Signed lower right: *Louis I. Kahn*
Collection of Sue Ann Kahn

With increasing impatience, but with a
sensitive eye for the character of the
scene, Kahn reduces practically all
elements of this composition to a
symbolic state. The fir trees in the
background are defoliated and reduced
to "shorthand" icons. It really matters
very little what individual forms look
like. The overall image, through this
newly acquired system of hieroglyphics,
is what counts the most. And in this,
Kahn succeeds remarkably well.

174
FISHERMAN'S CAMP, NO. 4, Saguenay
River, Quebec, Canada 1937
Watercolor on paper, 8 1/2 x 11 1/4 in.
(21.9 x 28.9 cm)
Verso of No. 257
Collection of Sue Ann Kahn

In painting this watercolor Kahn took
considerable liberties by departing from
the original travel sketch of this scene.
This, of course, is in keeping with artistic
license and especially with Kahn's
personal predilection for such changes.
In his article "The Value and Aim in
Sketching" (*T-Square Club Journal*, May
1931), Kahn stated: "I have learned to
regard it as no physical impossibility to
move mountains and trees, or change
cupolas and towers to suit my taste." The
rearrangement of elements in this
painting did not, however, result in a
composition superior to the original
sketch. But it did retain the freshness and
appearance of a painting made from
nature, even though Kahn painted it in
Philadelphia after his return from his
short vacation in Canada.

175
MOORED BOATS, NO. 1, Gaspe
Peninsula, Quebec, Canada 1937
Watercolor on bond paper, 5 9/10 x
8 3/5 in. (15.2 x 22.2 cm)
Collection of Sue Ann Kahn

There exist strong similarities in this
sketch to watercolor No. 174. Of
particular interest is Kahn's return to the
strong image of the fir tree on the left and
the placement of boats on the beach. The
fluid character of this sketch is derived to
some extent from the application of
watercolors to a smooth paper.

176
VILLAGE STREET, Gaspe Peninsula,
Quebec, Canada   1936–37
Charcoal pencil on paper,
size not available
Present whereabouts unknown

Kahn uses charcoal pencil here in the
clear, precise manner of architectural
rendering. Squiggly foliage and
shrubbery outlines are remarkably similar
to treatments of such subjects by Le
Corbusier in his sketches of this time.
There is, however, no evidence that Kahn
was either aware of or directly influenced
by the drawings of Le Corbusier's at this
point.

177
BACKYARD: DETAILS, Gaspe Peninsula,
Quebec, Canada   1936–37
Pencil on paper, 11 x 7 9/10 in.
(27.6 x 20.3 cm)
Color notations
Verso of No. 249
Collection of Sue Ann Kahn

There is a delightful order in this helter-
skelter grouping of buildings and shacks
which must have fascinated Kahn. Color
notations indicate that Kahn intended to
transform this sketch into a painting.

178
HARBOR WITH A SHELTER, NO. 1,
Gloucester, Massachusetts   1933–36
Charcoal on paper, size not available
Present whereabouts unknown

This, the first of three renditions of the
same scene (see Nos. 179 and 180),
was executed by Kahn on the spot. It
possesses all the characteristic
spontaneity of his direct sketches from
nature. Selecting a small portion of the
harbor, Kahn was able to create a
concentration of interest in the scene.
The angular arcade of the dock shelter
echoes the gables of harbor structures
and houses rising in the background.
The church spire at the top of the hill
anchors the composition and reflects the
verticality of the sailboat mast in the right
foreground.

179
HARBOR WITH A SHELTER, NO. 2,
Gloucester, Massachusetts   1933–36
Tempera on paper, size not available
Present whereabouts unknown

Kahn painted this scene from charcoal
study No. 178. Making only minor
compositional adjustments he hoped to
achieve an exciting painting of a very
interesting subject. However, the slow
and flat character of tempera robbed
Kahn of the vitality and character the
original sketch possessed. He was
obviously dissatisfied with the result and
abandoned the painting. His next effort
to salvage the on-the-spot character of
the charcoal original was watercolor
painting No. 180.

180
HARBOR WITH A SHELTER, NO. 3,
Gloucester, Massachusetts   1933–36
Watercolor on paper, 15 x 18 in.
(36.2 x 44.1 cm)
Collection of Sue Ann Kahn

This watercolor, a final effort at
producing a painting from charcoal
sketch No. 178 and tempera No. 179,
recaptures at least some of the immediacy
of the original sketch. This is due largely
to Kahn's proficiency with watercolors, a
medium which, by its very nature,
necessitates rapid production and
discourages overelaboration. While
employing the loose style typical of his
early efforts in watercolor, this work still
falls short of paintings made by Kahn
during his Italian sojourn.In particular,
the blocky handling of foliage and the
unconvincing orange building shades
lack his usual mastery.

181
BEACH HOUSES, NO. 1, Provincetown, Massachusetts 1934
Watercolor on paper, 8 2/5 x 11 1/10 in. (21.6 x 28.6 cm)
Signed lower right: *Louis I. Kahn*
Collection of Mr. and Mrs. Milton Abelson

This painting is the beginning of a series of rural and small town studies in which buildings acquire a dominance and where Kahn is able to demonstrate the architectural sensitivity at the center of his work. This is one of two watercolor paintings (see also No. 182) for which there is no apparent pencil or charcoal field sketch. Either one or both of these paintings were made in Philadelphia from travel sketches. They exhibit extraordinary similarities, almost as though Kahn wished to make two identical paintings. The only variation exists in the cloud formation. The color differences are most likely due to distortions in the reproduction of No. 182, which was photographed in 1972 in Kahn's office under adverse lighting conditions.

182
BEACH HOUSES, NO. 2, Provincetown, Massachusetts 1934
Watercolor on paper, size not available
Present whereabouts unknown

Kahn exhibits in these two paintings (Nos. 181 and 182) his complete control of the watercolor medium. In this version he succeeds in utilizing two diverse techniques—one for handling the sky and another for the remainder of the painting. The sky is washed and the high clouds are worked within the wet surface of blue pigment. Two pink clouds are left out in the wash, thus giving them the necessary highlights provided by dry paper. In the usual method of watercolor painting, boats, water, and houses are treated in such a way as to allow the white of the paper to show through and provide sparkle and highlights. Especially evocative are the houses, where Kahn, with his sensitive brushwork, creates the impression of a bright sunny day by the sea shore.

According to Esther Kahn, the scene in these paintings represents a view from their beach cottage bedroom window.

183
"MAGAZINE," Matane, Gaspe Peninsula,
Quebec, Canada   1936–37
Charcoal on paper, 4 9/10 x 7 9/10 in.
(12.7 x 20.3 cm)
Inscribed lower right: *Magazine Matane*
Collection of Sue Ann Kahn

This view is certainly a far cry from the
humble and romantic scenes which
Kahn sketched in Italy. However, the
unpretentious nature of this down-to-
earth North American simplicity
offered the essence of urbanity in an
unsophistcated setting.

184
BARN, NO. 1, Gaspe Peninsula,
Quebec, Canada   1936–37
Charcoal on paper, 4 9/10 x 7 9/10 in.
(12.7 x 20.3 cm)
Collection of Sue Ann Kahn

185
BARN, NO. 2, Gaspe Peninsula,
Quebec, Canada
Exact date unknown (c. 1940s)
Charcoal pencil on paper,
size not available
Present whereabouts unknown

This rendition of a barn scene was most
likely made in Philadelphia during the
1940s from a Canadian travel sketch (No.
184). This is one of a number of sketches
that demonstrate the development of
linearity in Kahn's drawings. This
tendency first appears in a few of his
crayon drawings (Nos. 107 and 108)
and a charcoal pencil sketch (No. 176),
and reaches a crystallization when
Kahn employs the pen-and-ink medium.
With this technique he adopts a Le
Corbusier–like linear mannerism and
establishes a new repertoire for his own
sketches. Through this method
uninterrupted lines carefully describe the
main subjects and the less important
elements are reduced to symbolic
simplicity. This technique is evident in
this sketch. The barn is handled with the
utmost linear care, while the
surroundings are treated in a casual
manner. Kahn departs here completely
from establishing shades and shadows
and relies exclusively on crisp lines as a
means of describing forms.

186
DUCKS BY THE BAY and COTTAGE,
Gaspe Peninsula, Quebec, Canada
1936–37
Charcoal on paper, 11 x 9 in.
(27.6 x 21.3 cm); top image: 4 x 7 in.
(9.5 x 17.1 cm); bottom image: 4 x 6 in.
(9.5 x 13.3 cm)
Color notations on bottom image
Collection of Sue Ann Kahn

187
BOATS ON A BAY, Gaspe Peninsula,
Quebec, Canada 1937
Watercolor on paper, 15 x 19 in.
(36.5 x 46.9 cm); cropped image:
11 1/4 x 15 3/5 (28.9 x 40.0 cm)
Collection of Sue Ann Kahn

Interestingly, Kahn decided to crop this
picture once he realized that the cloud in
the upper-left corner detracted from the
composition by creating a four-point
frame with the cloud on the right and the
two bottom boats.

188
MOUNTAIN VILLAGE, NO. 3,
Cape Breton Island, Nova Scotia,
Canada   1937
Watercolor on paper, 14 x 20 in.
(35.9 X 51.4 cm)
Collection of Mr. and Mrs. Milton
Abelson

In this color version of the top bordered
sketch in No. 191, Kahn adds and
reorganizes elements of the scene in
order to achieve a more defined
rendition of the village road. The small
building in the left foreground with two
men in front is actually taken from
another scene in the center sketch of No.
191. This allows for a more balanced
arrangement as compared to the original
sketch and the ink version (see No. 197).
Trees and building forms with solid color
washes lose their light appearance and
gain a heavy, rocklike character.

189
COVERED BRIDGE, Gaspe Peninsula,
Quebec, Canada   1936–37
Charcoal on paper, 4 9/10 x 7 9/10 in.
(12.7 x 20.3 cm)
Collection of Sue Ann Kahn

The linearity which became so prevalent
in Kahn's 1940s drawings appears very
infrequently during his 1930s travels. He
depended considerably on the use of
shades and shadows for the delineation
of forms and the establishment of depth.
This drawing, No. 186, and No. 190
demonstrate this point quite clearly. The
way Kahn draws trees and distant forms,
especially in No. 190, is reminiscent of
his European graphite-stick technique.

190
RURAL SCENES, Nova Scotia,
Canada   1937
Pencil on paper, 9 1/5 x 8 3/5 in. (23.8 x
22.5 cm); top left image: 3 9/10 x 3 in.
(10.2 x 7.9 cm); top right image: 4 4/5 x
3 in. (12.4 x 7.9 cm); bottom image:
6 1/5 x 8 7/10 in. (15.9 x 22.5 cm)
Verso of No. 273
Collection of Sue Ann Kahn

191
MOUNTAIN VILLAGE, NO. 1 AND
OTHER SKETCHES, Cape Breton Island,
Nova Scotia, Canada   1937
Pencil on paper, 13 9/10 x 10 in. (35.6 x
25.7 cm); bordered images: top left:
2 9/10 x 4 9/10 in. (7.6 x 12.7 cm); top
right: 2 2/5 x 2 9/10 in. (6.3 x 7.6 cm);

middle: 2 9/10 x 3 2/5 in. (6.3 x 8.9 cm);
bottom: 3 2/5 x 6 1/5 in. (8.9 x 15.9 cm)
Color notations
Private collection

The top-left bordered sketch served as
the model for one pen-and-ink drawing

(No. 197) and one watercolor (No. 188).
The bottom sketch was transformed into
pen-and-ink drawing No. 196. The other
sketches also must have been intended as
studies for ink or color interpretations.
There are, however, no other known
versions of these scenes.

192
STREET IN A COASTAL VILLAGE, NO. 1,
Isle Madame, Nova Scotia, Canada 1936
Watercolor on paper, 14 9/10 x 21
4/5 in. (38.4 x 55.9 cm)
Collection of Sue Ann Kahn

Of all the scenes from his Canadian
vacations, Kahn was fascinated by this
one enough to produce four watercolor
versions. Each one is almost identical to
the others. Only the right foreground
undergoes slight compositional
modifications. Except for No. 195, all the
paintings are executed in a very fluid
manner, with the plasticity of forms
dominating surface characteristics. In this
version the cattle and one of the human
figures are left unfinished, most probably
because of Kahn's dissatisfaction with the
overall outcome of the painting. No. 195
is the most developed version. It is
painted with more care in texture and
detail. However, the dense application of
pigments departs from watercolor's
immediacy and loses the freedom of the
other three renditions.

193
STREET IN A COASTAL VILLAGE, NO. 2,
Isle Madame, Nova Scotia,
Canada   1936
Watercolor on paper, 13 7/10 x
18 1/5 in. (35.2 x 46.7 cm)
Private collection

194
STREET IN A COASTAL VILLAGE, NO. 3,
Isle Madame, Nova Scotia,
Canada   1936
Watercolor on paper, 13 9/10 x
17 7/10 in. (35.8 x 45.4 cm)
Collection of Sue Ann Kahn

195
STREET IN A COASTAL VILLAGE, NO. 4
Isle Madame, Nova Scotia,
Canada   1936
Watercolor on paper, 7 9/10 x
10 1/10 in. (20.3 x 26.0 cm)
Collection of Mrs. Esther I. Kahn

196
VALLEY VILLAGE, Cape Breton Island,
Nova Scotia, Canada   1937
Pen and ink on paper, size not available
Signed lower right: Lou K '37
Present whereabouts unknown

This transformation of the small sketch at
the bottom of No. 191 follows Kahn's
newly acquired manner of handling pen
and ink. Staccato pen strokes contain the
contour lines of major forms and
combine to create a very credible
portrayal of a small village nestled in the
foothills. Kahn's shorthand notations for
trees are applied to buildings as well—
both stark symbols of reality.

197
MOUNTAIN VILLAGE, NO. 2,
Cape Breton Island, Nova Scotia,
Canada   1937
Pen and ink on paper, 9 1/3 x 12 1/3 in.
(24.1 x 31.7 cm)
Signed lower right: Lou K '37
Collection of Sue Ann Kahn

Drawn in Philadelphia from a small
sketch (No. 191), Kahn exhibits a change
in his application of pen to paper. While
in most of his previous pen-and-ink
sketches lines were predominantly
uniform in weight, Kahn in this drawing
changes pressure on his pen, allowing
the point to spread and produce lines
with variable thicknesses. This technique,
in a somewhat aggressive manner, allows
for the satisfactory modeling of forms
without a need for excessive linework.

198
RIVIERE-AU-RENARD, Gaspe Peninsula,
Quebec, Canada   1936
Charcoal on paper, 4 9/10 x 7 9/10 in.
(12.7 x 20.3 cm)
Color notations
Inscribed lower right: *Cap. Riviere au
Renard*
Collection of Sue Ann Kahn

199
STACKING HAY, Isle Madame,
Nova Scotia, Canada   1936
Pencil on bond paper, 5 9/10 x 8 7/10 in.
(15.2 x 22.5 cm)
Color notations
Collection of Sue Ann Kahn

This sketch is the first of a series of nine
renditions (Nos. 199–208) of a pastoral
scene in a coastal village on Gaspe
Peninsula. Upon his return to
Philadelphia, Kahn transformed this
simple sketch into several variations in
tempera and watercolors. Of interest are
the grazing cattle in the center
background. Taken from study No.
160—where they were detailed more
elaborately—they are repeated in study
Nos. 201 and 202.

200
HOUSES ON THE BAY, Isle Madame,
Nova Scotia, Canada   1936
Watercolor on paper, 5 1/2 x 8 1/10 in.
(14.3 x 20.9 cm)
Collection of Sue Ann Kahn

Kahn found the background houses in
watercolors Nos. 192–95 of special
interest. He zoomed in on them and
created a new composition which
comfortably stands on its own.

201
COASTAL VILLAGE, NO. 1,
Isle Madame, Nova Scotia,
Canada   1936
Tempera on paper, 8 4/5 x 11 3/5 in.
(22.8 x 29.8 cm)
Collection of Sue Ann Kahn

Borrowing essential elements from
his field sketches, Kahn composed a
scene that attempts to evoke a sense
of Arcadian beauty. However the
voluptuous rendition of the sky, with its
yellow glow, produces a disquieting
effect, as does the unclear delineation of
the sea.

202
COASTAL VILLAGE, NO. 2, Isle
Madame, Nova Scotia, Canada   1936
Tempera on paper, 8 4/5 x 11 3/5 in.
(22.8 x 29.8 cm)
Collection of Sue Ann Kahn

This painting and Nos. 203, 204, and
205 maintain the same arrangement of
buildings on the sea shore. The
changeable elements are people, cattle,
trees, and utility poles. With the
exception of the sky, water, and the
ground, most of the elements are treated
as solids or silhouettes—symbols of their
form.

203
COASTAL VILLAGE, NO. 3, Isle
Madame, Nova Scotia, Canada   1936
Tempera on paper, 8 9/10 x 10 9/10 in.
(18.1 x 27.9 cm)
Signed lower middle: *Lou K.*
Collection of Mrs. Esther I. Kahn

In this variation on the image of the Isle
Madame coastal village, Kahn wields an
expressionistic manner by outlining bare
trees in bright red. The composition of
the ghostlike trees is also strange and out
of place. The beautifully painted
background is thus contradicted by this
move, and the scene acquires an air of
mystery and foreboding.

204
COASTAL VILLAGE, NO. 4, Isle
Madame, Nova Scotia, Canada   1936
Watercolor on paper, 12 1/10 x 15 in.
(31.1 x 38.7 cm)
Collection of Sue Ann Kahn

This unfinished painting is another
variation on the theme begun in No. 201.
Kahn eliminates the grazing cattle and
two men, one with a wheelbarrow and
the other carrying a sack, and puts a
racing, horse-drawn carriage in their
place. The unfinished left side contains
only the outline of a house. Kahn
abandoned this painting, perhaps
because of his dissatisfaction with its
progress.

205
COASTAL VILLAGE, NO. 5, Isle
Madame, Nova Scotia, Canada   1936
Watercolor on paper, size not available
Present whereabouts unknown

This rendition from the series is by far the
loosest and most realistic. The buildings
are more believable and inviting, and the
inclusion of utility poles does not detract
from the overall presentation. The colors
are pleasantly fresh and cool, especially
the sprinkling of purple suggesting wild
flowers in the foreground. The horse-
drawn carriage to the right is left
unfinished in a probable endeavor to
balance the composition.

206
COASTAL VILLAGE, NO. 6, Isle
Madame, Nova Scotia, Canada   1936
Watercolor on paper, 15 x 21 4/5 in.
(38.7 x 55.9 cm)
Signed lower right: *Louis I. Kahn*
Collection of Sue Ann Kahn

Again, Kahn explores the general theme
of Nos. 201–204 with the houses pushed
to the middle and the mountains placed
in the background. The right foreground
is occupied by the familiar horse-drawn
carriage, but this time it moves more
slowly. Kahn's bold use of bright colors
and color contrasts allowed him to
explore artistic tendencies he was then
discovering in the work of the fauves and
expressionists.

207
COASTAL VILLAGE, NO. 7, Isle
Madame, Nova Scotia, Canada 1936
Pastels and watercolor on paper,
15 x 21 9/10 in. (38.7 x 56.2 cm)
Collection of Sue Ann Kahn

This pastel version of the coastal village
landscape is probably one of Kahn's
earliest works done in this medium. The
most successful parts of this sketch are
the distant hills and the transparent
shading of the houses.

208
COASTAL VILLAGE, NO. 8, Isle
Madame, Nova Scotia, Canada 1936
Watercolor on paper, 15 x 21 4/5 in.
(38.7 X 55.9 cm)
Collection of Sue Ann Kahn

Kahn left this rainbow-colored rendition
unfinished, most probably because the
running of pigments in the foreground
eliminated the possibility of salvaging the
painting.

209
VILLAGE AND WATERFRONT, Isle
Madame, Nova Scotia, Canada   1936
Pencil on paper, 13 3/5 x 9 9/10 in.
(34.9 x 25.4 cm); top and bottom images,
4 9/10 x 8 7/10 in. (12.7 x 22.5 cm) each
Color notations
Verso of No. 164
Collection of Sue Ann Kahn

The bottom sketch served as a direct
model for watercolor No. 211, while the
top sketch may have inspired a series of
four watercolors (Nos. 192–195). The
vantage point of the original sketch,
made at a normal eye level, is raised
considerably in the watercolor versions.
This was probably Kahn's method of
revealing the village's bay side. As in
other instances, Kahn uses artistic license
to rearrange and import elements to
enhance the composition.

210
BEACHED BOAT, Isle Madame, Nova
Scotia, Canada   1936
Oil on canvas, 15 3/10 x 19 2/5 in.
(39.4 x 49.8 cm)
Collection of Mrs. Esther I. Kahn

This is one of a few oil paintings that
Kahn attempted in his Philadelphia
studio. A medium requiring considerably
more patience than his favorite
watercolors, it robbed him of the
spontaneity which he preferred. But Kahn
compensated for it through an almost
cubist exploration of forms reduced to
their most common denominator. The
muted colors and the heavy sky, darker
than the background water, establish a
solemn mood in this waterfront
environment.

211
COASTAL HOUSES, Isle Madame,
Nova Scotia, Canada   1936
Watercolor on paper, 13 1/3 x 17 1/3 in.
(34.3 x 44.5 cm)
Collection of Sue Ann Kahn

This painting and No. 210 continue
Kahn's exploration of simple boxlike
houses and structures at seashore
locations. The elevated vantage point
provides a panoramic view of the water
with boats and landforms accentuating
the calmness of the bay.

212
GASPE PENINSULA, NO.1, Quebec,
Canada   1937
Pen, brush, and ink on paper,
4 3/5 x 7 2/5 in. (12.0 x 19.0 cm)
Shown at a traveling exhibition
organized by the Pennsylvania Academy
of the Fine Arts, 1978–1979, Catalogue
No. 38a–b., titled: *Sheets from a
Sketchbook of the Gaspe Peninsula, 1937*
Collection of Sue Ann Kahn

This is one of fourteen drawings in
Kahn's sketchbook from his 1937 trip to
Gaspe Peninsula. The sketches were
made on a boat ride down the St.
Lawrence and Saguenay rivers. Kahn
never used a camera and these hasty
sketches served as snapshots of scenery
which he desired to preserve for memory
and possible translation into paintings.
Using pen and regular fountain-pen ink,
he managed to soften selected forms with
a wet watercolor brush applied over the
ink lines. This gave the sketches a velvety
character reminiscent of Chinese and
Japanese landscapes.

213
GASPE PENINSULA, NO. 2, Quebec,
Canada   1937
Pen, brush, and ink on paper,
4 3/5 x 7 2/5 in. (12.0 x 19.0 cm)
Shown at a traveling exhibition
organized by the Pennsylvania Academy
of the Fine Arts, 1978–1979, Catalogue
No. 38a–b., titled: *Sheets from a
Sketchbook of the Gaspe Peninsula, 1937*
Collection of Sue Ann Kahn

214
GASPE PENINSULA, NO. 3, Quebec,
Canada   1937
Pen, brush, and ink on paper,
4 3/5 x 7 2/5 in. (12.0 x 19.0 cm)
Shown at a traveling exhibition
organized by the Pennsylvania Academy
of the Fine Arts, 1978–1979, Catalogue
No. 38a–b., titled: *Sheets from a
Sketchbook of the Gaspe Peninsula, 1937*
Collection of Sue Ann Kahn

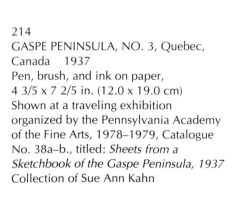

215
GASPE PENINSULA, NO. 4, Quebec,
Canada 1937
Pen, brush, and ink on paper,
4 3/5 x 7 2/5 in. (12.0 x 19.0 cm)
Shown at a traveling exhibition
organized by the Pennsylvania Academy
of the Fine Arts, 1978–1979, Catalogue
No. 38a–b., titled: *Sheets from a
Sketchbook of the Gaspe Peninsula, 1937*
Collection of Sue Ann Kahn

216
GASPE PENINSULA, NO. 5, Quebec,
Canada 1937
Pen, brush, and ink on paper,
4 3/5 x 7 2/5 in. (12.0 x 19.0 cm)
Color notations at lower left
Shown at a traveling exhibition
organized by the Pennsylvania Academy
of the Fine Arts, 1978–1979, Catalogue
No. 38a–b., titled: *Sheets from a
Sketchbook of the Gaspe Peninsula, 1937*
Collection of Sue Ann Kahn

217
GASPE PENINSULA, NO. 6, Quebec,
Canada 1937
Pen, brush, and ink on paper,
4 3/5 x 7 2/5 in. (12.0 x 19.0 cm)
Shown at a traveling exhibition
organized by the Pennsylvania Academy
of the Fine Arts, 1978–1979, Catalogue
No. 38a–b., titled: *Sheets from a
Sketchbook of the Gaspe Peninsula, 1937*
Collection of Sue Ann Kahn

218
GASPE PENINSULA, NO. 7, Quebec,
Canada   1937
Pen, brush, and ink on paper,
4 3/5 x 7 2/5 in. (12.0 x 19.0 cm)
Shown at a traveling exhibition
organized by the Pennsylvania Academy
of the Fine Arts, 1978–1979, Catalogue
No. 38a–b., titled: *Sheets from a*
Sketchbook of the Gaspe Peninsula, 1937
Collection of Sue Ann Kahn

219
GASPE PENINSULA, NO. 8, Quebec,
Canada   1937
Pen, brush, and ink on paper,
4 3/5 x 7 2/5 in. (12.0 x 19.0 cm)
Shown at a traveling exhibition
organized by the Pennsylvania Academy
of the Fine Arts, 1978–1979, Catalogue
No.38a–b., titled: *Sheets from a*
Sketchbook of the Gaspe Peninsula, 1937
Collection of Sue Ann Kahn

220
GASPE PENINSULA, NO. 9, Quebec,
Canada   1937
Pen, brush, and ink on paper,
4 3/5 x 7 2/5 in. (12.0 x 19.0 cm)
Shown at a traveling exhibition
organized by the Pennsylvania Academy
of the Fine Arts, 1978–1979, Catalogue
No. 38 a–b., titled: *Sheets from a*
Sketchbook of the Gaspe Peninsula, 1937
Collection of Sue Ann Kahn

221
GASPE PENINSULA, NO. 10, Quebec,
Canada 1937
Pen, brush, and ink on paper,
4 3/5 x 7 2/5 in. (12.0 x 19.0 cm)
Shown at a traveling exhibition
organized by the Pennsylvania Academy
of the Fine Arts, 1978–1979, Catalogue
No. 38a–b., titled: *Sheets from a
Sketchbook of the Gaspe Peninsula, 1937*
Collection of Sue Ann Kahn

222
GASPE PENINSULA, NO. 11, Quebec,
Canada 1937
Pen, brush, and ink on paper,
4 3/5 x 7 2/5 in. (12.0 x 19.0 cm)
Shown at a traveling exhibition
organized by the Pennsylvania Academy
of the Fine Arts, 1978–1979, Catalogue
No. 38a–b., titled: *Sheets from a
Sketchbook of the Gaspe Peninsula, 1937*
Collection of Sue Ann Kahn

223
GASPE PENINSULA, NO. 12, Quebec,
Canada 1937
Pen, brush, and ink on paper
4 2/5 x 7 1/2 in. (11.4 x 19.4 cm)
Color notations inscribed vertically on
the left
Shown at a traveling exhibition
organized by the Pennsylvania Academy
of the Fine Arts, 1978–1979, Catalogue
No. 38a–b., titled: *Sheets from a
Sketchbook of the Gaspe Peninsula, 1937*
Collection of Sue Ann Kahn

224

GASPE PENINSULA, NO. 13, Quebec,
Canada   1937
Pen, brush, and ink on paper, 4 1/2 x
7 2/5 in. (11.7 x 19.0 cm); image: 3 1/5 x
6 2/5 in. (8.3 x 16.5 cm)
Inscribed and signed lower right:
Perce a mist LIK
Shown at a traveling exhibition
organized by the Pennsylvania Academy
of the Fine Arts, 1978–1979, Catalogue
No.38a–b., titled: *Sheets from a
Sketchbook of the Gaspe Peninsula, 1937*
Collection of Sue Ann Kahn

This sketch stands out from the others in
this group due to Kahn's heavy use of
wash applied over the pen-and-ink lines.
It apparently served as a model for a
quick pen, brush, and ink rendition (No.
225), which Kahn most likely sketched
upon his return to Philadelphia.

225

VILLAGE BY THE BAY, NO. 1,
Cape Breton Island, Nova Scotia, Canada
1937
Pen, brush, and ink on paper, 11 9/10 x
13 9/10 in. (30.5 x 35.6 cm)
Signed lower right: *Lou K '37*
Private collection

This shorthand translation of travel sketch
No. 224 retains the general scenic drama
of the original without reliance on its
somewhat overworked washes.

226
BEACH WITH HILLS, Gaspe Peninsula,
Quebec, Canada   1936
Charcoal on paper, size not available
Signed lower right: *Lou K.*
Present whereabouts unknown

Compared with other sketches in the
Canadian series, this one falls somewhat
short in its quality of execution. Kahn's
reliance on fuzzy shading gives it an air
of indecision and a lack of focus. The
sharp, sure linework is absent with the
exception of the background outlines.
The scene resembles No. 224 in the
placement of shoreline, buildings,
background cliffs, and even the lonely
boat just off the beach.

227
CAP CHAT, Gaspe Peninsula, Quebec,
Canada   1936
Charcoal on paper, 4 9/10 x 7 9/10 in.
(12.7 x 20.3 cm)
Inscribed lower right: *Cap Chat*
Collection of Sue Ann Kahn

Compared with No. 226, this sketch
exhibits a more descriptive use of
charcoal. The perspective of the rolling
roadway is reinforced by a dark layer of
trees in the middle-ground and the
faintness of distant hills.

228
VILLAGE BY THE BAY, NO. 2,
Cape Breton Island, Nova Scotia,
Canada   1937
Tempera on paper, 8 2/5 x 11 1/10 in.
(21.6 x 28.6 cm)
Private collection

This painting appears to be a
combination of views derived from a
small sketch (No. 231) and a reversal of
the composition from No. 224. Kahn
handled the cumbersome tempera
medium quite well, without a significant
loss of the freshness so evident in his
watercolors.

229
"MAHONE BAY N.S.," Nova Scotia,
Canada   1936–38
Watercolor on paper, 11 9/10 x
10 3/4 in. (30.5 x 27.6 cm)
Title label on back: *Mahone Bay N.S.*
Exhibited at the 36th Annual
Philadelphia Watercolor Exhibition,
Pennsylvania Academy of the Fine Arts,
1938, Catalogue No. 2354
Collection of Sue Ann Kahn

This dramatic watercolor recalls Kahn's
stylized paintings from Italy. Missing,
however, are the soft colors and rhythmic
art-deco forms. Here the brush strokes
are much more turbulent and forms more
enigmatic.

230
ROCKY COVE, Nova Scotia, Canada
1936–37
Watercolor on paper, 9 x 7 2/5 in.
(23.3 x 19.0 cm)
Collection of Dr. David Alpers

This remarkable watercolor borders on
total abstraction. Water, shoreline, and
background foliage dissolve into a
harmony of subtle complementary
colors—green, purple, and the white
of exposed paper, suggesting a foaming
surf.

231
CLIFF ROAD, NO. 1, Cape Breton Island,
Nova Scotia, Canada   1937
Black crayon on paper, 4 4/5 x 8 in.
(12.5 x 20.5 cm)
Shown at a traveling exhibition
organized by the Pennsylvania Academy
of the Fine Arts, 1978–1979, Catalogue
No. 40a, titled: *Cape Breton Island, Nova
Scotia, 1937. Gaspe Sketchbook*
Collection of Sue Ann Kahn

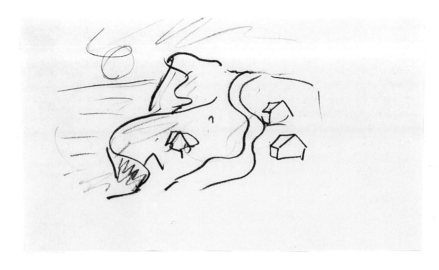

Kahn transformed this little crayon sketch
into two pen-and-ink drawings when he
returned to Philadelphia (see Nos. 232
and 233). In this simple, rapidly sketched
scene, Kahn captures the very essence of
a spectacular earth formation, humble
huts clinging to the bluff high above the
bay, and a snaky road diving beyond the
horizon's edge—all with minimal
linework. In No. 232 Kahn elaborates on
the original sketch by adding trees,
animals, and people. The harsh pen-and-
ink rendition, while capturing the overall
flavor of the scene, loses the purity of
form so striking in the original version. In
No. 233 the distillation of forms to their
essences reaches beyond the original
sketch. Here Kahn truly succeeds in what
appears to be an effortless conquest of
the spirit of the landscape.

232
CLIFF ROAD, NO. 2, Cape Breton Island,
Nova Scotia, Canada   1937
Pen and ink on paper, 8 1/3 x 10 9/10 in.
(21.4 x 28.0 cm)
Signed lower right: *Lou K/37*
Shown at a traveling exhibition
organized by the Pennsylvania Academy
of the Fine Arts, 1978–1979, Catalogue
No. 40b, titled: *Cape Breton Island, Nova
Scotia, 1937. Gaspe Sketchbook*
Collection of Sue Ann Kahn

233
CLIFF ROAD, NO. 3, Cape Breton Island,
Nova Scotia, Canada   1937
Pen and ink on paper, 8 1/3 x 10 9/10 in.
(21.4 x 28.0 cm)
Signed lower right: *Lou K '37*; Inscribed
lower right: *Dear Friend Ray. It's been
swell working with you, Xmas '46*
Shown at a traveling exhibition
organized by the Pennsylvania Academy
of the Fine Arts, 1978–1979, Catalogue
No. 40c, titled: *Cape Breton Island, Nova
Scotia, 1937. Gaspe Sketchbook*
Collection of Sue Ann Kahn

234
"ON THE WAY TO STOCKTON FROM
OAKLAND," California   1940–50
Charcoal pencil on paper, 11 3/4 x 8 3/5
in. (30.2 x 22.2 cm); top image: 3 1/5 x
6 9/10 in. (8.3 x 17.8 cm); bottom image:
2 9/10 x 5 1/10 in. (7.6 x 13.3 cm)
Inscribed on bottom of top image: *On
the way to Stockton from Oakland*
Color notations in left margin
Collection of Sue Ann Kahn

This is one of three sheets of sketches
Kahn made from a moving train during
his California visit (see also Nos. 235 and
236). With the exception of the bottom
image, Kahn abandons in these drawings
the linear representation so common in
his work of that time and models forms
with heavy charcoal shading.

235
SAN FERNANDO VALLEY FARMS,
California   1940–50
Charcoal pencil on paper, 11 2/10 x
8 3/5 in. (30.2 x 22.2 cm); image:
5 2/5 x 8 3/5 in. (14.0 x 22.2 cm)
Collection of Sue Ann Kahn

236
"SAN FERNANDO VALLEY," California
1940–50
Charcoal pencil on paper, 8 3/5 x
11 7/10 in. (22.2 x 30.2 cm)
Inscribed lower right: *San Fernando
Valley*
Collection of Sue Ann Kahn

237
ROCK FORMATION, NO. 1,
Garden of the Gods, Colorado 1948
Charcoal on paper, 8 3/5 x 11 9/10 in.
(22.2 x 30.5 cm)
Collection of Sue Ann Kahn

This is one of four charcoal sketches
(Nos. 237–240) devoted to the study of
unique rock formations in this
spectacular Colorado mountain setting.
They are executed with Kahn's usual
sense of the sublime with seemingly little
effort.

238
ROCK FORMATION, NO. 2,
Garden of the Gods, Colorado 1948
Charcoal on paper, 8 3/5 x 11 9/10 in.
(22.2 x 30.5 cm)
Collection of Sue Ann Kahn

239
ROCK FORMATION NO. 3,
Garden of the Gods, Colorado 1948
Charcoal pencil on paper, 8 3/5 x
11 9/10 in. (22.2 x 30.5 cm)
Collection of Sue Ann Kahn

240
SUSPENSION FOOTBRIDGE OVER
GORGE, Colorado   1948
Charcoal pencil on paper, 8 3/5 x
11 9/10 in. (22.2 x 30.5 cm)
Collection of Sue Ann Kahn

241

COAST and VILLAGE WITH CHURCH
STEEPLE, Gaspe Peninsula, Quebec,
Canada   1936–37
Charcoal pencil on paper, 10 9/10 x
8 1/2 in. (27.9 x 21.9 cm); top image:
1 7/10 x 3 7/10 in. (4.4 x 9.5 cm); bottom
image: 4 x 5 in. (10.5 x 13.0 cm)
Inscribed top right: *Canada*
Collection of Sue Ann Kahn

It is quite evident that Kahn maintained a
special fascination with vertical forms
such as towers and church steeples. His
European sketches are replete with
explorations of such structures. During
the 1930s, many of his sketches and
paintings featured church steeples as
distant accents in rural landscapes. The
series of drawings and paintings that
follow reveals Kahn's continual
exploration of religious structures and
towers.

In the bottom sketch the church steeple is
still handled as a distant element with no
significance other than to confirm its
existence in this little town. Of course, its
presence helps the composition by
adding verticality.

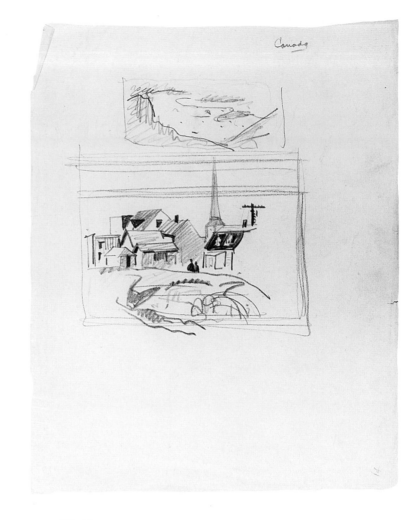

242

OLD CHURCH, NO. 1, New England
1936–37
Charcoal pencil on paper,
size not available
Proportion notations
Present whereabouts unknown

Kahn's interest in the architectural
qualities of this church took precedence
over any effort at preparing a sketch for a
painting. His markings of proportion
relate the width of the nave to parts of
the steeple. Kahn's fascination with this
church and especially its apse is reflected
in a watercolor rendition (No. 243) taken
from the opposite angle.

243
OLD CHURCH, NO. 2, New England
1936–37
Watercolor on paper, 12 4/5 x 9 1/2 in.
(33.0 X 24.4 cm)
Collection of Sue Ann Kahn

Kahn clearly elaborates here on the textural qualities of the wood sidings and shingles of the church and its adjoining structures. This contrasts with the very abstract rendition of the tree in the foreground. Also of interest is Kahn's buildup of gables and hips, culminating in the tip of the church's steeple, perfectly aligned with the unusual apse.

244
TOWERING CHURCH STEEPLES,
Gloucester, Massachusetts 1936
Watercolor on paper, 5 1/10 x 6 2/5 in.
(13.3 x 16.5 cm)
Collection of Sue Ann Kahn

Even though the church steeples are in
the far distance their prominence is
assured by a skillful rendition of the sky.
In a manner similar to No. 250, Kahn
dramatizes the towers by giving them an
aura of mysterious light. In this sketch,
however, the towers are silhouetted
against the glowing sky.

245
MAIN STREET BRIDGE, New England
1930–36
Watercolor on paper, 7 2/5 x 10 2/5 in.
(19.0 x 26.7 cm)
Collection of Sue Ann Kahn

246
CHURCH BEYOND THE BRIDGE,
New England 1930–36
Graphite and black crayon on paper,
6 3/5 x 6 in. (17.1 x 15.6 cm)
Collection of Sue Ann Kahn

This drawing has the appearance of a
lithograph. It was made in a manner
similar to Kahn's graphite-stick sketches
from Europe. However, the application of
crayon to paper in this drawing is harsher
and less exact. The church tower, on the
other hand, is portrayed with more
reverence. It stands bathed in light as a
bright element against the dark, brooding
buildings and trees, its features gently
revealed by only a few lines.

247
"ROCKLAND, MAIN," Rockland, Maine
1936–37
Charcoal pencil on paper, 4 9/10 x
7 9/10 in. (12.7 x 20.3 cm)
Inscribed middle right: Rockland Main
Collection of Sue Ann Kahn

A rural church becomes the focal point
of this quick sketch. It dominates the
scene and is accented by the dark form
of a tree to its right.

248
TOWNSCAPE WITH A CHURCH
STEEPLE, New England   1936–37
Charcoal pencil on paper,
size not available
Color notations
Present whereabouts unknown

This precise and crisp charcoal rendition
records a street scene for a future
painting. More importantly, it shows the
expert hand of an architect who
understands not only the building forms
but the spaces they define. The
compositional approach is similar to
Kahn's Italian townscapes (see No. 72),
even though the jagged shapes of the
New England architecture produce a
more disquieting skyline. As in the
European sketches, the tower assumes
the most prominent position.

249
STONE TOWER, Gaspe Peninsula,
Quebec, Canada   1936–37
Pencil on paper, 10 7/10 x 7 9/10 in.
(27.6 x 20.3 cm); image: 6 3/5 x 4 1/5
(17.1 x 10.8 cm)
Verso of No. 177
Collection of Sue Ann Kahn

This is a rather unusual looking tower
with a strange belfry window. The form
in the window is hard to comprehend
since the shadow cast by it gives us few
clues as to its nature.

250
THE WHITE CHURCH, NO. 4, 252
Rockport, Massachusetts   1930–36
Charcoal on paper, 5 4/5 x 6 4/5 in.
(14.9 x 17.5 cm)
Collection of Sue Ann Kahn

It would be hard to believe that Kahn did
not intend this scene to have some
symbolic meaning. The dichotomy
between the ghostlike brightness of the
church tower and the gloomy darkness of
the houses and figures on the street
suggests didactic intentions. The distant
church, however, is not accorded the
privilege of brightness, which it received
in Kahn's oil version of the scene.

251

THE WHITE CHURCH, NO. 1, Rockport,
Massachusetts   1930–36
Pencil on tracing paper, 13 7/10 x
19 1/3 in. (35.2 x 49.5 cm); image:
10 2/5 x 151/5 in. (26.7 x 39.1 cm)
Collection of Sue Ann Kahn

This pencil study served as a model for
three other versions of the same scene,
each in a different medium (Nos. 250,
252–53). Except for the starkness of the
bare trees, nothing in this sketch prepares
the viewer for the dramatic shock of its
later translations.

252

THE WHITE CHURCH, NO. 2, Rockport,
Massachusetts   1930–36
Watercolor on paper, 15 3/10 x 9 1/3 in.
(39.4 X 49.5 cm)
Collection of Sue Ann Kahn

In the portrayal of space and content, this
watercolor adheres quite faithfully to
pencil study No. 251. But the surprise is
Kahn's expressionistic use of primary
colors. This is not Kahn's usual painting
manner, in which he attempted to
capture the scene in a quick,
impressionistic manner. Here the mood
is conveyed through the use of coloration
and the mysterious transparency of trees.
Kahn's interest at that time was directed
toward the fauves and their predecessors.
His clip file contained numerous
reproductions of Gauguin, Van Gogh,
Matisse, Derain, Vlaminck and Dufy, cut
from journals and catalogues. This
watercolor and oil No. 253 were
produced under the strong influence of
these modern artists whom Kahn was
coming to appreciate.

253
THE WHITE CHURCH, NO. 3,
Rockport, Massachusetts   1930–36
Oil on canvas, 23 3/4 x 29 7/10 in.
(60.9 x 76.2 cm)
Collection of Mrs. Esther I. Kahn

In this oil version of pencil sketch No.
251, Kahn modifies elements of the
composition by adding another church
tower and by casting a mysterious light
on the otherwise desolate street. The
brightly lit tower against a dark gray sky
dominates the entire scene. Again, as in
the watercolor version (No. 252), trees
are bare and transparent, but do not
assume the importance of brightly
colored abstractions. Both of these
paintings fall away from Kahn's normal
mannerisms of the period. If anything,
they have a greater affinity to his
1950–51 pastels from Italy, Greece, and
Egypt.

254
CITY HALL, Philadelphia, Pennsylvania
1940–50
Pencil on perforated paper, 5 9/10 x
4 2/5 in. (15.2 x 11.4 cm)
Collection of Sue Ann Kahn

Kahn sketched the prominent position of
Philadelphia's City Hall on Broad Street
as a study of a refined urban space. This
drawing relates to his involvement at
the time with various projects for the
redevelopment of the city. The scale
of the tower is not compromised
significantly by the tall commercial
buildings framing the street. It is most
probably this relation that Kahn was
recording in this sketch. The plan outline
at the top of the sheet reveals the tower's
relation to the rest of the building.

255
COBBLESTONE STREET, Philadelphia
1949–50
Charcoal on tracing paper, 14 7/10 x
18 in. (37.8 x 46.4 cm)
Signed lower right: *Lou K*
Collection of Sue Ann Kahn

Kahn made this sketch as a study for the
Temple and Poplar Public Housing
Project, where the old church was to be
preserved and streets improved through
paving and landscaping. As in No. 254
this is a study of an urban space where a
significant building forms the focal point.
Even though this is not a pure artistic
work, the charcoal technique used in this
drawing is reminiscent of Kahn's sketches
of this period.

256
GOING TO CHURCH, NO. 1,
Gaspe Peninsula, Quebec,
Canada   1937
Charcoal on tracing paper, 18 3/5 x
23 1/2 in. (47.6 x 60.3 cm)
Collection of Sue Ann Kahn

This sketch explores a strange
perspective distortion in an almost
childlike manner. Kahn was obviously
less interested in the correct rendition of
this scene from a technical point of view
than in conveying an atmosphere of
innocent and peaceful community
activity. Kahn produced a watercolor
version of this sketch (No. 257).

257
GOING TO CHURCH, NO. 2,
Gaspe Peninsula, Quebec,
Canada   1937
Watercolor on paper, 8 1/2 x 11 1/4 in.
(21.9 X 28.9 cm)
Verso of No. 174
Collection of Sue Ann Kahn

By reducing the scope of sketch No. 256
to the church entrance and an adjoining
building, Kahn focuses attention on the
human component of the composition.
Perspective distortions present in
the charcoal sketch are significantly
reduced here by the removal of building
references. The highly reflective water in
the distance provides an exciting clue to
the location of the site.

258
JEWISH CEMETERY, NO. 1   1930–36
Watercolor on paper, 16 1/3 x
12 1/10 in. (41.9 x 31.1 cm); image:
15 1/3 x 9 3/5 in. (39.4 x 24.8 cm)
Collection of Sue Ann Kahn

This is one of two almost identical
watercolors (see also No. 259) of a
Jewish cemetery Kahn visited in Hungary
on his first European journey. They are
based either on a now-missing sketch or
they may have been painted from
memory. Kahn establishes the scene's
drama by casting light from behind the
gravestones and abstracting the forward-
pointing shadows. The mysterious purple
background is interrupted by ominous
and twisted branches from invisible trees.

259
JEWISH CEMETERY, NO. 2   1930–36
Watercolor on paper, 12 3/5 x 9 9/10 in.
(32.4 X 25.4 cm)
Private collection

260
FACTORY YARD, Philadelphia,
Pennsylvania   1930–35
Graphite on paper, size not available
Present whereabouts unknown

Kahn's technique of using the edges and
flat surfaces of a graphite stick, so
prevalent during the European trip from
which he had just returned, is still
evident in this sketch and in a more
heroic portrayal (No. 261). Shortly after
1930 he abandoned the use of this
technique in favor of a more linear
expression in pencil and charcoal.
The subject matter and compositional
characteristics of this drawing show
Kahn's continuing interest in representing
simple geometric forms found in
complex settings. He satisfied this interest
by choosing industrial subjects which he
managed to bring in line with more
familiar natural landscapes.

261
FACTORY, Philadelphia, Pennsylvania
1930–35
Graphite on paper, 8 7/10 x 6 7/10 in.
(22.3 X 17.2 cm)
Shown at a traveling exhibition
organized by the Pennsylvania Academy
of the Fine Arts, 1978–1979,
Catalogue No. 32.
Collection of the Philadelphia Maritime
Museum; Gift of Mrs. Esther I. Kahn

Like Fernand Léger, Charles Sheeler,
Charles Demuth, Ralston Crawford, and
Louis Lozowick, Kahn utilized the
confusion of modern industrial forms to
produce compositions which succeed by
the arranged harmony of elements
devoid of functional explanations. This
sketch borders on total abstraction.
Primary forms are arranged to produce a
pleasing pattern, a characteristic that
reveals the obvious architectural leaning
of the artist.

262
MEDICAL LECTURE 1930–35
Lithograph, 8 1/2 x 9 9/10 in.
(21.9 x 25.4 cm)
Signed lower right: *Louis I. Kahn*
Collection of Sue Ann Kahn

As in Kahn's portrayal of European
interiors, he concentrated on the play of
light in all its complexities during the
1930s. In this lithograph, reminiscent to
some extent of Thomas Eakins' *The Gross
Clinic*, Kahn investigates the scene's
difficult spatial organization and the
effect of light from the large window on
various surfaces—floors, furniture, and
people. This print and No. 264 are
among the very few lithographs Kahn
made in his lifetime.

263
"CAFE", NO. 1 1930–36
Graphite on paper, 8 7/10 x 12 in.
(22.5 x 31.0 cm)
Shown at a traveling exhibition
organized by the Pennsylvania Academy
of the Fine Arts, 1978–1979, Catalogue
No. 30, titled: *Study for a lithograph
entitled "Cafe," Philadelphia, 1930–35*
Collection of Sue Ann Kahn

This sketch is a study for lithograph
No. 264. Composition and shading are
rapidly conveyed in this study through
the graphite-stick method. In a way this
study maintains a life of its own in strong
competition with the finished lithograph.

264
"CAFE", NO. 2   1930–35
Lithograph on paper, 13 3/5 x 17 2/5 in.
(34.9 x 44.8 cm); image: 7 3/5 x
9 9/10 in. (19.7 x 25.4 cm)
Signed lower right: *Louis I. Kahn;*
inscribed lower left: *Cafe*
Shown at a traveling exhibition
organized by the Pennsylvania Academy
of the Fine Arts, 1978–1979,
Catalogue No. 31
Collection of Sue Ann Kahn

There are many possible sources of
inspiration for this work. American
scenes by John Sloan certainly come to
mind, as well as Van Gogh's *The Potato
Eaters.* But it is not the influence or, for
that matter, the technique that is
important in assessing the value of this
lithograph. It is, without any doubt,
Kahn's fascination with the nuances of
illumination that establishes this print's
vitality. This scene and *Medical Lecture*
(No. 262), apart from being credible
works of art, are undeniably important in
Kahn's development as an architect and
a master of light.

265
"IN THE CABIN," NO. 1, Indian Harbor,
Nova Scotia, Canada 1938
Pencil on paper, size not available
Inscribed lower right: *In the Cabin,
Indian Harbor, Nova Scotia, 1938*
Present whereabouts unknown

Kahn used this sketch to produce an oil
painting upon his return from Canada
(see No. 267). The seated man and the
woman outside are most probably Mr.
and Mrs. Jacob Sherman, with whom the
Kahns frequently traveled and shared
accommodations.

266
NUDE IN A DOORWAY, Halifax,
Nova Scotia, Canada 1937
Tempera on paper, 9 1/4 x 8 7/10 in.
(23.8 x 22.5 cm); image: 6 9/10 x
5 3/4 in. (17.8 x 14.6 cm)
Collection of Sue Ann Kahn

Kahn painted this somewhat whimsical
and voyeuristic scene to commemorate
the meager accommodations his wife
and he shared with the Shermans.
According to Esther Kahn, they did not
even have indoor plumbing.

267
"IN THE CABIN," NO. 2, Indian Harbor,
Nova Scotia, Canada 1938
Oil on canvas, 21 4/5 x 24 7/10 in.
(55.9 x 63.5 cm)
Collection of Sue Ann Kahn

Borrowing from cubism and purism,
Kahn translates Canadian travel sketch
No. 265 into this intriguing painting.
Kahn manages to strike a balance
between all the elements in the
composition. Forms are defined by color
planes; the seated man, the chair, and
the newspaper are presented in linework,
with colors sliding past the forms,
allowing some parts to appear
transparent; and the diagonals of various
planes direct the eye toward the red
female figure on the yellow plane.
Compared with *Child's Room* and
Artist in a Studio (Nos. 272 and 273,
respectively) this painting is a sophisti-
cated understanding of modernist
concerns in representation.

268
LEOPOLD KAHN, Philadelphia 1932
Scratchboard, 5 1/3 x 4 1/5 in.
(13.6 x 10.8 cm)
Exhibited at the 30th Annual
Philadelphia Watercolor Exhibition,
Pennsylvania Academy of the Fine Arts,
1932, Catalogue No. 2719
Shown at a traveling exhibition
organized by the Pennsylvania Academy
of the Fine Arts, 1978–1979, Catalogue
No. 35, titled: *Black and White, 1932*
Collection of Sue Ann Kahn

This is the only known portrait that Kahn
made of his father. There appears to be a
slight hint of inspiration from Picasso's
1920 pencil portrait of Stravinski, even
though the techniques are different. Yet
there are similarities, especially in the
manner in which hands are rendered.
Kahn's use of scratchboard here and in
No. 291 would indicate that both these
portraits were made at about the same
time.

269
SELF-PORTRAIT WITH A PIPE,
Philadelphia 1930
Graphite on paper, 10 9/10 x 8 2/5 in.
(27.9 x 21.6 cm); image: 5 3/5 x 8 2/5 in.
(14.6 x 13.6 cm)
Collection of Sue Ann Kahn

During the Depression and on through
the 1940s, Kahn produced numerous
portraits. Besides himself, his subjects
were predominantly family and friends.
Kahn made this portrait study in a
manner similar to the graphite self-
portrait from 1928–1929 (see No. 90).
The graphite-stick technique, which
Kahn abandoned after the early 1930s, is
used here with less sharpness than in his
earlier work. The sculpted appearance is
replaced with softer modeling and less
heroic glamorization. Kahn used the
stationery of the law offices of Bernard
Harris of Philadelphia for this sketch.

270
SELF-PORTRAIT WITH A CIGARETTE,
Philadelphia 1946
Pen and ink on tracing paper, 10 9/10 x
8 2/5 in. (27.9 x 21.6 cm)
Signed lower right: *Lou K.\46*
Present whereabouts unknown

This sketch and No. 271 constitute a set
of drawings executed most probably in
Kahn's architectural office. Both sketches
are of the same size and technique and
are on a paper characteristic of a drafting
room. In addition, both sketches were
stored together. All of this would indicate
that Kahn drew them at about the same
time and that he meant them to be a set.
Kahn's elegant and economical use of
lines, reminiscent of sketches by Picasso
and Matisse, is in character with his
handling of landscapes of this period.

271
ANNE G. TYNG, Philadelphia 1946
Pen and ink on tracing paper, 10 9/10 x
8 2/5 in. (27.9 x 21.6 cm)
Present whereabouts unknown

This is a companion portrait to No. 270,
made in Kahn's office at the same time.

272
CHILD'S ROOM   1930–36
Watercolor on paper, 13 1/10 x
16 1/2 in. (33.6 X 42.5 cm); image:
 8 9/10 x 12 3/5 in. (18.1 x 32.7 cm)
Signed lower right: *L.I.K.*
Verso of No. 110
Collection of Sue Ann Kahn

This is a totally invented scene that Kahn painted as a token of his new awareness of Bauhaus-inspired architecture. It represents his admiration of this movement's advocacy for simplicity, openness, light, and transparency. Simple furniture, geometric lighting fixtures, and a large plate-glass window are the symbols which Kahn employs to demonstrate his emerging understanding of this new architecture. To Kahn, this sketch, in spite of its technical shortcomings, had a great significance. It represented a point of departure from architectural references which he had accumulated during his Beaux-Arts training. This painting was preceded by a little study sketch in pencil at the bottom of No. 121.

273
"ARTIST IN A STUDIO"   1930–36
Oil on canvas, 8 1/3 x 11 1/4 in.
(21.3 x 28.9 cm)
Signed lower right: *Louis I. Kahn*
Collection of Mrs. Esther I. Kahn

This appears to be a companion piece to No. 272. There are similarities in the uncluttered, simple spaces illuminated by a large modern window. The light entering this room, however, is clear and casts sharp shadows; the colors are rendered more intensely. The scene possesses a peculiar defiance of gravity, which might be associated with the modern movement's challenge of this force.

274
SELF-PORTRAIT, NO. 1
Exact date unknown (c. 1949)
Pencil on paper, 11 7/10 x 8 7/10 in.
(30.0 x 22.5 cm)
Shown at a traveling exhibition
organized by the Pennsylvania Academy
of the Fine Arts, 1978–1979, Catalogue
No. 43, titled: *Self-portrait, ca. 1949*
Collection of Sue Ann Kahn

This is one of three self-portraits Kahn
completed most probably at the same
time. All of them are on the same type
and size of paper. The set appears,
in fact, to be an exercise in the
representation of various moods and
attitudes. The first one, faintly suggesting
facial features, presents Kahn in a
contemplative mood. The second one
(No. 275) is aggressive and distorted,
revealing inner conflict. The third one
(No. 276), reminiscent of Francis Bacon's
self-portraits, is a grotesque distortion,
which, even if intended as a caricature,
comes through as an unsettling portrayal
of a man in turmoil. For Kahn, 1949 was
a year of great transition. As a professor
of architectural design at Yale he was
emerging from the struggle of reconciling
his Beaux-Arts training with his
understanding of the modern movement.

275
SELF-PORTRAIT, NO. 2
Exact date unknown (c. 1949)
Charcoal on paper, 11 7/10 x 8 7/10 in.
(30.0 x 22.5 cm)
Shown at a traveling exhibition
organized by the Pennsylvania Academy
of the Fine Arts, 1978–1979, Catalogue
No. 44, titled: *Self-portrait, ca. 1949*
Collection of Sue Ann Kahn

276
SELF-PORTRAIT, NO. 3 ca. 1949
Charcoal on paper, 11 7/10 x 8 7/10 in.
(30.0 x 22.5 cm)
Shown at a traveling exhibition

organized by the Pennsylvania Academy
of the Fine Arts, 1978–1979, Catalogue
No. 45, titled: *Self-portrait, ca. 1949*
Collection of Sue Ann Kahn

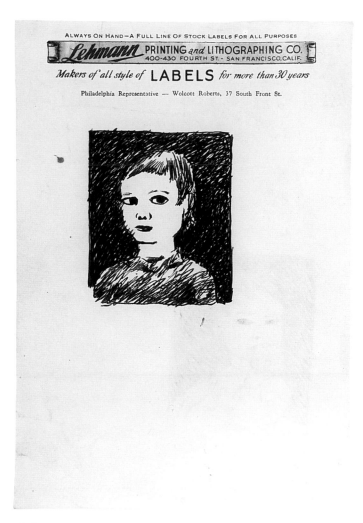

277
PORTRAIT OF A BOY 1941
Pen and ink on stationery paper, 6 9/10 x
4 4/5 in. (17.8 x 12.4 cm); image:
6 9/10 x 4 4/5 in. (6.0 x 5.1 cm)
Collection of Sue Ann Kahn

It is not clear who posed as a model for
Kahn's three portrait sketches of a little
boy. This version and No. 278 may have
served as studies for a more refined
pencil drawing of the boy holding a toy
duck (No. 279). Even though the two
small portraits were drawn rapidly and
without special care, they are filled with
a great tenderness and understanding of
the boy's mischievousness. The large
pencil portrait, on the other hand, is
neatly drawn, but seems in the end to be
overly cute and doll-like.

278
PORTRAIT OF A BOY WITH AN APPLE
1941
Pen and ink on bond paper, 6 9/10 x
4 4/5 in. (17.8 x 12.4 cm); image:
2 1/3 x 1 9/10 in. (6.0 x 5.1 cm)
Inscription at top not by the artist; no
relevance to the sketch
Verso of No. 277
Collection of Sue Ann Kahn

279
PORTRAIT OF A BOY WITH A TOY
DUCK 1941
Pencil on paper, 13 7/10 x 10 9/10 in.
(35.2 x 28.0 cm)
Collection of Sue Ann Kahn

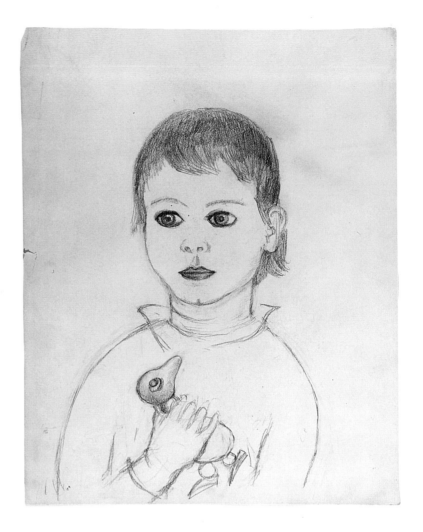

280
THE GIRL WITH A PAPER HAT 1941
Black crayon on paper, 3 1/5 x 2 1/3 in.
(8.3 x 6.0 cm)
Collection of Sue Ann Kahn

This whimsical little sketch may have
been a study for a Halloween pirate
costume. Kahn probably used his
neighbor's children as models for these
drawings.

281
ESTHER IN A HAT
Exact date unknown (c. 1930s)
Charcoal on tracing paper, 8 x 8 1/3 in.
(20.6 x 21.3 cm)
Collection of Sue Ann Kahn

This is one of eight known portraits Kahn made of his wife over approximately a twenty-year period; most of them date from the 1930s. In a pose which may have been inspired by Matisse's *The Red Madras Hat*, Kahn captures the youthful beauty of his bride draped in a feather boa and topped with a cocky saucer hat.

282
ESTHER IN A WINDOW
Exact date unknown (c. 1930s)
Charcoal on paper, 24 x 18 1/4 in.
(61.6 X 46.9 cm); image: 12 3/4 x
14 2/5 in. (32.7 x 37.1 cm)
Signed lower right: *Louis I. Kahn*
Collection of Sue Ann Kahn

Kahn here used soft charcoal shades to depict Esther's statuesque grace with the appearance of sculptural relief. Her very expressive eyes, so aptly captured by Kahn, communicate a melancholy mood.

283
ESTHER WITH A CAT, NO. 1 1931
Charcoal on paper, 8 3/4 x 7 2/5 in.
(22.5 x 19.0 cm); image: 5 7/10 x
4 9/10 in. (14.6 x 12.7 cm)
Collection of Sue Ann Kahn

This sketch and No. 284, apparently
made in one sitting, capture Esther
Kahn's reflective mood while coddling a
cat in a highback easy chair, a treasured
wedding gift from a close friend. While
Kahn was still concerned with the correct
modeling of forms during the early
1930s, he managed here to reduce some
forms to a mere suggestion by using
strongly accented lines.

284
ESTHER WITH A CAT, NO. 2 1931
Charcoal on paper, 11 3/4 x 8 9/10 in.
(30.2 x 22.9 cm); image: 6 1/5 x
5 1/10 in. (15.9 x 13.3 cm)
Collection of Sue Ann Kahn

285
ESTHER 1931
Charcoal on paper, 9 1/10 x 7 1/2 in.
(23.5 X 19.4 cm); center image: 6 1/3 x
5 1/10 in. (16.2 x 13.3 cm); upper left
image: 2 2/5 x 1 1/2 in. (6.3 x 4.1 cm)
Signed lower right (after 1972):
Louis I. Kahn 31

Upper left: Outline sketch
Collection of Sue Ann Kahn

This sketch is by far the most sensitive of
Kahn's attempts at portraiture. In this
drawing, he reached deep into the soul
of his subject and captured Esther's

melancholy beauty with a well-modeled
handling of the charcoal medium. Of
special interest is Kahn's exaggeration of
the eyes in order to convey his wife's
mood. The little sketch at upper left is a
study for portraits of *Esther with a Cat*
(Nos. 283 and 284).

286
PORTRAIT OF ESTHER 1935
Watercolor on paper, 7 1/2 x 4 3/5 in.
(19.4 x 12.0 cm)
Collection of Mrs. Esther I. Kahn

This watercolor and oil painting No. 287
are the only two known portraits of
Kahn's wife made in color. This loose
and semiabstract painting has definite
technical similarities to his European
watercolors. This is especially evident in
the overall color tonality and the manner
in which Esther's hair is painted.

287
ESTHER IN PINK 1939
Oil on canvas, 9 3/5 x 7 3/5 in.
(24.7 x 19.7 cm)
Collection of Mrs. Esther I. Kahn

This is Kahn's last known portrait of his
wife. Made nine years after they were
married and while Esther was pregnant,
this oil painting is Kahn's most elaborate
portrait of her. Kahn placed her in a very
plain space devoid of any details, which
Kahn at that time associated with the
approaching modern movement in
architecture. Esther's expressive eyes,
combined with a blue, stark background,
set a tender yet melancholy mood for
the painting.

288
OLIVIA WITH A GRAPE 1939
Oil on canvas, 22 x 18 3/5 in.
(56.5 x 47.6 cm)
Collection of Mr. and Mrs. Milton
Abelson

Many influences affected the
development of Kahn's paintings at this
time. Kahn collected numerous clippings
from news magazines, journals, and art
reproduction catalogues. The large folder
in which he carefully collected these
clippings contained mostly the work of
the European avant-garde, then creating
a stir in this country. Judging by the
selection in the folder, the paintings of
Cézanne, Matisse, Picasso, Dufy, and
Derain must have been of special interest
to Kahn. In this portrait of his sister-in-
law, several influences play a role.

289
OLIVIA
Exact date unknown (c. 1930s)
Pastel and charcoal on brown paper,
15 1/2 x 10 2/5 in. (39.8 x 26.7 cm)
Signed lower right: *Louis I. Kahn*
Private collection

Working in pastels, Kahn departs here
from the stony rigidity of his oils.
However, he retains the classical
detachment so evident in the faces of his
subjects.

290
ESTHER, STUDY
Exact date unknown (c. 1930s)
Charcoal on paper, 5 9/10 x 4 1/3 in.
(15.2 X 11.1 cm)
Collection of Mrs. Esther I. Kahn

291
OLIVIA WITH A CIGARETTE 1932
Scratchboard, 10 9/10 x 8 2/5 in. (28.0 x
21.6 cm); image: 7 1/10 x 5 9/10 in.
(18.4 x 15.2 cm)
Collection of Mr. and Mrs. Milton
Abelson

This portrait was made using
scratchboard, a technique similar to
woodcut except that no carving is
required; black ink is applied over a layer
of white paint on paper, and has only to
be scraped to achieve the character of a
woodcut. Even though Kahn made only a
few works using this technique, he
demonstrates here his mastery of it.

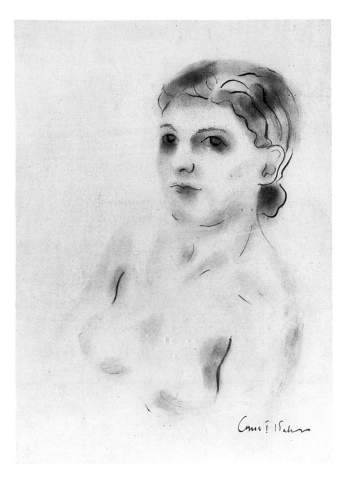

292a
REGINA, NO. 1 1930–34
Charcoal on paper, 23 2/5 x 20 3/10 in.
(60.0 x 52.0 cm)
Collection of the Architectural Archives,
University of Pennsylvania, Catalogue
No. 950.1, titled: *Portrait of Regina
Israeli*; Gift of Regina Israeli Soopper

When comparing Kahn's two portraits of
his sister-in-law Regina, this rather
academic rendition appears at first
glance to contrast greatly with No. 292b.
While the elaborate modeling of No.
292a is distinct from the frugality of lines
and modeling in No. 292b, this does not
necessarily reflect distinctly different
artistic approaches. Picasso's influence
on Kahn is quite evident in both works,
but especially when one compares No.
292b to Picasso's 1923 painting *Woman
in White*. There are many uncanny
parallels between the two works: the
soft veil-like rendition of form, the
calligraphic accents of selected features,
and the overall statuesque serenity of the
figures. There is little doubt that Picasso's
classical period had a significant impact
on Kahn, and many of Kahn's portraits in
this series display Picasso's characteristic
calm, repose, dignity, and objective
detachment in portraiture.

292b
REGINA, NO. 2 1930–34
Charcoal on paper, 10 1/10 x 7 2/3 in.
(26.0 x 19.7 cm)
Signed lower right: *Louis I. Kahn*
Private collection

293
ESTHER/OLIVIA, NO. 1 1932
Pencil and charcoal on paper,
7 1/10 x 5 1/10 in. (18.4 x 13.3 cm)
Private collection

This is one of two studies for an oil
portrait (No. 295) that depicts the
combined features of Esther Kahn and
her sister Olivia. There are absolutely no
clues as to why he attempted such an
unusual metamorphosis.

294
ESTHER/OLIVIA, NO. 2 1932
Colored pencil on paper, 11 1/10 x
8 1/10 in. (28.6 x 21.0 cm)
Private collection

295
ESTHER/OLIVIA, NO. 3 1932
Oil on canvas, 25 1/5 x 19 1/3 in.
(64.7 x 49.5 cm)
Collection of Mrs. Esther I. Kahn

An important change of setting takes place in Kahn's transformation of study No. 293 into this finished painting. The drapery background in No. 293 becomes a swooping, modern interior in study No. 294, which then becomes a distinct International Style interior with all the requisite symbols of architectural modernism in the final oil version. From several portraits and interiors he painted during this period, it is obvious that Kahn was exploring modern architecture through the medium of painting. What is truly remarkable is the way Kahn combined his interest in modern art, with which he was more familiar, and the vocabulary of modern architecture, in an attempt to reconcile them.

296
FOUR WOMEN
Exact date unknown (c. 1940s)
Pen and ink on paper, 7 3/5 x 8 2/5 in.
(19.7 x 21.6 cm)
Signed lower right: *Lou K*
Collection of Sue Ann Kahn

In mood and technical character, this
sketch differs greatly from the rest of the
works in this group. The sketch contains
intentional ambiguities created to trick
the observer's eye. What at first glance
appear to be the shoulders and back of
the woman on the left actually form the
back of the head of another woman; and
in the middle, peering out from the three
heads, is the partial face of a fourth
woman. One can only assume that Kahn
made this sketch to amuse himself and
others and that it had no additional
significance.

297
ABSTRACT OF FIGURES   1948–50
Pen and ink on paper, 11 7/10 x
15 7/10 in. (30.0 x 40.3 cm)
Signed lower right: *Lou K*
Shown at a traveling exhibition
organized by the Pennsylvania Academy
of the Fine Arts, 1978–1979,
Catalogue No. 52
Collection of Sue Ann Kahn

Kahn made this unusual sketch several
years after the end of World War II. Yet
news reports and photographs of the
destruction caused by the war, and
especially the annihilation of millions in
concentration camps, were still fresh in
Kahn's mind and served as probable
stimuli for this sketch. Much inspiration,
in any case, came from Picasso's
Guernica. There are many similarities in
the agonizing gestures and contortions.
However, Kahn managed to convey the
tragic mood through deceitfully simple
linework and perspectives suggesting the
endless horror of war.

298
ON THE TRAIN TO NEW HAVEN
1949–50
Pencil on paper, 4 9/10 x 7 9/10 in.
(12.6 x 20.3 cm)
Shown at a traveling exhibition
organized by the Pennsylvania Academy
of the Fine Arts, 1978–1979,
Catalogue No. 46
Collection of Sue Ann Kahn

While Kahn was teaching architectural
design at Yale he did not live in New
Haven and had to commute by train from
Philadelphia. It was during one of these
frequent trips that he sketched this
"snapshot" scene of his fellow
commuters. This sketch was probably
never intended as anything but a
personal notation.

299
COMMUTERS   1949-50
Brushed india ink on onionskin paper,
8 2/5 x 10 9/10 in. (21.6 x 27.9 cm)
Collection of Sue Ann Kahn

Kahn captured a moment in the life of
commuters in this energetic sketch,
which he most likely made from
memory. By tightly packing the
entire picture surface with faces, he
successfully conveys the crowded
environment of a commuter. Bold
calligraphic lines give the work a spirit
reminiscent of the expressionist works of
Ensor and Munch, but with less ominous
overtones.

300
GIRL WITH A DOLL
Exact date unknown (c. 1930s)
Watercolor on paper, 16 9/10 x
13 1/5 in. (43.5 x 33.9 cm)
Collection of Sue Ann Kahn

The energetic watercolors Kahn used in
his landscapes from the 1930s found
their way into his representation of
people. This watercolor and No. 301
stand in drastic contrast to the portraits of
his wife and her sister Kahn made in oil.
But more than medium separates these
works. These two watercolors draw on
the emotionalism and energy of Matisse,
Ensor, Kirchner, and Derain, while the
former were inspired by a sense of
controlled repose and order. Kahn's
swing from one attitude to the other was
not so much a matter of evolutionary
development, but rather an enthusiastic
probing and searching for the underlying
theories of art through actual
experimentation.

301
GIRL WITH HER PET
Exact date unknown (c. 1930s)
Watercolor on paper, 17 1/5 x
14 1/10 in. (44.1 x 36.2 cm)
Collection of Sue Ann Kahn

302
ESTHER READING
Exact date unknown (c. 1930s)
Tempera on paper, 9 9/10 x 11 1/10 in.
(27.9 x 28.6 cm); image: 9 3/5 x
11 1/10 in. (24.8 x 28.6 cm)
Collection of Sue Ann Kahn

The awkward anatomical distortions in
this tempera do not qualify this as one of
Kahn's better works. However, his
attention to patterns, textures, and colors
makes this painting important as an
indicator of the influences to which he
was subjected at that time. Ernst Ludwig
Kirchner (a former architecture student)
and other expressionists must have left a
strong imprint on Kahn, because he
carried many of their daring spectral
explorations and distortions into his
paintings all the way through 1951.

303
TYPING SESSION
Exact date unknown (c. 1930s)
Tempera and watercolor on paper,
12 x 10 1/2 in. (31.0 x 27.0 cm)
Private collection

304
ANIMALS 1940–50
Black crayon on paper, 4 2/5 x 5 4/5 in.
(11.4 x 14.9 cm)
Private collection

This is a study Kahn made for a wall
decoration in a kindergarten. His
portrayal of each animal's nature is
more visible than any slight anatomical
inaccuracies. Kahn became a father in
1940, and this must have increased his
sensitivity to a child's perception of
things, particularly animals.

305
CAT
Exact date unknown (c. 1930s)
Pastel and charcoal pencil on brown
paper, 8 3/5 x 11 3/5 in. (22.2 x 29.8 cm)
Private collection

Kahn employed the same pastel
technique in this sketch that he used in
his portraits of Regina (No. 292a–b).
The brown paper permits accenting of
selected features with white or light
colors. In this instance, the cat's eyes
become powerful magnets. It is not clear
whether the cat is sleeping or blind. The
absence of pupils and the luminescence
of the eyes add to the enigma of this
feline.

306
STILL LIFE, STUDY   1930–35
Pencil on paper, 23 1/2 x 17 1/2 in.
(60.3 x 45.1 cm); image: 10 2/5 x
8 2/5 in. (26.7 x 21.6 cm)
Signed lower right: *Louis I. Kahn*;
inscribed lower left: *Pencil study for
lithograph*
Collection of Sue Ann Kahn

This is a study for the lithograph *Still Life*
(No. 307), of which Kahn made thirty
signed prints. Inspired by Cézanne, this is
a fairly good composition in which
objects are arranged in a pyramid
formation, thus displaying an interest in
all parts of the composition with
dominance given to the stein. Slight
perspective distortions add to the success
of the composition by allowing a greater
display of objects on the table. Kahn's
handling of light and shade, as well as
transparency, is carried out with an
expert touch.

307
STILL LIFE   1930–35
Lithograph on paper, 11 x 8 2/5 in.
(28.3 x 21.6 cm); image: 10 2/5 x
8 2/5 in. (26.7 x 21.6 cm)
Signed lower right: *Louis I. Kahn*;
inscribed lower left: *1/30 - Still Life*
Private collection

One signed (untitled, un-numbered)
lithograph is in the collection of Sue Ann
Kahn. Another one, signed, titled, and
numbered "2/30," is in the collection of
Mr. and Mrs. Milton Abelson. This
sketch, as well as Nos. 44, 56, 59, and
69, were published originally in Kahn's
article "The Value and Aim in Sketching"
in the *T-Square Club Journal* (May 1931).

308
STILL LIFE WITH APPLES AND A VASE,
NO. 1   1930–35
Watercolor on paper, 11 9/10 x
14 3/5 in. (30.5 x 37.5 cm)
Collection of Mrs. Esther I. Kahn

This is one of two variations (see No.
309) on the same theme in which a
porcelain vase forms the center of the
composition. These watercolors have
more in common with Matisse than
Cézanne. Forms are not clearly
constructed but exist by the sheer
suggestion of loosely applied colors.

309
STILL LIFE WITH APPLES AND A VASE,
NO. 2   1930–35
Watercolor on paper, 14 22/5 x
18 1/3 in. (37.1 x 47.0 cm); image:
12 1/3 x 15 1/3 in. (31.7 x 39.4 cm)
Collection of Sue Ann Kahn

310
STILL LIFE WITH A GLASS VASE
1930–35
Watercolor on paper, 16 1/5 x 11 1/3 in.
(41.6 x 29.2 cm)
Collection of Sue Ann Kahn

This is by far the most successful still life
in watercolor Kahn attempted. The forms
and gentle colors are in harmony. It is
hardly important that the forms are not
clearly legible. The charm of the painting
is in the way subtle suggestions substitute
for descriptive renditions.

311
POTTED PLANTS   1930–35
Watercolor on paper, 14 4/5 x 19 4/5 in.
(38.1 x 50.8 cm)
Collection of Sue Ann Kahn

312
STILL LIFE WITH APPLES AND
ORANGES   1930–35
Oil on canvas, 17 4/5 x 21 4/5 in.
(45.7 x 55.9 cm)
Collection of Sue Ann Kahn

The fluidity with which Kahn produced
most of his watercolors deserted him in
this unfinished oil painting. His initial
moves suggest similarities to the
watercolor medium, but the layers of
light, shades, and highlights do not come
as freely or as quickly as the whiteness of
paper in watercolors.

313
STILL LIFE WITH APPLES AND A
CHROME JUG   1930–35
Watercolor on paper, 13 1/10 x
16 4/5 in. (33.6 x 43.2 cm)
Collection of Sue Ann Kahn

In this watercolor Kahn undertook the
very difficult task of representing the
reflection of fruit in a highly polished
chrome jug. The attention given to
achieving this effect seems to have
robbed him of any serious attempt at
rendering the table and the background.

314

MODERN SKYSCRAPER 1930
Graphite on tracing paper, 11 1/2 x
8 7/10 in. (29.5 x 22.5 cm)
Collection of Deutsches
Architekturmuseum, Frankfurt am Main,
Germany, Catalogue No. 275, titled:
*Design for a Skyscraper, Bird's Eye View,
1927–29*

The placement of this drawing among
Kahn's non-architectural work may seem
strange. However, because of the
graphite-stick technique he employed
here and the critical period in Kahn's
development that this sketch represents,
it deserves scrutiny in a nonarchitectural
context. It also indicates Kahn's attitudes
towards the emergence of modern
architecture in the United States. The
building in the drawing is clearly
Raymond Hood's Daily News Building in
New York of 1930. Kahn probably
copied an aerial photograph of the
structure for his sketch. His interest in
this building was triggered most likely by
the proposal in 1929 and construction
through 1932 of the P.S.F.S. Building in
Philadelphia by Howe and Lescaze. Most
of Kahn's architectural interests in the
1930s were still bound by the Beaux-Arts
tradition. His fascination with modernism
after his return from Europe is significant
in the way it influenced his paintings of
interiors and portraits at this time.

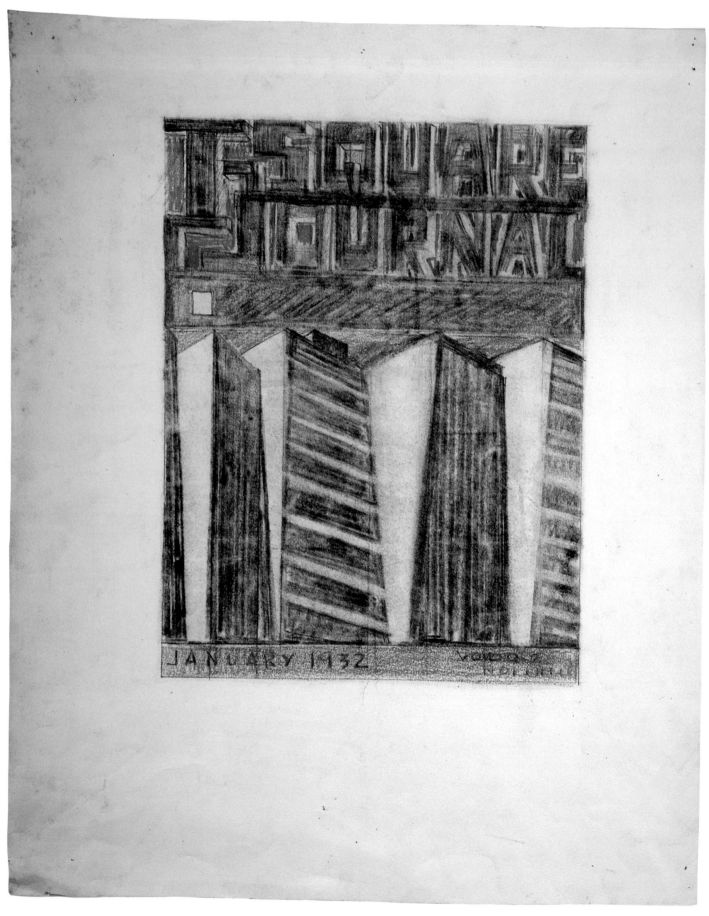

315
T-SQUARE JOURNAL, JANUARY 1932,
COVER DESIGN   1931
Charcoal and pastel on paper, 18 7/10 x
14 7/10 in. (47.9 x 37.8 cm); image:
11 4/5 x 8 9/10 in. (30.5 x 22.9 cm)

Verso of No. 13
Collection of Sue Ann Kahn

The following are various examples of
Kahn's graphic and decorative art. The

blocky, stylized lettering and truncated
pyramidal skyscrapers are derived from
Kahn's early brushes with the modern
movement in architecture and graphics.

230

316
"GREETINGS, ESTHER KAHN"
CHRISTMAS CARD   1931
Woodcut, 5 1/10 x 4 in. (13.3 x 10.5 cm)
Signed lower left: *Louis I. Kahn*
Collection of Mrs. Esther I. Kahn

This card and No. 317 are very rare examples of Kahn's experiments in woodcut. In this case, he used the method to produce Christmas cards which he and Esther sent in 1930 and 1931. Woodcuts were ideal for this purpose and Kahn exhibited considerable proficiency using this method without any indication of previous experience. Of special interest is Kahn's portrayal of a sculptor in classical garb creating a Bauhaus-inspired building. It is a prophetic drawing and could be considered a self-portrait: Kahn, the classically trained architect producing a work of modernism.

Woodcut created by Louis I. Kahn.
Reproduction of Christmas
card used by Esther and
Louis Kahn in 1931

317
CHRISTMAS CARD, RUSSIAN MOTIF
1930
Woodcut, 3 7/10 x 5 9/10 in.
(9.5 x 15.2 cm)
Signed lower left: *Louis Kahn*
Collection of Mrs. Esther I. Kahn

This is another Christmas card the Kahns used in 1930. It is not clear where he found the source for this allegorical scene, especially since the setting he chose is unrelated to customary Christmas portrayals.

318
TRANSPARENCY, NO. 1   1948–50
Pen and ink on paper, 15 3/5 x 11 1/2 in.
(40.0 x 29.5 cm)
Signed lower right: *Lou K.*
Shown at a traveling exhibition
organized by the Pennsylvania Academy
of the Fine Arts, 1978–1979, Catalogue
No. 49, titled: *Abstract, 1948–50*
Collection of Sue Ann Kahn

This sketch and an almost identical one
(No. 319) continue to explore modern
architecture's simplicity, purity, and
transparency, but from a more space-
conscious point of view. Because these
concepts are presented in a dramatic
perspective view, these drawings belong
more to the realm of Kahn's visual art
than his architectural studies.

319
TRANSPARENCY, NO. 2   1948–50
Pen and ink on paper, 11 1/3 x 15 3/5 in.
(29.2 x 40.0 cm)
Signed lower right: *Lou K*
Private collection

320
ABSTRACT OF PLANES AND STEPS
1948–50
Pen and ink on paper, 11 7/10 x
15 4/5 in. (30.0 x 40.5 cm)
Signed lower right: *Lou K*
Shown at a traveling exhibition
organized by the Pennsylvania Academy
of the Fine Arts, 1978–1979,
Catalogue No. 48
Collection of Sue Ann Kahn

This sketch represents components or
"orders" of modern architecture. The
transparent slab appears again, but this
time occupies a three-dimensional space
shared with the scattered symbols of
modern buildings.

321
ALLEGORICAL LANDSCAPE, NO. 1
1930–33
Watercolor on brown paper, 13 7/10 x
11 3/10 in. (35.2 x 28.9 cm); image:
6 3/5 x 8 2/5 in. (17.1 x 21.6 cm)
Signed lower right: *Louis I. Kahn*
Collection of Sue Ann Kahn

This design, and Nos. 322 and 323, were
preparatory studies for bedroom door
panels to be executed in oil at Kahn's
residence at 5243 Chester Avenue in
Philadelphia. The allegorical nature of
these sketches represents a strange
departure from Kahn's customary subject
matter and style. Reminiscent of art
nouveau illustrations, these studies
contain elements which also bring them
close to the works of artists like Matisse
and Delaunay. The predominance of
purples and reds, reinforced by the
sinuous forms, creates a sentimental
sensation.

322
ALLEGORICAL LANDSCAPE, NO. 3
1930–33
Watercolor on canvas, 7 1/2 x
11 1/10 in. (19.4 x 28.6 cm); image:
7 1/2 x 8 1/2 in. (19.4 x 21.9 cm)
Shown at a traveling exhibition
organized by the Pennsylvania Academy
of the Fine Arts, 1978–1979, Catalogue
No. 37, titled: *Abstract, ca. 1930-33*
Collection of Sue Ann Kahn

323
ALLEGORICAL LANDSCAPE, NO. 2
1930–33
Watercolor on paper, 10 7/10 x 8 1/3 in.
(27.6 x 21.3 cm)
Signed lower right: *Louis I. Kahn*

Shown at a traveling exhibition
organized by the Pennsylvania Academy
of the Fine Arts, 1978–1979, Catalogue
No. 36, titled: *Abstract, ca. 1930-33*
Collection of Sue Ann Kahn

324
ABSTRACT WITH A DUCK AND A
LAMP   1948–50
Black crayon with scratched lines on
paper, 9 1/3 x 12 in. (24.1 x 30.8 cm);
6 1/5 x 5 3/5 in. (image: 15.9 x 14.6 cm)
Collection of Sue Ann Kahn

In a series of studies, starting with this
sketch and running through oil paintings
Nos. 328 and 329 (see also Nos.
318–320), Kahn explored the relationship
of abstract forms to three-dimensional
space in a manner totally different from
his traditional constructs. He examined
shapes and forms, their immaterial
nature, the challenge of gravity, space,
and shadows. All of this seemed to be a
response to his struggle with the concepts
of modern architecture and its relation to
modern art. These sketches reveal a
range of possible influences, from Hans
Arp's amorphous forms to Marc Chagall's
floating figures and childlike innocence.
Considering Kahn's evolving theories of
design at the time, it would appear that
some of this experimentation was related
to his search for the eternal essence of
what he called "form."

325
ABSTRACT WITH FIGURES   1948–50
Pen and ink on paper, 11 3/5 x 15 3/5 in.
(29.8 x 40.0 cm)
Signed lower right: Lou K
Shown at a traveling exhibition
organized by the Pennsylvania Academy
of the Fine Arts, 1978–1979, Catalogue
No. 51
Collection of Sue Ann Kahn

326
ABSTRACT   1948–50
Pen and ink on paper, 10 7/10 x
14 7/10 in. (27.6 x 37.8 cm)
Signed lower right: Lou K
Shown at a traveling exhibition
organized by the Pennsylvania Academy
of the Fine Arts, 1978–1979,
Catalogue No. 50
Collection of the Pennsylvania Academy
of the Fine Arts, Acc. No. 1978.2.2. Gift
of Mrs. Louis I. Kahn

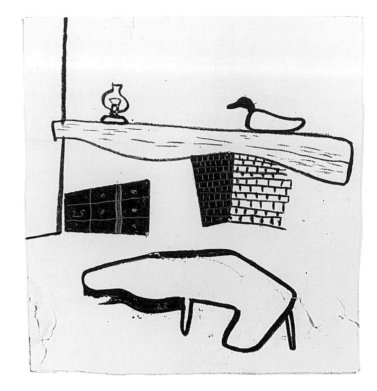

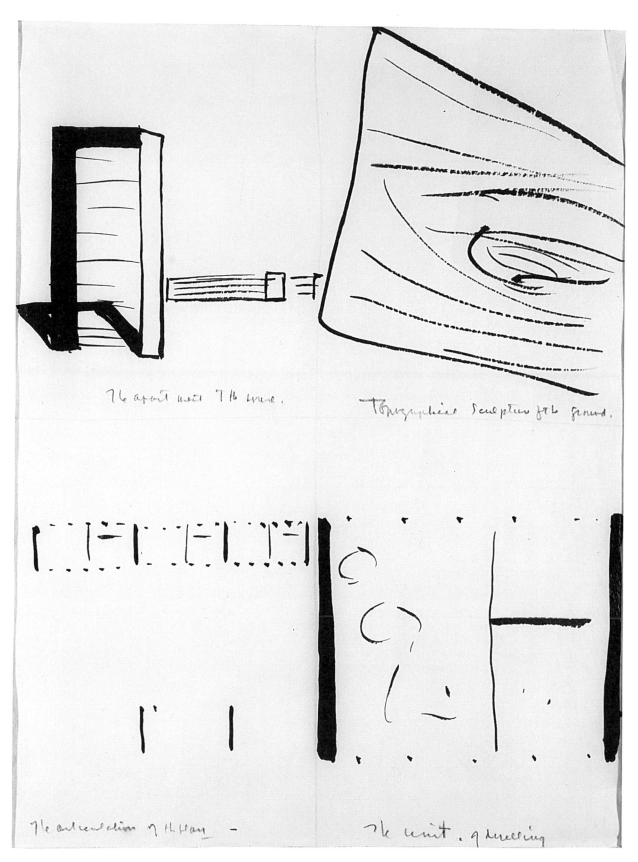

The apart ment The house.

Topographical Sculpture of the ground.

The articulation of the Plan —

The unit of dwelling

327
THE APARTMENT, THE HOUSE
1949–50
Pen, ink, and pencil on onionskin paper,
10 9/10 x 8 2/5 in. (28.0 x 21.6 cm)
Inscribed under each of the four images;
upper left: *The apartment The house*;
upper right: *Topographical sculpture of the ground*; lower left: *The articulation of the plan*; lower right: *The unit of dwelling*

Shown at a traveling exhibition organized by the Pennsylvania Academy of the Fine Arts, 1978–1979, Catalogue No. 47
Collection of Sue Ann Kahn

Decidedly more architectonic than previous studies, these sketches explore the nature of modern architecture as inspired by Mies van der Rohe and

Le Corbusier. Kahn investigates the hierarchical relation of the essential components of design. In this case, the transparency of a vertical building slab, casting only a shadow of the outer frame, is directly related to the openness of the building's plan and is contrasted with the materiality of the ground.

328
ABSTRACT OF PLANES AND FORMS
1948–50
Oil on masonite, 15 4/5 x 21 4/5 in.
(40.6 x 55.9 cm)
Collection of Sue Ann Kahn

Two unfinished oil paintings, this one
and No. 329, are clearly derived from the
pen-and-ink transparency studies Nos.
318 and 319. They obviously transcend
architectonic boundaries and belong in
the domain of fine art production. As
abstractions, they have common roots in
surrealism and suprematism, and also
exhibit certain characteristics of Stuart
Davis' work. Of special interest is a
bright yellow horizontal bar which, while
resting on a receding white wall, splits
the picture into two rectangles. Distant
mountains define the space of the lower
rectangle, where building forms compete
visually with a strange red tree growing
from an orange ground. The upper
rectangle's deep blue sky is almost
undisturbed, save for a few branches

from the abstract tree. Kahn may
have wanted to express a symbolic
relationship between the modern forms
of architecture and the eternal forms
of nature.

329
ABSTRACT OF PLANES IN LANDSCAPE
1948–50
Oil on canvas, 15 3/5 x 19 1/3 in.
(40.0 x 49.5 cm)
Collection of Mrs. Esther I. Kahn

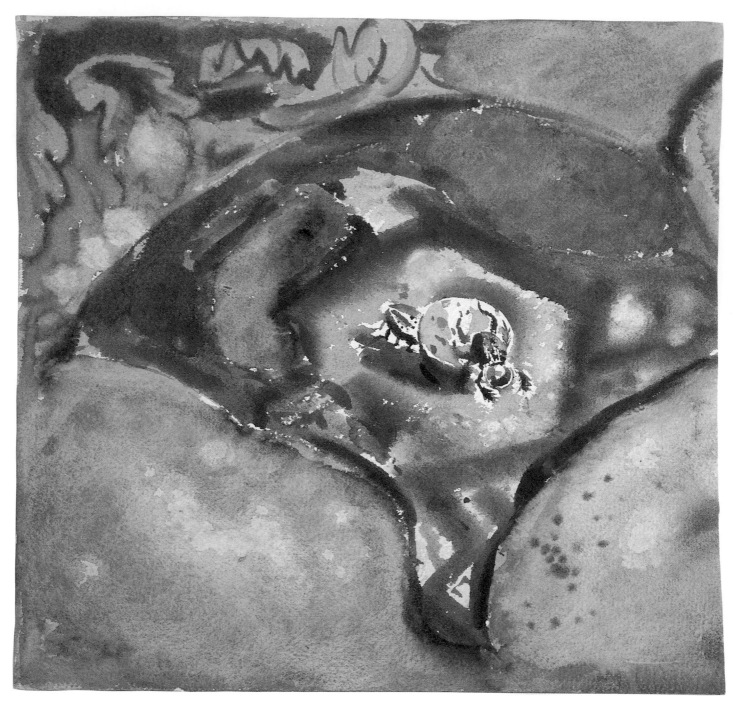

330
BEETLE   1930–33
Watercolor on paper, 10 x 10 3/5 in.
(25.7 x 27.3 cm)
Verso of No. 167
Collection of Sue Ann Kahn

This watercolor was painted in a manner
very similar to still life No. 310. With the
exception of the beetle—the focus of
attention—all forms are softened by
harmonious pigments applied to a wet
paper surface. The resulting image is
successful in conveying the cozy and
intimate world of the wilderness at a
small scale.

PERIOD IV
1950–51

SECOND EUROPEAN TRIP

In 1950, Kahn was chosen to be the Resident Architect at the prestigious American Academy in Rome. This honor became his great chance to revisit the Italian cities and countryside he recorded so lovingly in his sketches nearly twenty years before. In addition, the residency at the Academy offered him the opportunity to travel to Egypt and Greece, places he had not had a chance to see before. Arriving in Rome in the fall of 1950, Kahn began to explore the city and to make short trips to Pompeii, Siena, Florence, Pisa, and Venice. In 1951, along with a small group of Fellows and Residents of the Academy, he embarked on an extended trip to Egypt and Greece. Among his companions were William H. Sippel, recipient of the Lloyd Warren Rome Prize, whom Kahn met at the Academy; architects Joseph Amisano and his wife, Spiro Daltas; and landscape architect George Patton, with whom Kahn later developed a long professional relation.

According to Sippel, the trip began in January after a short delay caused by Kahn's difficulty in obtaining an entry visa from the Egyptian government. They flew from Rome to Cairo, where Sippel contended with a bout of malaria, landing him in a local hospital. Kahn and the rest of the travelers decided to stay in Cairo until Mr. Sippel got better. This delay of almost a week allowed Kahn to spend a considerable amount of time exploring and sketching the pyramids.

From Cairo the group went by train to Aswan and worked their way back down the Nile on a boat for over a week, stopping along the way at important temple sites. From Egypt they traveled to Greece. Encountering cold and wet February weather, several members of the party decided to visit some of the Greek islands. Kahn and Sippel remained and traveled for three weeks by train, bus, donkey, and on foot, exploring sites of Greek antiquity. Kahn always carried a sketch pad and a box of charcoal and pastels which he used to make on-site sketches. He worked very rapidly, taking no more than twenty minutes to complete a pastel picture.

The residency at the Academy and his various trips left a powerful legacy of artistic production. It was the last period in which Kahn employed color. He had abandoned the use of watercolors even prior to this trip, yet interestingly, of all his drawings and paintings, it was the pastels of which he was the most proud and which he treasured the most. They are, indeed, a remarkable body of artistic production, no longer experimental or dependent on other artists' work. They display a genuinely unique character. Kahn loved to show the pastels in his illustrated lectures and he sent them out, along with design sketches and photographs of completed projects, to architectural journals for publication. These pastels, therefore, are his best-known artworks and are thought to be Kahn's chief artistic accomplishment.

From the standpoint of his development as an architect, this short period (1950–51) allowed Kahn to realize the long-sought crystallization of his design theories. Italian cities and the ruins of Greek and Egyptian monuments provided Kahn with the missing clues necessary to make the connection between the traditional and modern worlds. His early confusion about that relationship was finally eliminated and he was able to employ his theories by applying the timeless ingredients of past monuments to contemporary pragmatic challenges. The legacy of this late awakening resulted in an architecture of great influence and an embodiment of his creative genius.

The organization of Kahn's artwork in this section is based mainly on the relationship of locations and does not necessarily follow the travel itinerary. The work from Greece, in fact, is presented ahead of that from Egypt— the reverse order of his travels—to make a better architectural connection between the Italian and Greek sites. The end of this section presents Kahn's graphic designs related to the 1950–51 travels, executed back in Philadelphia up until 1959.

331
POMPEII, Pompeii, Italy 1951
Charcoal and pastel on brown paper,
6 3/5 x 8 1/10 in. (17.1 x 21.0 cm)
Present whereabouts unknown

During his 1950–51 travels in Italy,
Greece, and Egypt, Kahn began using
pastels, a medium he seldom employed
before. Pastels offered him greater
convenience for outdoor use without
sacrificing the spontaneity he enjoyed
with watercolors. This quick sketch,
which uses only brown pastel with
charcoal, is one of the subtlest of the
series. Forms are suggested by minimum
shading or lines. With the exception
of the smoking Vesuvius, the natural
elements and ruins are almost
indistinguishable.

332
"ITALIAN LANDSCAPE, " Italy 1951
Pastel on paper, 7 2/5 x 8 1/2 in.
(19.0 x 22.0 cm)
Signed middle right: *Lou K '51*
Shown at a traveling exhibition
organized by the Pennsylvania Academy
of the Fine Arts, 1978–1979,
Catalogue No. 54
Collection of Sue Ann Kahn

Strangely distorted forms reminiscent of
Kahn's earlier experiments in black
and white (Nos. 325–26) reappear as
landscape elements in this pastel and in
charcoal drawing No. 334. In this sketch
clearly defined patches of solid colors are
organized in harmony with outlined
volumes. Colors in this sketch seem
purposely subdued in order not to detract
from the formal composition. This scene,
with its scattered ruins and cypresses,
may have been sketched by Kahn at
either Pompeii or Ostia.

333
CLASSICAL SCULPTURE,
Rome-Ostia, Italy 1951
Pastel on paper, 7 2/5 x 8 1/2 in.
(19.0 x 21.9 cm)
Signed middle right: *Lou K '51*
Collection of Sue Ann Kahn

Using relics of the past, Kahn produces a
Mondrian-like composition, even to the
point of employing primary colors. It is
no coincidence that Kahn combined
forms separated by two millennia in
this sketch.

334
RUINS, Rome-Ostia, Italy 1951
Charcoal on paper, 8 1/2 x 9 3/5 in.
(21.9 x 24.8 cm)
Signed middle right: *Lou K '51*
Collection of Sue Ann Kahn

Kahn's fascination with ruins is
developed in this sketch to a surreal
level. There is a dreamlike ambivalence
in this study, caused by the reciprocal
transformation of natural and man-made
elements. Forms are unintelligible and
ominous in appearance. This is further
bolstered by the "nostriled" black mass
on the right, while antlike human forms
provide a surprising hint of the scale of
this unusual formation.

335
ROMAN WALL, Rome-Ostia, Italy 1951
Charcoal on paper, 11 1/9 x 14 7/10 in.
(28.9 x 37.8 cm)
Signed lower right: *Louis I. Kahn '51*
Private collection

Kahn's interest in Roman architecture,
especially in the construction methods of
masonry walls, found its way a few years
later into his own architectural designs.
Open brick arches and reinforcing
arches, as sketched by Kahn in Italy,
appear in the Fine Arts Center, Fort
Wayne, Indiana; the Institute of
Management in Ahmedabad, India; and
the National Capital Ministers Hostels
and the Ayub National Hospital in
Dacca, Bangladesh. Roman brick
construction offered Kahn an opportunity
to explore the timeless qualities of simple
geometric forms and their power of
expression.

336
"ROME, 1951," Rome, Italy 1951
Pastel on paper, 7 2/5 x 8 1/2 in.
(19.0 x 22.0 cm)
Signed lower right: *Lou K*
Shown at a traveling exhibition
organized by the Pennsylvania Academy
of the Fine Arts, 1978–1979, Catalogue
No. 53, titled: *Rome, 1951*
Collection of Sue Ann Kahn

Kahn's five pastel sketches of Italian
piazzas (Nos. 336–340) demonstrate
his unique perception of major urban
settings through angular spatial views
defined by strong sunlight. He uses broad
areas of color to give solidity to enclosing
planes. Those planes abstract the
complexities of architectural facades and
focus attention on public spaces.

This pastel, with its unusual viewpoint,
shows Kahn's remarkable perception of
Rome. It reveals his interest in Rome's
spatial mysteries and in discovering the
uncommon in the most familiar.
Interestingly, this drawing reflects the
work of Giorgio de Chirico, who found
the architecture of Italian cities to be
highly metaphysical settings. Here Kahn
consciously eliminates details and
concentrates on the presence of light as a
modifier of space.

337
PIAZZA CAMPIDOGLIO,
Rome, Italy 1951
Pastel on paper, 10 3/5 x 13 3/5 in.
(27.3 x 34.9 cm)
Private collection

Again, as in No. 336, Kahn chooses a
more picturesque angle over one which
is more familiar. Here he captures the
convergence of two stepped ramps, one
leading to Santa Maria Aracoeli and the
other to the piazza. Apart from this
sketch's unique perspective, it is the
color—the brilliant red of the church,
the deep blue shadows, and the outlines
of details in orange and brown
backgrounds—that make this pastel
so remarkable.

338
PIAZZA DEL CAMPO, NO. 1,
Siena, Italy 1951
Pastel on paper, 11 1/3 x 14 3/5 in.
(29.0 x 37.5 cm)
Inscribed on back at lower left: *Siena I*
Shown at a traveling exhibition
organized by the Pennsylvania Academy
of the Fine Arts, 1978–1979, Catalogue
No. 55, titled: *Siena I. 1951*
Collection of Sue Ann Kahn

This is one of two views (see also No.
339) of the piazza. This view is taken
from the east side looking toward the
cathedral, with Palazzo Pubblico on the
left. Rendered in the golden tones of
Siena, with only the palazzo in brown,
the concave piazza is bathed in bright
red shadows produced by the late-
afternoon winter sun. Similarities to the
paintings of de Chirico are very tempting
to consider, especially the emptiness of
the space and the advancing shadows,
but Kahn's scene is devoid of any
foreboding atmosphere. In many ways it
conveys just the opposite mood.

339
PIAZZA DEL CAMPO, NO. 2,
Siena, Italy 1951
Pastel on paper, 11 1/3 x 14 3/5 in.
(29.0 x 37.5 cm)
Private collection

This view is taken from the opposite side
of the piazza looking east. Standing now
on high ground with the sun behind him,
Kahn casts the shadows in hues much
cooler than those in No. 338. As in the
previous view, there are no architectural
details; only general forms are provided
to delineate space. But in order to
convey the concavity of the piazza's
floor, Kahn develops the paving pattern
by showing joints in colors
complementary to the surface: blue-
green on orange in the first view, and
orange on blue-green in the second.

340
BAPTISTRY OF SAN GIOVANNI,
Siena, Italy 1951
Pastel on paper, 11 3/4 x 15 in.
(29.0 x 38.5 cm)
Inscribed on the back at lower left:
Siena III
Shown at a traveling exhibition
organized by the Pennsylvania Academy
of the Fine Arts, 1978–1979, Catalogue
No. 56, titled: *Siena III. 1951*
Collection of Sue Ann Kahn

This pastel concentrates on the Baptistry
facade, which Kahn renders with more
detail than in any of the previous
buildings. The whiteness of the building
against the dark tone of its surroundings,
as well as its central position in the
composition, establishes it as a dramatic
focal point. In spite of the flat color areas,
there is a wonderful sense of perspective
generated by the lines of pavement,
shadows, and, above all, the sensation of
distance created through the archway at
left.

341
PIAZZA DELLA SIGNIORIA, NO. 1,
Florence, Italy 1950
Crayon on paper, 6 4/5 x 9 9/10 in.
(17.5 x 25.4 cm)
Color notations
Present whereabouts unknown

Kahn made this sketch and others of
Florence, Pisa and Venice (Nos. 342–352)
in a spiral pad, drawing on both sides of
the paper. They were made most
probably upon his arrival at the American
Academy in Rome, in the latter part of
1950, before he produced pastels Nos.
331–340. The attitude toward urban
spaces Kahn exhibited in his pastels was
already present in these sketches and
may be further compared with his 1929
graphite drawings such as *The Plaza* in
San Gimignano (No. 93). Even though
twenty-one years separate these works,
Kahn's lively interest in large public
spaces persisted. He preferred squares
with varied and exciting rooflines, and
monuments or fountains which acted as
anchoring devices holding the space
together. While his techniques differed
over time, the quality of the spaces was
always captured by Kahn's expert choice
of views, prudent featuring of selected
forms, hints of textures, and masterful use
of shadows.

342
PIAZZA DELLA SIGNIORIA, NO. 2,
Florence, Italy 1950
Crayon on paper, 6 4/5 x 9 9/10 in.
(17.5 x 25.4 cm)
Present whereabouts unknown

343
PALAZZO VECCHIO, NO. 1,
Florence, Italy 1950
Crayon on paper, 6 4/5 x 9 9/10 in.
(17.5 x 25.4 cm)
Present whereabouts unknown

344
PALAZZO VECCHIO, NO. 2,
Florence, Italy 1950
Crayon on paper, 6 4/5 x 9 9/10 in.
(17.5 x 25.4 cm); image: 6 4/5 x 7 4/5 in.
(17.5 x 20.0 cm)
Inscribed lower right: *18 paces short
600 ft. + steps 30 paces*
Present whereabouts unknown

Even though Kahn's fascination with
urban spaces did not change greatly from
the time of his first European trip, the
romantic perception of his youth was
replaced in 1950 with more seasoned
and analytical objectives. Color notations
became less frequent and were replaced,
as in this sketch, with dimensional
characteristics of the space. Sketches
became more architecturally referential,
and not merely studies for paintings.
However, one should not conclude that
Kahn had turned his back on his beloved
pastime. He obviously still planned and
continued to produce notable artworks.
But by 1950, Kahn's art ceased to exist
predominantly for art's sake and began to
substantially integrate with his design
concerns.

345
DUOMO AND GIOTTO'S CAMPANILE,
Florence, Italy 1950
Crayon on paper, 6 4/5 x 9 9/10 in.
(17.5 x 25.4 cm); image: 6 4/5 x
6 9/10 in. (17.5 x 17.8 cm)
Present whereabouts unknown

346
PALAZZO STROZZI, Florence, Italy 1950
Crayon on paper, 2 9/10 x 3 1/5 in.
(7.6 x 8.3 cm)
Inscribed lower left: *Strozzi*
Present whereabouts unknown

In this very rapid gesture sketch, Kahn
manages to capture the siting of the
palace and to convey, with only a few
energetic strokes, the textural character
of the rusticated masonry.

347
DUOMO, Florence, Italy 1950
Crayon on paper, 6 4/5 x 9 9/10 in. (17.5 x 25.4 cm); image: 6 4/5 x 5 1/10 in. (17.5 x 13.3 cm)
Color notations
Present whereabouts unknown

Kahn's seven sketches (Nos. 341–347) of Florence's famous architectural sites express his perennial interest in dramatic views of towers and other dominant architectural forms. In this drawing, the bulk of the cathedral and its famous dome are spotted through the slot of a narrow adjoining street. It is characteristic of Kahn's dramatic compositional staging.

348
PIAZZA DEL DUOMO, Pisa, Italy 1950
Crayon on paper, 7 9/10 x 11 1/10 in.
(20.3 x 28.6 cm)
Color notations
Present whereabouts unknown

In this view of the baptistry, cathedral
and tower ensemble in Pisa, Kahn
concentrates on the geometry of
forms, ignoring the fine Romanesque
articulations. The double image of the
dome at left resulted from an attempt at
correcting the improperly scaled baptistry
with the help of a guide line relating to
the leaning tower.

349
DOGE'S PALACE, Venice, Italy 1950
Crayon on paper, 5 9/10 x 9 9/10 in.
(15.2 x 25.4 cm)
Present whereabouts unknown

A comparison of this drawing to Kahn's
1929 sketch of the same view (No. 97)
points to the artist's evolution from a
romantic youth struck by the beauty of
Venice to a mature architect who
recognizes the importance of relating
architecture and urban spaces to a
natural environment. While this later
sketch is not devoid of romanticism, it
abandons excessive sentimentality for a
dramatic representation of reality. Thus,
the proportions of all the elements are
intact and the excitement is achieved by
a careful choice of viewpoint with
detailed emphasis on chosen elements.

350
PIAZZETTA DI SAN MARCO,
Venice, Italy 1950
Crayon on paper, 5 9/10 x 9 9/10 in.
(15.2 x 25.4 cm)
Present whereabouts unknown

This drawing should be compared with
Kahn's sketch of the same scene made in
1929 (No. 101). In the early rendition, in
an obviously emotional overemphasis of
its importance, the basilica looms out of
scale with the piazzetta. In this later
version, Kahn gives the true character
to the overall space and the basilica
becomes one of many buildings forming
the "walls" of the Piazza di San Marco
and the piazzetta. While the early sketch
represented the piazzetta in a semi-
silhouette fashion, this drawing dwells on
the textural character of the surroundings.

351
BASILICA DI SAN MARCO, NORTH
FACADE, Venice, Italy 1950
Crayon on paper, 5 9/10 x 9 9/10 in.
(15.2 x 25.4 cm)
Present whereabouts unknown

This little square on the approach to the
piazza, with the basilica on the left and
the clocktower on the right, is not one
of the spots for which Venice is known.
However, Kahn's artistic eye and
architectural sense relished it and he
found the need to record it in this
exquisite sketch.

352
PIAZZA DI SAN MARCO,
Venice, Italy 1950
Crayon on paper, 5 9/10 x 9 9/10 in.
(15.2 x 25.4 cm)
Signed lower right: *Lou K*
Color notations lower left and center
Present whereabouts unknown

Almost all of Kahn's sketches from
Venice (Nos. 349–354) exhibit an
attitude toward urban space similar to his
Florentine drawings (Nos. 341–347).
They pay greater attention to details,
however, and have more concern for
texture. There is also an added emphasis
on the presence of city life through the
casual indication of pedestrians. Finally,
using loose fragments of lines on the
ground and in the sky, Kahn reflects the
expanse of the piazza's pavement and
fills the entire scene with a dynamic
atmosphere.

353
BASILICA DI SAN MARCO,
Venice, Italy 1951
Pastel on paper, 12 1/3 x 15 1/3 in.
(31.7 x 39.4 cm)
Shown at a traveling exhibition
organized by the Pennsylvania Academy
of the Fine Arts, 1978–1979,
Catalogue No. 58, titled: *Venice, 1951*
Collection of Sue Ann Kahn

Temporarily abandoning his architectural
concerns, Kahn plunges into artistic
ecstasy with this jubilant abstraction of
the Basilica di San Marco. Blending
impressionistic and expressionistic
tendencies he produces a composition
which, through its emotional explosion
of colors and forms, might be compared
to an exuberant musical orchestration.

354
CA' D'ORO, Venice, Italy 1951
Pastel on paper, 12 x 9 9/10 in.
(30.8 x 25.4 cm)
Shown at a traveling exhibition
organized by the Pennsylvania Academy
of the Fine Arts, 1978–1979, Catalogue
No. 58, titled: *St. Mark's Cathedral,
Venice. 1951*
Collection of Sue Ann Kahn

Kahn's fascination with Venetian
architecture is transformed here into an
exciting abstraction. Rather than using
solid planes of color, he translates the
building into independent lines of
primary hues, which, due to their
separation, create the impression of
transparency characteristic of Venetian
Gothic architecture. The bottom of the

picture—completely integrated with the
building—depicts gondolas and candy-
striped lantern poles. Of all Kahn's
artwork, this sketch comes closest to a
total abstraction and is in step with the
abstract expressionism sweeping the
American art world at that time.

355
"ARACOVA," Greece 1951
Crayon on paper, size not available
Inscribed lower right: *Aracova*
Present whereabouts unknown

Touring through Greece on the road to
Delphi, Kahn was struck by the violent
beauty of its mountain ranges. The bare,
rocky, and jagged forms were in great
contrast to the soft rolling mountains and
valleys he sketched back home. Kahn
recorded this furious natural setting in
this study and a triple crayon sketch (No.
360). Several years later he translated
them into brush and ink sketches (see
Nos. 356, 358, and 359).

356
PEAK OF ARAKHOVA, NO. 1,
Greece 1951/55
Brush and india ink on paper, 12 1/2 x
17 in. (32.1 x 43.8 cm)
Collection of Sue Ann Kahn

Kahn made this sketch in Philadelphia in
1955 from crayon drawing No. 355. The
strong impression that this mountain
range made on him is apparent from
the emotional manner in which he
composed this sketch four years later.
There is an impatient reliance on
brushwork controlled only by Kahn's
feelings and his awareness of the scene's
overall composition.

357
PANORAMA, Delphi, Greece 1951
Pastel on paper, 10 x 14 1/5 in.
(25.7 x 36.5 cm)
Inscribed on the back at upper right:
Delphi III
Shown at a traveling exhibition
organized by the Pennsylvania Academy
of the Fine Arts, 1978–1979, Catalogue
No. 68, titled: *Delphi III, 1951*
Collection of Sue Ann Kahn

Kahn took ample time to create this
rendition of a breathtaking view. It is one
of his most refined pastels. He did not
have to resort here to his usual selective
notations and abstractions; the scenery,
with its natural grandeur, revealed its
spirit quite openly. In this way, the sketch
harks back to the romanticism of the
Hudson River School.

358
PEAK OF ARAKHOVA, NO. 2,
Greece 1951/55
Brush and india ink on paper, 12 2/5 x
16 4/5 in. (31.8 x 43.2 cm)
Signed lower right: *Louis I. Kahn '51-55*
Exhibited at Max Protetch Gallery, New
York, June 1981, Catalogue No. 15,
titled: *1955 Peak of Arachova, Greece*
Collection of the Architectural Archives,
University of Pennsylvania, Catalogue
No. 945.23, titled: *Travel Sketch, Peak of
Arachova, Greece* ; Gift of Richard Saul
Wurman

359
PEAK OF ARAKHOVA, NO. 3,
Greece 1951/55
Brush and india ink on onionskin paper,
5 9/10 x 9 9/10 in. (15.2 x 25.4 cm)
Shown at a traveling exhibition
organized by the Pennsylvania Academy
of the Fine Arts, 1978–1979,
Catalogue No. 42, titled: *Landscape with
Mountains, 1946–7*
Collection of Sue Ann Kahn

Like No. 358, this is a 1955 rendition of
drawing No. 360. Kahn varies the style of
this sketch significantly by employing
controlled abstractions and stylization.
He combines shades into patches of solid
black, floating in areas delineated by
strong outlines. Again, the mountains
in the center assume the shapes of
pyramids, but the violence of the jagged
landscape appears somewhat subdued.

360
PEAK OF ARAKHOVA, ON THE ROAD
TO DELPHI, Greece 1951
Crayon on paper, 10 2/5 x 7 9/10 in.
(26.7 x 20.3 cm)
Present whereabouts unknown

The bottom of these three sketches
served as the base for ink renditions Nos.
358 and 359, executed in 1955. The hills
in the center of the bottom sketch exhibit
an uncanny resemblance to Kahn's

sketches of pyramids (Nos.
410–21), structures which deeply
affected him on his recently completed
trip through Egypt.

361
ROCKS AND TREES, Greece 1951
Crayon on paper, size not available
Present whereabouts unknown

This sketch has the character of an
artwork made in Kahn's studio from field
sketches. There is a stiffness which is
absent in his work direct from nature.
The crayon is used here in a rigid,
decisive manner reminiscent of his ink
sketches from this period.

362
RUINS WITH DEAD TREES,
Greece 1951
Crayon on paper, size not available
Present whereabouts unknown

Ruins, because of their timeless qualities,
intrigued Kahn as much as the sublime
fury of Greek mountains or the spirit
of survival revealed in old gnarled trees.
There was a beauty in the ruins from
their having outlived their original
purpose and because, stripped of
utilitarian function, they could be
enjoyed for their purity of form. Kahn
pursued this beauty in his own
architectural designs, even though
he had to fulfill strict functional
requirements. In this sketch and in No.
332, Kahn created compositions in
which elements of ruins assume unique
forms accented by the sharp contrast of
light and shadows. The abstract quality of
these sketches highlights Kahn's interest
in conveying the very spirit of the
subject, rather than its obvious external
appearance. The visual harmony of the
dead trees and the architectural ruins in
this sketch dramatize this point very
clearly.

363
THE ORACLE, NO. 1, Delphi,
Greece 1951
Charcoal pencil on paper, 11 2/10 x
14 3/5 in. (28.9 x 37.5 cm)
Signed lower right: *Louis I. Kahn '51*
Collection of Sue Ann Kahn

This is one of three sketches depicting
the sanctuary of Apollo at Delphi. Kahn's
renditions of these ruins are quite
different from the semiabstract sketches
of other incidental and little-known ruins.
He allowed himself no artistic license to
rearrange elements of the composition.
His choice of views, however, is of
interest. Rather than use a view which
would clearly explain the nature of the
monument, as would be expected of
most architects, Kahn chose the most
dramatic and picturesque angles. His
desire to express the environmental
quality of the ruins within their setting
was of greater importance to Kahn than
the formal or structural characteristics of
the monument.

365
THE ORACLE, NO. 3, Delphi,
Greece 1951
Charcoal pencil on paper, 11 2/10 x
14 1/10 in. (28.9 x 36.2 cm)
Inscribed lower right: *Delphi '51*
Shown at a traveling exhibition
organized by the Pennsylvania Academy
of the Fine Arts, 1978–1979, Catalogue
No. 67, titled: *Delphi, Greece, 1951*
Collection of Sue Ann Kahn

This sketch is almost identical to No.
364. It exhibits simplified textures and
details, which indicate that it may have
been made in Philadelphia from the
original field sketch.

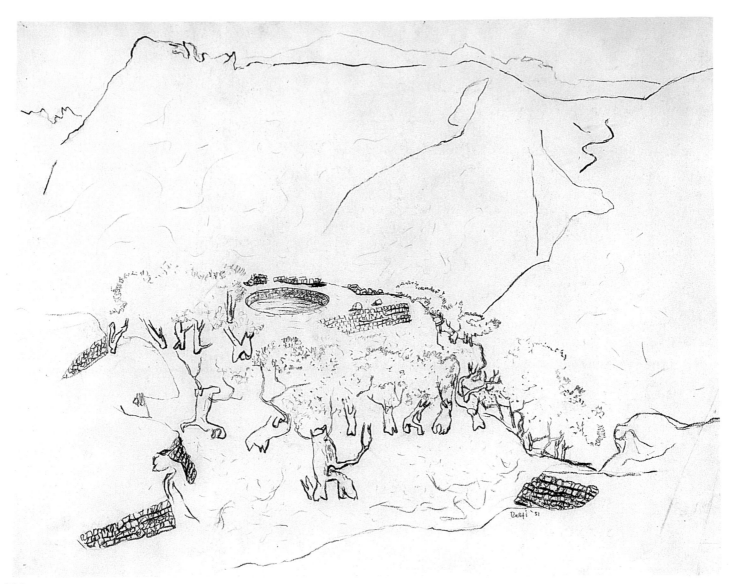

364
THE ORACLE, NO. 2, Delphi,
Greece 1951
Charcoal pencil on paper, 11 1/5 x
14 1/10 in. (28.9 x 36.2 cm)
Present whereabouts unknown

366
TREE STUDY, Greece 1951
Charcoal pencil on paper, 11 1/5 x
14 3/5 in. (28.9 x 37.5 cm)
Collection of Sue Ann Kahn

This sketch analyzes one of the scraggly
trees found at the Delphi ruins. Besides
the exquisite rendition of the trunk and
the sparse branches, this drawing
portrays the symbolism of rebirth. The
young, fragile leaves bearing twigs rise
Phoenix-like from the ruin of the
decaying tree.

367
SANCTUARY OF APOLLO,
Delphi, Greece 1951
Charcoal pencil on paper, 11 1/5 x
14 1/10 in. (28.9 x 36.2 cm)
Exhibited at Max Protetch Gallery, New
York City, June 1981, Catalogue No. 16,
titled: *1951 Delphi from Marmaria
Greece*
Collection of the Architectural Archives,
University of Pennsylvania, Catalogue
No. 945.22; titled: *Travel Sketch, Delphi
from Marmaria, Greece.* Gift of Richard
Saul Wurman

Kahn judiciously eliminates from this
view those elements he deems
nonessential. Thus, the foreground is
left blank and attention is directed
immediately to the ruins. The carefully
drawn forward wall, with each stone in
detail, provides perspective clues to this
layered set of elements. The background
trees and rocks are made an integral part
of the ruins, while a delicate hint of hills
beyond establish the majesty of the site.

368
"DELPHI FROM MARMARIA,"
Delphi, Greece 1951
Charcoal on paper, 11 1/3 x 14 1/3 in.
(29.2 x 36.8 cm)
Present whereabouts unknown

Looking north toward the sanctuary of
Apollo with the tholos in the foreground,
Kahn develops the striking contrast of
airy ruins against dark mountains. The
brilliant light flooding the site causes
deep shadows that heighten the dramatic
effect.

369
"MYCENAE" and ACROPOLIS,
Mycenae and Athens, Greece 1951
Charcoal pencil on sketchbook paper,
size not available
Inscribed lower right: *Mycenae*
Present whereabouts unknown

This and several other drawings from
Greece (Nos. 370–72) appeared in
Kahn's spiral sketchbook, many
straddling the spiral binding in order to
accommodate a panoramic view. This
double page spread shows a view of the
Mycenaen ruins on the left page and
the Acropolis in Athens, viewed from
the southeast, on the right page. As in
Kahn's drawing of the Lion Gate at
Mycenae (No. 370), these are faithful
recordings of physical reality, with
careful attention paid to scale, proportion,
and texture.

370
LION GATE, Mycenae, Greece 1951
Charcoal pencil on sketchbook paper,
size not available
Present whereabouts unknown

The massive stonework and simple
construction of this gateway must have
appealed to Kahn's sense of order and
inspired him to render these ruins with
the utmost accuracy and faithfulness.
There is no attempt at dramatization or
glorification in this sketch, due mainly to
the site's inherently sublime character.

371
ACROPOLIS, APPROACH FROM THE
WEST, NO. 1, Athens, Greece 1951
Charcoal pencil on sketchbook paper,
size not available
Present whereabouts unknown

The placement of this sketch in the spiral
pad points to the possibility that Kahn
either started sketching from the right
side—an unusual procedure for a right-
handed person—or that in order to
utilize the full height of the paper, the
proportions of the view required him to
begin on the left side of the spiral binding
and then bridge over to the right page.
This mode of composition occurs again
in another view of the Acropolis (No.
372).

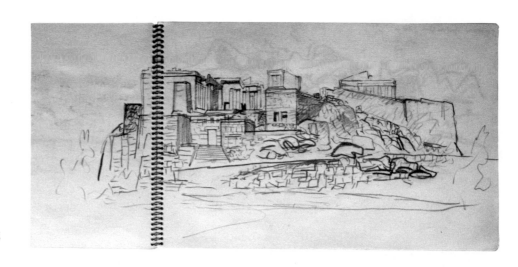

372
ACROPOLIS, APPROACH FROM THE
WEST, NO. 2, Athens, Greece   1951
Charcoal pencil on sketchbook paper,
size not available
Present whereabouts unknown

373
PROPYLAEA, ACROPOLIS,
Athens, Greece 1951
Pastel on paper, 11 3/5 x 9 1/10 in.
(29.8 x 23.5 cm)
Shown at a traveling exhibition
organized by the Pennsylvania Academy
of the Fine Arts, 1978–1979, Catalogue

No. 62, titled: *Propylaea, Parthenon,
Acropolis, Athens, 1951*
Collection of Sue Ann Kahn

Kahn's interest in the relationship of
walls to columns is explored in this
closeup view of the ruins of the

Propylaeum. The solid-void contrast is
amplified by the superimposition of pale
structure against the brilliant blue sky.
While Kahn explores tectonic concerns,
the resulting composition borders on
pure abstraction.

374
"ACROPOLIS," Athens, Greece 1951
Pastel and charcoal pencil on
paper, 11 1/10 x 14 3/5 in.
(28.5 x 37.5 cm)
Signed lower right: *Louis I. Kahn '51*;
inscribed on the back at lower left:
Acropolis, Athens
Shown at a traveling exhibition
organized by the Pennsylvania Academy
of the Fine Arts, 1978–1979, Catalogue
No. 60, titled: *Acropolis, Athens, 1951*
Collection of Sue Ann Kahn

In a rare departure from employing colors
for expressionistic ends, Kahn follows in
this drawing a rather faithful depiction of
forms, more characteristic of his charcoal
sketches of the Acropolis. With the
exception of a bright blue portion of
the sky and small red shadows cast on
the Erechtheion and a barely visible
Parthenon, all the colors are realistically
restrained. The great variety of shades,
set off by deep shadows and contrasted
against the blue of the sky, help to
delineate the crystalline forms immersed
in a bright sunlight. And, as in so many

of Kahn's color scenes, portions of the
composition are left unfinished, assuring
the prominence of the fully rendered
forms.

375
ACROPOLIS FROM THE OLYMPIEION,
Athens, Greece 1951
Pastel and charcoal pencil on
paper, 10 9/10 x 13 4/5 in.
(28.0 x 35.5 cm)
Shown at a traveling exhibition
organized by the Pennsylvania Academy
of the Fine Arts, 1978–1979, Catalogue
No. 61, titled: *Acropolis, Athens, 1951*
Collection of Sue Ann Kahn

When employing pastels in this series,
Kahn released his expressive energies, in
contrast to the sober accuracy of his
charcoal drawings of the same period.
Colors allowed him to explore the
emotional and spiritual dimensions of
these sites. Thus, in this pastel, the
Corinthian columns of the Olympieion
and the distant Acropolis are rendered in
color, leaving the city and trees as mere
charcoal outlines. Forms are reduced to
simplified abstractions and colors are
used symbolically. In this drawing, a late
afternoon winter sun touches the sides of
columns and walls with its golden light.
A flutter of luminescent clouds connects
the foreground colonnade with the
distant citadel.

376
ACROPOLIS FROM SOUTHEAST,
Athens, Greece 1951
Pastel on paper, 5 x 7 4/5 in.
(13.0 x 20.0 cm)
Signed lower right: *Lou K '51*
Private collection

Viewed from about the same angle as
No. 375, but from a closer vantage point,
this work captures the last rays of the
evening sun illuminating the southern
slopes of the Acropolis and the crowning
ruins of the Parthenon.

377
VIEW FROM THE PARTHENON,
ACROPOLIS, Athens, Greece 1951
Charcoal on paper, 10 3/5 x 13 1/4 in.
(27.3 x 34.0 cm)
Private collection

This spectacular view demonstrates
Kahn's love for picturesque organization
in his drawings. Standing on the north
stylobate of the Parthenon and looking
directly west past the Propylaea, the
colonnade of the Parthenon becomes a
vertically striped plane. The resulting
sharp perspective does not glorify the
beauty of the Parthenon but the
important part it plays in the overall
physical setting of the Acropolis.

378
ACROPOLIS, FRANKISH WALLS,
Athens, Greece 1951
Charcoal and black crayon on paper,
11 1/3 x 14 1/10 in. (29.0 x 36.3 cm)
Signed lower right: *Louis I. Kahn '51*;
inscribed on the back at lower left:
Acropolis Walls
Shown at a traveling exhibition
organized by the Pennsylvania Academy
of the Fine Arts, 1978–1979, Catalogue
No. 59, titled: *Frankish Walls, Acropolis,
Athens, Greece, 1951*
Collection of Sue Ann Kahn

In spite of its prominent position, the
Parthenon is not of interest to Kahn in
this drawing. His fascination with the
reinforced south wall of the Acropolis
is evident in the contrasting shadows
cast by the buttresses and the sharp
demarcation of the wall against the sky.
The composition, layered horizontally
with broken relics in he foreground, is
reminiscent of Delphi sketch No. 367.

379
ERECHTHEION AND PARTHENON,
ACROPOLIS, Athens, Greece, 1951
Pastel and charcoal pencil on paper,
size not available
Signed lower right: *Louis I. Kahn '51*
Present whereabouts unknown

In a manner similar to No. 374, this
pastel sketch concentrates more on an
accurate portrayal of architectural
features than an expressionistic mood.
The inclusion of human figures in the
Parthenon gives the site scale, while a
sense of depth is provided by loose
marble blocks in the foreground. Kahn
unites the composition with a spectacular
sky, where the giant pink cloud reflects
secondary light onto the north side of
Parthenon and the low wall of the old
temple of Athena.

380
INTERIOR, PARTHENON, ACROPOLIS,
Athens, Greece 1951
Pastel on paper, 11 1/10 x 13 9/10 in.
(28.6 x 35.6 cm)
Shown at a traveling exhibition
organized by the Pennsylvania Academy
of the Fine Arts, 1978–1979,
Catalogue No. 63
Collection of Sue Ann Kahn

With fewer tectonic concerns and a
departure from the subdued colors he
used in No. 379, Kahn here explores the
power of complementary hues to achieve
both contrast and harmony. The warm
burnt sienna and browns of the columns
and the architraves stand out against
the deep blue of the sky, providing a
strong sense of depth. The blending of
these colors in the foreground and in the
sky unifies the composition and allows
the eye to blend the colors in an
impressionistic manner.

381
TEMPLE OF APOLLO, NO. 1 and NO. 2,
Corinth, Greece 1951
Charcoal pencil on sketchbook paper,
size not available
Present whereabouts unknown

This study of architectural ruins viewed
from opposite angles presents two
variations of the effect of sunlight on
forms. The sketch on the left explores the
more common illumination in which
sunlight reveals forms with highlights,
shades, and shadows. The sketch on the
right is an unusual analysis of forms
silhouetted against oncoming sunlight.
Kahn made a similar double sketch in
Pompeii on his first European trip in
1928–29 (No. 86). Of interest is Kahn's
change in style. Forms outlined in sharp
linework replace broad strokes of
graphite stick in the later sketches.

382
TEMPLE OF APOLLO, NO. 3, Corinth,
Greece 1951
Pastel and charcoal on paper, 10 7/10 x
10 1/10 in. (27.5 x 26.0 cm)
Shown at a traveling exhibition
organized by the Pennsylvania Academy
of the Fine Arts, 1978–1979, Catalogue
No. 66, titled: *Columns, Temple of
Apollo, Corinth, Greece, 1951*
Collection of Sue Ann Kahn

In addition to his explorations of light,
Kahn applies his very personal sense of

coloration in these sketches. In contrast
to the earthy tones of the two left
columns, Kahn colors the remaining
three blue, green, and red, all silhouetted
against a yellow sky. This expressionistic
stroke is very personal and hard to
interpret. However, the ravages of time
on the ruins are easily read through the
casual, yet effective, distortions and
texturing.

383
TEMPLE OF APOLLO, NO. 4, Corinth,
Greece 1951
Pastel and charcoal on paper, 11 1/10 x
14 1/3 in. (28.6 x 36.8 cm)
Shown at a traveling exhibition
organized by the Pennsylvania Academy
of the Fine Arts, 1978–1979, Catalogue
No. 65, titled: *Temple of Apollo, Corinth,
Greece, 1951*
Collection of Sue Ann Kahn

This sketch recalls Kahn's rendition of the
interior of the Parthenon (No. 380). But
this pastel employs stronger tones and a
more precise representation of columns
and lintels. Details of the columns from
the base up are abandoned at the ground
level; only quick blue scribbles denote
the setting for outlines of broken
masonry.

384
TEMPLE OF APOLLO, NO. 5,
Corinth, Greece 1951
Pastel and charcoal on paper, 11 1/10 x
14 3/5 in. (28.6 x 37.5 cm)
Signed lower right: *Louis I. Kahn '51*
Shown at a traveling exhibition
organized by the Pennsylvania Academy
of the Fine Arts, 1978–1979, Catalogue
No. 64, titled: *Temple of Apollo,
Corinth, Greece, 1951*
Collection of Sue Ann Kahn

This color rendition of the temple ruin in
Nos. 381, 382, and 383, is one of Louis
Kahn's best pastel drawings. It combines
the best elements of his work throughout
his career. The soft, warm light on the
columns is reminiscent of his 1929
sketch of the Temple of Poseidon
(No. 88). The judiciously unfinished
foreground is similar to his view of the
monastery in Assisi (No. 37). The
semiabstract handling of incidental
portions of the ruins is close to the
renditions of such subjects in No. 379.
More importantly, the placement of
the ruins in relation to their environment
exhibits Kahn's concern with
architectural issues more than with
picturesque settings.

385
GRANITE QUARRIES, NO. 1,
Aswan, Egypt 1951
Charcoal pencil on paper,
8 3/4 x 11 7/10 in. (22.5 x 30.1 cm);
image upper left: 3 1/5 x 4 2/5 in. (8.3 x
11.4 cm); image lower center: 2 1/3 x
4 3/5 in. (6.0 x 12.0 cm)
Color notations
Collection of Sue Ann Kahn

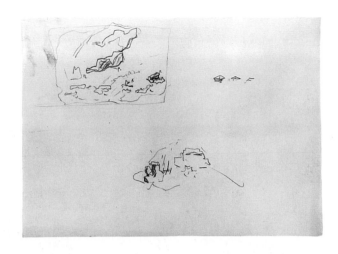

The sketches and drawings from Kahn's
Egyptian journey are presented here not
in the order of his travels, but rather by
subject matter as they relate to the
exposure of his theoretical concerns.
Thus, even though his trip originated in
Cairo, the drawings of the pyramids are
placed at the end of this group in order to
emphasize Kahn's attitudes toward their
forms and their influence on his
subsequent architectural work.

In this series of nine sketches (Nos.
385–393) depicting various views of
stone quarries at Aswan, Kahn imbues his
drawings with the mysterious wonder he
maintained for architectural ruins (see
No. 362). In a way, Kahn manages to
exceed his reverence for ruins by
presenting the potential for these
random blocks of stone to transform
themselves into architecture. Through
a masterly manipulation of powerful
lines and definitive shadows, Kahn
imbues the stones with immense
potency. The formations, bordering on
total abstractions, supply a hint of
architectural form, but they are more
suggestive of ruins, the final cycle of their
potential existence.

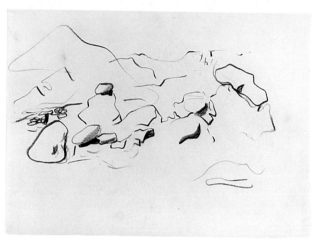

386
GRANITE QUARRIES, NO. 2,
Aswan, Egypt 1951
Charcoal pencil on paper, 8 7/10 x
11 7/10 in. (22.5 x 30.1 cm)
Collection of Sue Ann Kahn

387
GRANITE QUARRIES, NO. 3,
Aswan, Egypt 1951
Charcoal pencil on paper, 7 2/5 x
8 1/2 in. (19.0 x 21.9 cm)
Collection of Sue Ann Kahn

388
GRANITE QUARRIES, NO. 4A,
Aswan, Egypt 1951
Charcoal pencil on paper,
7 2/5 x 8 1/2 in. (19.0 x 21.9 cm)
Collection of Sue Ann Kahn

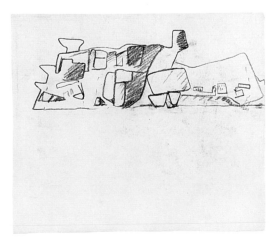

389
GRANITE QUARRIES, NO. 4B,
Aswan, Egypt 1951/1951–59
Brush and india ink on textured bond
paper, 7 9/10 x 9 9/10 in.
(20.3 x 25.4 cm)
Collection of Sue Ann Kahn

Kahn made this sketch back in
Philadelphia using charcoal pencil study
No. 388. The brush-and-ink echnique
employed here and the resulting
abstractions were characteristic of Kahn's
returning to travel sketches to produce
new versions, sometimes several almost
identical ones (see also Nos. 390–93).

390
GRANITE QUARRIES, NO. 5A,
Aswan, Egypt 1951
Charcoal pencil on paper,
7 2/5 x 8 1/2 in. (19.0 x 21.9 cm)
Verso of No. 382
Collection of Sue Ann Kahn

391
GRANITE QUARRIES, NO. 5B,
Aswan, Egypt 1951
Brush and india ink on paper,
11 1/5 x 14 3/5 in. (28.9 x 37.5 cm)
Collection of Sue Ann Kahn

This is a fairly faithful ink rendition of
charcoal pencil drawing No. 390, even
to the point of almost totally isolating the
scene from its context.

392
GRANITE QUARRIES, NO. 6A,
Aswan, Egypt 1951
Charcoal pencil on paper,
7 2/5 x 8 1/2 in. (19.0 x 21.9 cm)
Collection of Sue Ann Kahn

This panoramic view is rendered with a
considerable reliance on modeling
techniques reminiscent of Kahn's
graphite sketches from his first European
trip. The scene is imbued with tension
created by the contrast of prismatic
quarried stone and soft and curving hills.

393
GRANITE QUARRIES, NO. 6B,
Aswan, Egypt 1951
Brush and india ink on paper,
7 9/10 x 9 9/10 in. (20.3 x 25.4 cm)
Present whereabouts unknown

This very loose rendition of charcoal
pencil study No. 392 borders on pure
abstraction. Kahn creates calligraphic
symbols which mask the physical reality
of the scene, but also convey dreamlike
messages in a manner reminiscent of
Joan Miró .

394

HYPOSTYLE HALL, TEMPLE OF
AMMON, Luxor, Egypt 1951
Charcoal pencil on sketchbook paper,
5 1/10 x 7 3/5 in. (13.3 x 19.7 cm)
Present whereabouts unknown

Kahn's sketches of Egyptian temple ruins
fall into the same category of work as
the Greek temple series (Nos. 362–384).
They are studies of the mysteries of
ancient monuments for the purpose of
extracting their timeless essences. It
was in Egypt that Kahn came upon the
forms that were closest to his ideas and
aspirations. Through these sketches he
was able to make the important
connection between his Beaux-Arts
training and the modern movement.

One of the significant ingredients of
Kahn's sketches throughout his career
was his rendition of the play of light and
shadow on architectural forms. In Egypt
this inclination stimulated him beyond
anything he had experienced before.
He was subjected to the strong African
sunlight which combined with the clear
desert air to generate shadows of utmost
clarity. It was a lesson of light and
architecture which had to be preserved
and treasured.

395

COURT OF RAMSES II, TEMPLE OF
AMMON, Luxor, Egypt 1951
Charcoal pencil on sketchbook paper,
5 1/10 x 7 3/5 in. (13.3 x 19.7 cm)
Color notations
Present whereabouts unknown

Kahn made charcoal pencil sketches
Nos. 394–397 in a spiral sketchbook
which he also used in Greece (see Nos.
369–72 and 381). The sketchbook was
photographed in Kahn's office in
Philadelphia in December 1972.
Unfortunately, like so many of Kahn's
drawings, this sketchbook cannot be
located and is presumed lost.

396
HYPOSTYLE HALL AND PYLON OF
RAMSES II, TEMPLE OF AMMON NO. 1,
Luxor, Egypt 1951
Charcoal pencil on sketchbook paper,
5 1/10 x 7 3/5 in. (13.3 x 19.7 cm)
Present whereabouts unknown

397
HYPOSTYLE HALL AND PYLON OF
RAMSES II, TEMPLE OF AMMON,
NO. 2, Luxor, Egypt 1951
Charcoal pencil on sketchbook paper,
5 1/10 x 7 3/5 in. (13.3 x 19.7 cm)
Present whereabouts unknown

Viewed at an angle slightly different than
No. 396, this sketch served as a study for
pastel drawing No. 398. Probably in
anticipation of making a color rendition
of this scene, Kahn omitted the deep
shadows of No. 396 here to reveal in
detail the tectonic characteristics of
the ruins.

398

HYPOSTYLE HALL AND PYLON OF
RAMSES II, TEMPLE OF AMMON,
NO. 3, Luxor, Egypt 1951
Pastel on paper, 11 1/4 x 14 3/5 in.
(28.9 x 37.5 cm)
Signed lower right: *Louis I. Kahn '51*
Shown at a traveling exhibition
organized by the Pennsylvania Academy
of the Fine Arts, 1978–1979, Catalogue
No. 72, titled: *Luxor, Egypt, 1951*
Collection of Sue Ann Kahn

Using No. 397 as a model for this pastel,
Kahn propelled the drama of this site
with a burst of brilliant colors. Green
shadows are cast by the late-afternoon
sun on the purple-brown foreground, on
the remnants of a brightly lit temple wall,
on the red columns and pylon, and on
the yellow walls in the background. The
complementary color phenomena of
shadows and reflected light fascinated
Kahn for quite some time. However, the
choice of primary colors, such as red for
the pylon and columns, indicates an
expressionistic rather than impressionistic
tendency. This is quite evident in many
of his pastels from this period.

399

SOUTHEAST PYLONS, TEMPLE OF
AMMON, Karnak, Egypt 1951
Pastel on paper, 8 1/10 x 14 3/10 in.
(21.0 x 36.8 cm)
Signed lower right: *Lou K '51*
Collection of Sue Ann Kahn

In a much more subdued mood than in
No. 398, Kahn concentrates on a fairly
accurate representation of the ruins in his
composition and use of colors. Siennas
and ochers now dominate the picture,
with only palm trunks in the distance
brandishing pure red. Kahn captures the
brightness of light and the clarity of air by
making little distinction between shades
and shadows, and by playing up the
great contrast between illuminated and
shaded surfaces.

400
PYLON, PTOLEMAIC TEMPLE,
Edfu, Egypt 1951
Pastel on paper, 7 x 8 2/5 in.
(18.1 x 21.6 cm)
Private collection

Reverting back to expressionistic
colorations, Kahn juxtaposes naturally
hued forms against surroundings that are
subjected to his heightened perception of
light. Thus, the tan pylon set against a
clear blue sky seems realistic, while the
red shadow on the blue ground evokes a
sense of mystery.

401
COURT, TEMPLE OF KHONS,
Karnak, Egypt 1951
Pastel and charcoal pencil on paper,
7 1/5 x 12 in. (18.5 x 31.0 cm)
Shown at a traveling exhibition
organized by the Pennsylvania Academy
of the Fine Arts, 1978–1979, Catalogue
No. 78, titled: *Temple Ruins, Egypt, 1951*
Collection of Sue Ann Kahn

This is a masterful study of architectural
forms revealed in light. Kahn's
Beaux-Arts training clearly influenced
its black-and-white foundation. However,
Kahn also provides us with a most erudite
essay on the representation of shades and
shadows in color. Even though he does
not rely on his usual complementary
colors for reflected light, he does
emphasize the warmth of secondary
illumination by the use of bright yellows,
reds, and oranges. Of particular interest
is Kahn's rendition of the wall, where the
dark brown shadow cast by the broken
entablature becomes red as it reaches the
ground level and picks up its reflection.
In a similar manner, the side of the
column closest to the sunlit wall picks up
a red reflection, as do the masonry joints
on the shaded wall.

402
HYPOSTYLE HALL, TEMPLE OF
AMMON, Karnak, Egypt, 1951
Charcoal on paper, 11 1/3 x 14 3/5 in.
(29.2 x 37.5 cm)
Signed lower left: *Louis I. Kahn '51*
Shown at a traveling exhibition
organized by the Pennsylvania Academy
of the Fine Arts, 1978–1979,
Catalogue No. 75,
titled: *Hypostyle Hall, Karnak, Egypt,
1951*
Collection of Sue Ann Kahn

The drama of shadows and light played
out on the basic forms of architecture can
hardly be presented better than in this
unusual sketch. Kahn forgoes the
rendering of cylindrical forms through
modeling and resorts to a sharp contrast
of black shadows against white columns.
The resulting composition becomes an
abstract pattern which retains interest
without becoming strictly descriptive of
the subject.

403
COMPOSITION, TEMPLE OF AMMON,
Luxor, Egypt 1951
Charcoal on paper, 10 4/5 x 9 1/3 in.
(27.9 x 24.1 cm)
Signed lower right: *Lou K 51*
Private collection

Kahn's prolific repertoire of techniques
emerges here in a drawing completely
opposite in manner to No. 402. Reverting
back to his graphite-stick method of the
1920s, he models forms with soft and
gentle shades and sets them up against
mysterious and dark background
shadows.

404
MORTUARY TEMPLE OF HATSHEPSUT,
Deir el-Bahari, Egypt 1951
Pastel on paper, 11 1/3 x 15 3/10 in.
(29.2 x 39.4 cm)
Shown at a traveling exhibition
organized by the Pennsylvania Academy
of the Fine Arts, 1978–1979, Catalogue
No. 77, titled: *Tomb Temple of
Hatshepsut, Nile River, Egypt, 1951*
Collection of Sue Ann Kahn

This sketch, in its composition and
technical execution, recalls Kahn's 1929
Amalfi coast watercolor *Fisherman's
Huts, No.1* (No. 60). In both, Kahn leaves
the sky outside the picture frame and
uses sharp decisive strokes to delineate
forms in strong sunlight. The almost
monochromatic palette also links the
two works. It is as if Kahn had made a
full cycle in his compositional and
technical development, but with a
greater sophistication and power of
abstraction in the later work.

405
COLUMN CAPITALS, NO. 1,
Karnak, Egypt 1951
Pastel on paper, 11 1/10 x 14 1/10 in.
(28.6 x 36.2 cm)
Present whereabouts unknown

Kahn's three pastels of column capitals (Nos. 405–407) are semiabstract renditions of architectural forms. In these sketches Kahn uses the pattern of sunlight as an abstract form in its own right. All three sketches utilize the dramatic angle and deep blue of the sky, which complement in color and form the pattern of lintels and capitals. In No. 406, Kahn ventures into abstraction through the introduction of a black outline separating shade from sunlight on the background capital. In No. 407 the move toward abstraction is almost completed. The three-dimensional quality of the columns and lintels is reduced to a two-dimensional color pattern of white, red, yellow-orange, green, and black. Patches of sunlight on columns and capitals are outlined boldly again. The right column was probably left unfinished in Kahn's usual attempt at dramatization by contrast.

406
COLUMN CAPITALS, NO. 2,
Karnak, Egypt 1951
Pastel on paper, 11 1/10 x 14 1/10 in.
(28.6 x 36.2 cm)
Present whereabouts unknown

407
COLUMN CAPITALS, NO. 3,
Karnak, Egypt 1951
Pastel on paper, 11 1/10 x 14 1/10 in.
(28.6 x 36.2 cm)
Signed lower right: *Louis I. Kahn '51*
Shown at a traveling exhibition
organized by the Pennsylvania Academy
of the Fine Arts, 1978–1979, Catalogue
No. 76, titled: *Temple Interior,
Karnak, Egypt, 1951*
Collection of Sue Ann Kahn

408
INTERIOR VIEW WITH STATUE
1951/1959
Charcoal on tracing paper, 10 7/10 x 13
9/10 in. (27.6 x 35.7 cm)
Shown at a traveling exhibition
organized by the Pennsylvania Academy
of the Fine Arts, 1978–1979, Catalogue
No. 73, titled: *Interior, Egypt, 1951*
Collection of the Art Institute of Chicago.;
Gift of Centennial Fund and Three Oaks
Wrecking Company by exchange,
1986.1055; Catalogue No. E 8891, titled:
*Louis Kahn, Travel Sketch: Egypt, Interior
View with Statue, 1951*

This drawing and No. 409 drastically
depart from the rest of the Egyptian travel
sketches. They are the only ones which
deal with interior spaces and were
executed in a manner more characteristic
of Kahn's work during the decade
following his return to the United States.
This charcoal drawing, more likely of a
Roman than an Egyptian subject, appears
to have been composed from memory or
invented. This drawing rightly belongs in
the category of architectural fantasy, with
strong indications of Kahn's search for
the beginning of form, its meaning, and
its relationship to light.

409
INTERIOR VIEW 1951/1959
Ink or watercolor paper, 12 1/5 x 17 in.
(32.0 x 43.8 cm)
Collection of the Art Institute of Chicago;
Gift of Centennial Fund and Three Oaks
Wrecking Company by exchange,
1986.1056; Catalogue No. E 8990, titled:
*Louis Kahn, Travel Sketch: Egypt, Interior
View, 1951*

Since Kahn did not use pen and ink or
watercolors during his 1950–51 travels, it
must be assumed that he made this
sketch upon returning home. The subject
and the manner of execution also appear
to place this work, like No. 408, in the
category of architectural fantasy, but this
time with more restraint and precision.
The work also explores the issue of
transparency—a guiding principle of
modernism—in a nonmodern setting,
primarily through the rendering of space
with telescoping frames.

410
PYRAMIDS ACROSS THE NILE,
Egypt 1951
Pastel on paper, 7 2/5 x 8 1/2 in.
(19.0 x 21.9 cm)
Collection of Sue Ann Kahn

Twelve sketches and drawings from Kahn's Egyptian vist (Nos. 410–421) concentrate on the subject of pyramids. As in his drawings of ancient classical ruins, Kahn demonstrates his fascination with the sublime quality of these famous sites. His prolific production of sketches and later elaborations on the subject for mural studies points to the importance pyramids played in his understanding of architecture—formally, spiritually, and symbolically. In pyramids Kahn finally found the means to make a connection between his Beaux-Arts training and modernism's principles of simplicity and detachment.

411
STEPPED PYRAMID, NO. 1, Saqqara,
Egypt 1951.
Charcoal on paper, 11 1/5 x 14 3/5 in.
(28.9 x 37.5 cm)
Shown at "Collectors' Choice Exhibition," Rosa Esman Gallery, New York City, December 1985–January 1986
Collection of Sue Ann Kahn

In most cases, Kahn produced a single rendition of a scene that he sometimes translated into another version (see Nos. 414–17). But because of delays in his travel plans he had more time to study the pyramids. This allowed him to develop two renditions of this scene in two different media. To express different moods, Kahn produced this detailed charcoal sketch and a more abstract pastel drawing (No. 412). This charcoal rendition, through its articulation of stonework, conveys the solidity and weight of the pyramids rising from the softly shaped, ephemeral sand dunes.

412
STEPPED PYRAMID, NO. 2, Saqqara,
Egypt 1951
Pastel and charcoal on paper,
11 1/5 x 14 3/5 in. (28.9 x 37.5 cm)
Shown at "Collectors' Choice
Exhibition," Rosa Esman Gallery, New
York City, December 1985–January 1986
Collection of Sue Ann Kahn

The awesome presence of the ruins is
dramatized in this drawing by the
contrast of the eerily illuminated stepped
pyramid against the blackened sky. The
heaviness in charcoal sketch No. 411
now becomes a pale and integral part of
the desert's fleeting nature.

413
PYRAMID STUDIES, Egypt, 1951
Pastel on paper, 11 1/3 x 14 3/5 in.
(29.0 x 37.5 cm); upper left image:
4 x 6 1/5 in. (10.5 x 16.0 cm); upper right
image: 2 1/10 x 3 1/3 in. (5.5 x 8.5 cm);
bottom image: 3 1/3 x 4 3/5 in.
(8.5 x 12.0 cm)
Signed lower right: *Lou K '51*
Shown at a traveling exhibition
organized by the Pennsylvania Academy
of the Fine Arts, 1978–1979,
Catalogue No. 69
Present whereabouts unknown

Kahn must have signed this pastel
drawing sometime after 1972, since the
photograph of this sketch taken in
December 1972 did not contain a
signature. This is also true of a number of
other drawings Kahn probably signed as
gifts to relatives and friends. These three
small sketches of pyramids viewed from
different angles appear to have been
made from a moving vehicle. They are
rapid notations using a limited number
of colors. Of particular interest is the
varied rendition of each pyramid in the
top left sketch.

414
PYRAMIDS, NO. 1, Giza, Egypt
1951/1955
Ink brushed on paper, 12 1/2 x 16 4/5 in.
(32.3 x 43.2 cm)
Signed lower right: *Louis I. Kahn 51–55*
Private collection

Kahn painted this ink rendition of the
pyramids in 1955. This sketch was
modeled after pastel drawing No. 417,
clarifying the relationship of the pyramids
to the surrounding ruins. It was at this
time that Kahn introduced pyramidal
forms to his architectural projects for
the Yale University Art Gallery in New
Haven, Connecticut, and the Jewish
Community Center in Trenton, New
Jersey.

415
PYRAMIDS, NO. 2, Giza, Egypt
1951/1955
Ink brushed on paper, 11 7/10 x
16 2/5 in. (30.0 x 42.2 cm)
Signed lower right: *Louis I. Kahn 51–55*
Private collection

Again, as with No. 414, this is a 1955
version of the pyramids modeled after an
original pastel drawing (No. 418). The
detailed texture of stones, absent in the
original drawing, is now brought to life.

416
PYRAMIDS, NO. 3, Giza, Egypt 1951
Pastel on paper, 6 4/5 x 9 9/10 in.
(17.5 x 25.4 cm)
Private collection

Employing a semiabstract composition
and a more daring color scheme than in
previous pastels of this site, Kahn
captures the varied illumination of the
pyramids caused by passing clouds. In
this case, the Chephren pyramid stands
out as a shaded volume complementing
rhythmically the pyramids of Mykerinos
and Cheops. The realistic rendition of the
sky contrasts strongly with the brown and
yellow surfaces of the pyramids, but does
not detract from the powerful presence of
their volumes.

417
PYRAMIDS, NO. 4, Giza, Egypt 1951
Pastel and charcoal pencil on paper,
size not available
Signed lower right: *Lou K '51*
Present whereabouts unknown

The abstracted and distorted pyramids,
with heavily textured and warmly
colored surfaces, are imbued with an
organic vitality that contrasts with the
lifeless outlines of walls and rocks in the
foreground. Reverting to his usual
method of emphasizing the primary
subject, Kahn applies color only to the
pyramids, but manages to maintain the
completeness of the composition through
the judicious placement of rocks in the
right foreground.

418
PYRAMIDS, NO. 5, Giza, Egypt 1951
Pastel and charcoal pencil on paper,
11 1/5 x 14 3/5 in. (28.9 x 37.5 cm)
Collection of Sue Ann Kahn

In a manner similar to *Pyramids Across
the Nile* (No. 410), the sky becomes an
extension of the desert. The gold sky and
the brown ground unite to form a setting
for the three pyramids. In turn, the brown
and orange colors of the pyramids
reinforce their role as an integral part
of the setting.

298

419
PYRAMIDS, NO. 6, Giza, Egypt 1951
Pastel and charcoal pencil on paper,
7 2/5 x 8 4/5 in. (19.0 x 22.6 cm)
Signed lower right: *Lou K*
Shown at a traveling exhibition
organized by the Pennsylvania Academy
of the Fine Arts, 1978–1979, Catalogue
No. 70, titled: *Pyramids, Egypt, 1951*
Collection of Sue Ann Kahn

This is one of Kahn's most unusual
pastels. He departs completely from
his typical technique of applying colors
in large planes or in multidirectional
jabs. This drawing is an exercise in
the blending of colors. The various
color areas are outlined and become
abstract patterns which blend only
when viewed from a distance. This
impressionistic technique produces a
shimmering effect. Except for slight color
variations, the pyramids are reduced to
two-dimensional patterns with hardly any
discernable hints of their solidity. It is not
clear whether Kahn left the foreground
unfinished in order to bring attention
to the main subject or if he simply
abandoned the drawing.

420
PYRAMIDS, NO. 7, Giza, Egypt 1951
Pastel and charcoal pencil on paper,
6 4/5 x 9 9/10 in. (17.5 x 25.4 cm)
Collection of Mrs. Esther I. Kahn

This pastel drawing is similar to No. 417,
except that here Kahn renders the sky
and the foreground in pale hues and
shows the pyramids in a more revealing,
three-dimensional manner through a
clear definition of their sides. Even
though this drawing is more refined than
No. 417, the energy imparted to the
pyramids is not compromised by the
additional coloration of the surroundings.

421
PYRAMIDS, NO. 8, Giza, Egypt 1951
Pastel and charcoal pencil on paper,
4 3/5 x 6 1/10 in. (11.8 x 15.7 cm)
Shown at a traveling exhibition
organized by the Pennsylvania Academy
of the Fine Arts, 1978–1979, Catalogue
No. 71, titled: *Pyramids, Egypt, 1951*

In contrast to all other renditions of
the pyramids this pastel is the most
expressionistic. Kahn charges the picture
with a high degree of emotionalism
through the use of striking colors and
dynamic lines. Because this drawing
was so representative of Louis Kahn's
deep reverence for the pyramids, it was
selected by Esther Kahn for reproduction
as a postcard.

422
STUDY FOR A MURAL BASED ON
EGYPTIAN MOTIFS, NO. 4, 1955
Ink on paper, 12 1/10 x 15 7/10 in.
(31.1 x 40.3 cm)
Shown at a traveling exhibition
organized by the Pennsylvania Academy
of the Fine Arts, 1978–1979, Catalogue
No. 82, titled: *Study for a Mural,
ca. 1955*
Collection of Sue Ann Kahn

Upon his return from Europe, Kahn
worked on a mural for the already
completed Weiss house. The house's
location motivated Kahn to produce a
theme based on the Pennsylvania Dutch
countryside, but his fascination with
pyramids and Egyptian subjects
continued to haunt him for a very long
time and he managed to weave Egyptian
motifs into the mural. This is one of a
series of studies for the mural in which
the entire work was to be composed of
small panels, each an image in its own
right. The combined effect was to
produce an overall picture based on the
principle of "giant pointillism."[1]
The 130 images in this study, while
difficult to read individually, blend
together into a mosaic of temple
ruins—hypostyle columns visible
against a rectangular opening with little
articulation. Individual panels represent
various architectural forms and spaces
revealed through black shadows.

1. As described by Anne Tyng in
Alessandra Latour, *Louis I. Kahn: l'uomo,
il maestro* (Rome: Edizioni Kappa, 1986),
43.

423
STUDY FOR A MURAL BASED ON
EGYPTIAN MOTIFS, NO. 5 1955
Photostatic print of ink brushed on paper,
12 1/10 x 15 7/10 in. (31.1 x 40.3 cm)
Present whereabouts unknown

A negative of No. 422, this mounted
photostatic print was probably produced
by Kahn in order to study the effect of
reversed blacks and whites. The overall
image visible in No. 422 does not
materialize in this negative because of
reversed shadows.

424
STUDY FOR A MURAL BASED ON
EGYPTIAN MOTIFS, NO. 6 1955
Charcoal on paper, 11 1/5 x 14 3/5 in.
(28.9 x 37.5 cm)
Collection of Sue Ann Kahn

This drawing consists of 221 pieces,
some repeating earlier pyramid studies,
and includes transparencies of modern
apartment building slabs. All of these
panels unite to produce a very distinct
pharoah's head. The arrangement of
shadows in each piece suggests a three-
dimensional mosaic. However, the
overall effect is more reminiscent of
sunken reliefs so common in Egyptian
architecture. Kahn reverted in this study
to the use of grays, finding it difficult to
produce the necessary modeling by
relying only on black-and-white
contrasts. Considering this design's
Egyptian theme, it was probably meant
only as an exercise or a mural study.

425
STUDY FOR A MURAL BASED ON
EGYPTIAN MOTIFS, NO. 1 1951
Pastel and charcoal on paper,
11 1/5 x 14 3/5 in. (28.9 x 37.5 cm)
Shown at a traveling exhibition
organized by the Pennsylvania Academy
of the Fine Arts, 1978–1979, Catalogue
No. 79, titled: *Four Pyramid Studies,
Egypt, 1951*
Collection of Sue Ann Kahn

This sketch, exploring the powerful
shade and shadows characteristic of the
pyramids when viewed from above, is
one of only two mural studies executed
in color.

426
STUDY FOR A MURAL BASED ON
EGYPTIAN MOTIFS, NO. 2 1951
Charcoal on paper, 11 1/5 x 14 3/5 in.
(28.9 x 37.5 cm)
Signed lower right: *Louis I. Kahn 51*;
inscribed (on original mount):
Detail-Mural
Shown at a traveling exhibition
organized by the Pennsylvania Academy
of the Fine Arts, 1978–1979, Catalogue
No. 81, titled: *Detail-Mural (Based on
Egyptian Motives), 1951*
Collection of Sue Ann Kahn

These four panels are much less
figurative than those in No. 425. The
reduction of form to absolute black-and-
white evokes the very essence of these
forms when subjected to light. The real
drama occurs in the black shadows, or
"the Sanctuary of Art," Kahn's expression
of the "Silence" in his frequent and
famous "Silence and Light"
pronouncements.[1]

1. Louis I. Kahn, "Architecture: Silence
and Light." In *On the Future of Art* (New
York: The Viking Press, 1970).

427
STUDY FOR A MURAL BASED ON
EGYPTIAN MOTIFS, NO. 3 1951–53
Ink on paper, 11 4/5 x 15 4/5 in.
(30.5 x 40.6 cm)
Inscribed (on original mount): *Study for
Mural Based on Egyptian Motives*
Shown at a traveling exhibition
organized by the Pennsylvania Academy
of the Fine Arts, 1978–1979, Catalogue
No. 80, titled: *Study for a Mural Based
on Egyptian Motives, 1951–53*
Collection of Sue Ann Kahn

428
STUDY FOR A MURAL BASED ON
URBAN MOTIFS, NO. 1 1951/1955
Ink brushed on paper, 18 x 23 1/2 in.
(46.4 x 60.3 cm)
Shown at a traveling exhibition
organized by the Pennsylvania Academy
of the Fine Arts, 1978–1979, Catalogue
No. 83, titled: *A City Plan, ca. 1951–55*
Collection of Sue Ann Kahn

Still showing strong Egyptian influences,
this abstraction of a city in a mosaic form
is very difficult to grasp. An enigmatic
order appears to govern the arrangement
of each element, but the overall pattern
defies comprehension.

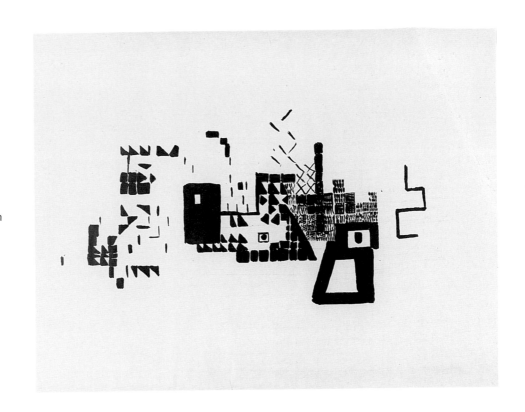

429
STUDY FOR A MURAL BASED ON
URBAN MOTIFS, NO. 2 1955
Oil on canvas, 21 4/5 x 27 3/5 in.
(56.0 x 71.0 cm)
Private collection

In a daring attempt to transcend the
black-and-white panel approach in
realizing a unified mosaic image, Kahn
employs color and achieves a very
exciting study for a mural depicting a
city. The "giant" pointillism of the work
does generate the images and energy of a
modern city, while individual pieces
display symbolic images in bright
primary colors. This is most likely Kahn's
last artwork executed in color. From
1955 until 1959, his non-architectural
sketching was done in pen and ink. He
did, however, continue to utilize color in
his design sketches, for which he used
pastels on yellow tracing paper.

430
STUDY FOR A MURAL FOR THE
TRENTON BATH HOUSE 1956
Ink on tracing paper, 12 1/3 x 16 9/10 in.
(31.7 x 43.5 cm); mural image: 10 4/5 x
8 3/5 in. (27.9 x 22.2 cm)
Collection of Sue Ann Kahn

Using standard exposed concrete blocks
on the exterior wall of a bath house as
the "tiles" for a mural, Kahn created arc-
generated images. The resulting forms—
waves, fish, and flowers—were not
meant to combine into a larger image, as
was the case with Kahn's other murals. In
the actual mural the arc-generated
shapes were subdued and a series of dark
triangles, recalling pyramids and their
shadows, invaded the mural at several
carefully selected locations.

431
STUDY FOR A MURAL ON THE THEME
OF CIVILIZATION
Exact date unknown
Charcoal on tracing paper,
4 1/3 x 18 1/4 in. (11.1 x 46.9 cm);
image: 3 1/2 x 17 1/10 in. (9.1 x 44.1 cm)
Collection of Sue Ann Kahn

This study for a mural conveys mixed
messages of creation and destruction.
The figure on the right seems to be using
a battering ram, while the two figures on
the left are either building a structure
or trying to protect their space from
the figure on the right. Kahn's angular
division of space and rendition of human
figures reveal the strong influence of
Picasso's *Guernica*.

432
STUDY FOR A MURAL—"LIFE AND
TRAFFIC ON THE MISSISSIPPI"
Exact date unknown
Charcoal on tracing paper, 8 2/5 x 21 in.
(21.6 x 53.9 cm); image: 2 2/5 x
15 1/3 in. (6.3 x 39.4 cm)
Collection of Sue Ann Kahn

Joseph Burton[1] has suggested that Kahn's
possession of the 1962 edition of
Egyptian Wall Paintings by C.D.
Noblecourt inspired him to include
cryptic Egyptian emblems in this mural.
Thus, images of fish represent the
pharaoh's dead and resurrected souls.
Pyramids are prominent in the panel on
the right; and a chronological
progression from hunting to the creation
of cities is depicted. Kahn separates
different panels with abstract trees.

1. Joseph Burton, "Castles of Eternity. The
Architectural Hieroglyphics of Louis I.
Kahn," in *Rassegna* VII 21/1 (March
1985): 68-73.

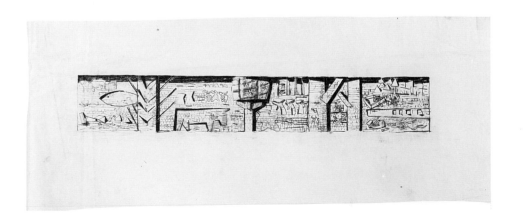

PERIOD V
1959

SHORT EUROPEAN TRIP

Kahn made a brief trip to Europe in 1959 to deliver the closing remarks at the Tenth C.I.A.M. (Congrès Internationaux d'Architecture Moderne) meeting in Otterlo, The Netherlands. The trip resulted in a small, but very significant group of pencil and pen-and-ink sketches. A number of them were actually made back in Philadelphia using field sketches as models. After 1959 the increasing demand for his architectural talents left him no time to devote to his artwork. He ceased making travel sketches, but he continued to use his drawing abilities to produce beautiful charcoal and pastel architectural design studies and renderings. Thus, this small group of drawings from the 1959 trip represents the finale of an incredibly rich and varied volume of artistic production. This series is exclusively black and white. Gone are the heavily shaded charcoals and expressionistic pastels from the 1950–51 trip. The manner in which Kahn made these sketches shows his impatience with details and a strong drive to reveal the very essence of form through gestures of minimal linearity. Their character recalls the sketching mannerisms of Le Corbusier. However, Kahn's work was affected to a great extent by his impaired vision, which required him to wear eyeglasses with very thick lenses.

433
TREE ROWS, France 1959
Pen and ink on paper, size not available
Present whereabouts unknown

Kahn organized this sketch as if it were
an architectural composition. Not only
are the tree groupings fitted into neat
rectangles, but the spatial arrangement is
reminiscent of urban plazas. In both this
sketch and No. 436, the suggestion of
trees is achieved through very energetic
and stenographic linework.

434
VILLAGE, Carcassonne, France 1959
Pen and ink on notebook paper,
8 1/10 x 10 1/10 in. (21.0 x 26.0 cm)
Exhibited at Max Protetch Gallery,
New York, June 1981, Catalogue No. 8,
titled: *1959 Carcassonne, France*
Collection of the Architectural Archives,
University of Pennsylvania, Catalogue
No. 945.4, titled: *Travel Sketch,
Carcassonne, France*; Gift of Richard Saul
Wurman

435
BIRD'S-EYE VIEW,
Carcassonne, France 1959
Pen and ink on paper, 6 2/5 x 9 1/3 in.
(16.5 x 24.1 cm)
Exhibited at Max Protetch Gallery, New
York, June 1981, Catalogue No. 3b,
titled: *1959 Carcassonne, France*
Collection of Richard Saul Wurman

Kahn probably sketched this view from a
postcard. In order to clearly examine the
configuration and organization of the
defensive walls and towers he eliminated
all hints of the city within the walls and
the country outside. What remains is the
abstracted, double-fortification system of
the city. The misleading simplicity of this
sketch recalls medieval drawings of
European cities.

436
APPROACH TO THE CITY,
Carcassonne, France 1959
Pen and ink on paper, 6 2/5 x 7 9/10 in.
(16.5 x 20.3 cm)
Private collection

This view of Carcassonne's western
entrance is drawn with great attention to
the mounting layers of walls and
buildings, but with no great concern for
establishing correct proportions among
them. What occupied Kahn, in contrast
to his earlier European sketches, was not
the heaviness of masses but the
articulation of edges and openings.

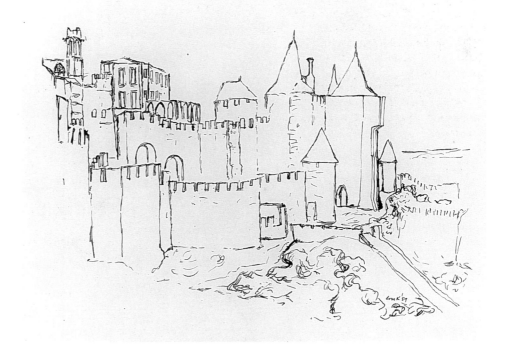

437
CASTLE ENTRANCE, NO. 1,
Carcassonne, France 1959
Pencil on notebook paper,
6 3/5 x 8 1/2 in. (17.0 x 22.0 cm)
Proportion markings
Exhibited at Max Protetch Gallery,
New York, June 1981, Catalogue No. 6,
titled: *1959 Sketch Book on Carcassonne
(12 Drawings)*
Collection of the Architectural Archives,
University of Pennsylvania, Catalogue
No. 945.8, titled: *Travel Sketch,
Sketchbook: Carcassonne, France*; Gift of
Richard Saul Wurman

Kahn produced four versions of the east
entrance to the castle (Nos. 437–40), two
of them in pencil and two in pen and ink.
It is clear that the pencil drawings were
made on the spot and that the ink
sketches were translations of the field
drawings, probably made back in
Philadelphia. In this view the gate is seen
from the bridge, almost straight on.
Pencil lines are sparse and faint and
Kahn made no attempt to create an
elegant composition. Crudely rendered
figures provide a sense of scale and a
double-headed arrow on the wall
adjacent to the gate indicates the proper
proportions of the fortification.

438
CASTLE ENTRANCE, NO. 2,
Carcassonne, France 1959
Pencil on notebook paper,
6 3/5 x 8 1/2 in. (17.0 x 22.0 cm)
Exhibited at Max Protetch Gallery, New
York, June 1981, Catalogue No. 6, titled:
*1959 Sketch Book on Carcassonne
(12 Drawings)*
Collection of the Architectural Archives,
University of Pennsylvania, Catalogue
No. 945.10, titled: *Travel Sketch,
Sketchbook: Carcassonne, France*; Gift of
Richard Saul Wurman

This sketch became the model for the
two subsequent pen-and-ink drawings
(Nos. 439–40). This view, more removed
than No. 437 and from a more exciting
angle, leads the eye down the side of the
bridge to the gate. The sketch is devoid
of details; only the major forms are
depicted in a very hurried manner.

439
CASTLE ENTRANCE, NO. 3,
Carcassonne, France 1959
Ink on notebook paper,
8 1/10 x 10 1/10 in. (21.0 x 26.0 cm)
Signed lower right: *Lou K 59*
Exhibited at Max Protetch Gallery,
New York, June 1981, Catalogue No. 3,
titled: *1959 Carcassonne, France*
Collection of the Architectural Archives,
University of Pennsylvania, Catalogue
No. 945.5, titled: *Travel Sketch,
Carcassonne, France*; Gift of Richard
Saul Wurman

The energetic and scratchy penmanship
of this sketch makes it a typical example
of Kahn's artwork at this time. He
subjected his sketchbook to violent pen-
and-ink attacks in order to extract
the essence of forms without relying on
shades and shadows. In this way the
subject becomes vibrant and imbued
with sense of life, which would have
been lost through accurate outlines or
elaborate renditions. Kahn utilized this
technique earlier, but with less violence
and in different media (see Nos. 348–50
and 421).

440
CASTLE ENTRANCE, NO. 4,
Carcassonne, France 1959
Ink on notebook paper,
8 1/10 x 10 1/10 in. (21.0 x 26.0 cm)
Signed lower right: *Lou K '59*
Collection of Sue Ann Kahn

This is an almost identical version of the
previous pen-and-ink sketch (No. 439),
but it is more carefully composed and
drawn. The gate towers on the left have
moved in, away from the edge of the
picture, and the hash marks on the
approach to the bridge fill the right side
of the composition, reflecting the sky.
The fact that Kahn produced four
versions of this scene demonstrates his
attraction to the monumental nature of
these very simple geometric forms.

441
BETWEEN OUTER AND INNER WALLS,
Carcassonne, France 1959
Pen and ink on paper, 7 9/10 x 9 3/5 in.
(20.3 x 24.8 cm)
Signed lower right: *Lou K '59*
Exhibited at Max Protetch Gallery,
New York, June 1981, Catalogue No. 3a,
titled: *1959 Carcassonne, France*
Collection of Richard Saul Wurman

This sketch portrays a set of double
fortifications with their walls and towers
in a sharp perspective. In an effort to
concentrate on formal and proportional
issues, Kahn provided no clues to
masonry textures and details.

442
CITY WALLS, Carcassonne, France 1959
Pen and ink on paper, 9 1/2 x 12 1/3 in.
(24.5 x 31.7 cm)
Inscribed lower right: *Carcassone*
Shown at a traveling exhibition
organized by the Pennsylvania Academy
of the Fine Arts, 1978–1979, Catalogue
No. 88, titled: *Carcassonne, France, 1959*
Collection of Sue Ann Kahn

The calm and poise of sketch No. 443 is
replaced here with purely emotional
gestures. Building forms are reduced to
traces of motion in a desperate search for
the spirit of the fortifications rather than
their physical attributes. This sketch
comes close to what Kahn was teaching:
to put on paper the first "realization" or
"form drawing," where form does not
refer to the physical reality but to "what a
thing wants to be," or the "existence
will." In a sense, this is an expressionistic
drawing, but the search does not concern
the artist's feelings but the inner soul of
the subject.

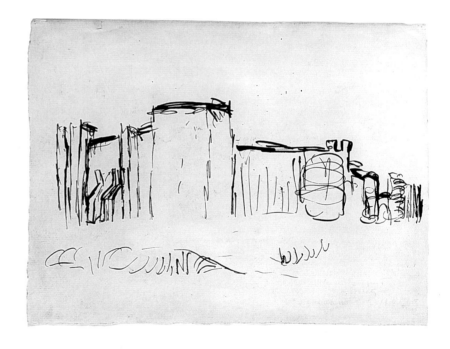

443
INSIDE THE WALLS, NO. 1,
Carcassonne, France 1959
Pencil on notebook paper,
8 3/5 x 13 1/3 in. (22.2 x 34.3 cm)
Exhibited at Max Protetch Gallery, New
York, June 1981, Catalogue No. 6, titled:
1959 Carcassonne, France
Collection of the Architectural Archives,
University of Pennsylvania, Catalogue
No. 945.13, titled: *Travel Sketch,
Sketchbook: Carcassonne, France*; Gift of
Richard Saul Wurman

Kahn translated this field study into two
pen-and-ink sketches (Nos. 444–45).

444

INSIDE THE WALLS, NO. 3,
Carcassonne, France 1959
Pen and ink on paper, size not available
Signed lower right: *Lou K '59*
Present whereabouts unknown

This pen-and-ink version of No. 445
faithfully retains all the elements of the
scene in a fairly accurate portrayal.
However, Kahn allows himself some
freedom in the execution of the linework.

445

INSIDE THE WALLS, NO. 2,
Carcassonne, France 1959
Pen and ink on paper, 9 1/3 x 12 1/3 in.
(24.1 x 31.7 cm)
Signed lower right: *Lou K '59*
Collection of the Architectural Archives,
University of Pennsylvania, Catalogue
No. 945.3.1, titled: *Travel Sketch,
Carcassonne, France*; Gift of Jack
McAllister

This second transformation of pencil
drawing No. 443 turned a rather ordinary
sketch into an exciting, quivering
arrangement of masses delineating an
enticing urban space. Kahn removed the
gabled structure in the middle and the
nondescript forms in the foreground,
freeing the composition of confusion and
providing a flow of space into the depth
of the picture. The linework also
becomes more energetic and exciting.

446
CASTLE WALLS, NO. 1,
Carcassonne, France 1959
Pen and ink on notebook paper,
9 1/3 x 7 9/10 in. (24.1 x 20.3 cm)
Signed lower right: *Lou K '59*; inscribed
lower right: *Carcassonne*
Shown at a traveling exhibition
organized by the Pennsylvania Academy
of the Fine Arts, 1978–1979, Catalogue
No. 90, titled: *Carcassonne, France, 1959*
Exhibited at Max Protetch Gallery, New
York, June 1981, Catalogue No. 3f, titled:
1959 Carcassonne, France
Collection of the Architectural Archives,
University of Pennsylvania, Catalogue
No. 945.3.3, titled: *Travel Sketch,
Carcassonne, France*; Gift of Richard
Saul Wurman

Kahn demonstrates his versatility in
presenting the same scene in a
completely different manner in these two
sketches of the southern approach to the
castle (Nos. 446–47). Judging by its
scratchy technique, this sketch would
appear to have been made at the site. It
is loaded with the implied power of
masses expressed through roughly
textured forms. The age and crustiness
of the walls and towers are conveyed
through Kahn's intentionally nervous
penmanship. In contrast, No. 447 is an
abstracted rendition of the original, full
of freely arranged elements, invasive
clouds, and a mysterious grouping of
people in the center—all executed with
fluid and carefree linework.

447
CASTLE WALLS, NO. 2,
Carcassonne, France 1959
Pen and ink on notebook paper,
10 1/10 x 8 1/10 in. (26.0 x 21.0 cm)
Exhibited at Max Protetch Gallery, New
York, June 1981, Catalogue No. 7,
titled: *1959 Carcassonne, France*
Collection of the Architectural Archives,
University of Pennsylvania, Catalogue
No. 945.5, titled: *Travel Sketch,
Carcassonne, France*; Gift of Richard
Saul Wurman

448
CASTLE WALLS, NO. 3, Carcassonne,
France 1959
Pen and ink on paper, 9 9/10 x 7 9/10 in.
(25.4 x 20.3 cm)
Collection of William S. Huff

This sketch is unusual in the way it
isolates its subject from its surroundings.
The walls appear to float as a single unit
of tightly packed structures.

449
CASTLE WALLS, NO. 4, Carcassonne,
France 1959
Pen and ink on paper, 10 1/5 x 8 1/2 in.
(26.2 x 21.8 cm)
Signed lower right: *Lou K '59*
Shown at a traveling exhibition
organized by the Pennsylvania Academy
of the Fine Arts, 1978–1979, Catalogue
No. 89, titled: *Carcassonne, France,
1959*
Collection of William S. Huff

As in Nos. 446–48, Kahn creates a
drastic change of mood through yet
another presentation technique. Here the
castle and the ramparts are modeled in a
most unusual manner. The forms acquire
heavily textured dark tones produced by
ink lines of different thicknesses. This
dramatic effect, resembling a woodcut, is
produced when the point of Kahn's pen
is subjected to varied pressures and
changes of directions. Likewise, the sky,
with its rhythmically twisting lines,
acquires a vibrating dynamism.

450
FORTIFICATIONS, NO. 1,
Carcassonne, France 1959
Pencil on notebook paper, 8 3/5 x
13 1/3 in. (22.2 x 34.3 cm)
Color notations
Exhibited at Max Protetch Gallery,
New York, June 1981, Catalogue No. 6,
titled: *1959 Sketchbook on Carcassonne,
(12 Drawings)*
Collection of the Architectural Archives,
University of Pennsylvania, Catalogue
No. 945.9, titled: *Travel Sketch,
Sketchbook: Carcassonne, France*; Gift of
Richard Saul Wurman

These four pencil sketches (Nos. 450–53)
of fortifications accurately capture the
spatial and formal characteristics of the
structures. Using pencil lines of varied
thicknesses, Kahn establishes depth and
the heaviness of masses. Kahn's desire to
produce color versions of these sketches
is documented by notations on the
drawing.

451
FORTIFICATIONS, NO. 2,
Carcassonne, France 1959
Pencil on notebook paper, 6 3/5 x
8 3/5 in. (17.1 x 22.2 cm)
Collection of the Architectural Archives,
University of Pennsylvania, Catalogue
No. 945.12, titled: *Travel Sketch,
Sketchbook: Carcassonne, France*; Gift of
Richard Saul Wurman

452
FORTIFICATIONS, NO. 3,
Carcassonne, France 1959
Pencil on notebook paper, 8 3/5 x
13 1/3 in. (22.2 x 34.3 cm)
Exhibited at Max Protetch Gallery,
New York, June 1981, Catalogue No. 6,
titled: *1959 Sketch Book on Carcassonne
(12 Drawings)*
Collection of the Architectural Archives,
University of Pennsylvania, Catalogue
No. 945.11, titled: *Travel Sketch,
Sketchbook: Carcassonne, France*; Gift of
Richard Saul Wurman

In a slight departure from the linear
manner of drawing that dominated his
work on this trip, Kahn applies shading to
express the formal characteristics of the
fortifications. Clearly the eye of an
architect is at work here. These sketches,
while made by Kahn for artistic
conversions, are nevertheless replete
with material for future architectural
designs.

453
FORTIFICATIONS, NO. 4,
Carcassonne, France 1959
Pencil on note paper, 10 2/5 x 8 2/5 in.
(26.7 x 21.6 cm)
Notations not by the artist
Exhibited at Max Protetch Gallery,
New York, June 1981, Catalogue No. 6,
titled: *1959 Sketch Book on Carcassonne
(12 Drawings)*
Collection of the Architectural Archives,
University of Pennsylvania, Catalogue
No. 945.7, titled: *Travel Sketch,
Carcassonne, France*; Gift of Richard
Saul Wurman

454

TOP OF BATTLEMENTS, NO. 1,
Carcassonne, France 1959
Pencil on notebook paper,
8 3/5 x 6 3/5 in. (22.2 x 17.1 cm)
Collection of the Architectural Archives,
University of Pennsylvania, Catalogue
No. 945.17, titled: *Travel Sketch,
Sketchbook: Carcassonne, France*; Gift of
Richard Saul Wurman

Kahn faithfully converted a set of three
pencil sketches from the top of the
Carcassonne battlements (Nos. 454, 456,
and 458) into three pen-and-ink drawings
(Nos. 455, 457, and 459). All three of
the ink translations are filled with the
spontaneity of sketches made in the
field and they even provide more
detail than the original drawings. The
conversions once again capture the
weather-beaten character of masonry
through the varied line weights produced
by Kahn's quill pen.

455

TOP OF BATTLEMENTS, NO. 2,
Carcassonne, France 1959
Pen and ink on notebook paper,
10 1/10 x 8 1/10 in. (26.0 x 21.0 cm)
Verso of No. 458
Signed lower right: *Lou K Sept '59*
Exhibited at Max Protetch Gallery,
New York, June 1981, Catalogue No.
11., titled: *1959 Carcassonne, France*
Collection of the Architectural Archives,
University of Pennsylvania, Catalogue
No. 945.3, titled: *Travel Sketch,
Carcassonne, France*; Gift of Richard
Saul Wurman

456
BATTLEMENTS STAIRS, NO. 1,
Carcassonne, France 1959
Pencil on notebook paper,
8 3/5 x 6 3/5 in. (22.2 x 17.1 cm)
Collection of the Architectural Archives,

University of Pennsylvania, Catalogue
No. 945.12, titled: *Travel Sketch,
Sketchbook: Carcassonne, France*; Gift of
Richard Saul Wurman

457

BATTLEMENTS STAIRS, NO. 2,
Carcassonne, France 1959
Pen and ink on notebook paper,
9 9/10 x 7 9/10 in. (25.4 x 20.3 cm)
Signed lower right: *Lou K '59*
Exhibited at Max Protetch Gallery, New
York, June 1981, Catalogue No. 3c,

titled: *1959 Carcassonne, France*
Collection of the Architectural Archives,
University of Pennsylvania, Catalogue
No. 945.3.4, titled: *Travel Sketch,
Carcassonne, France*; Gift of Richard
Saul Wurman

458
VIEW FROM THE BATTLEMENTS,
NO. 1, Carcassonne, France 1959
Pencil on notebook paper,
8 2/5 x 10 2/5 in. (21.6 x 26.7 cm)
Verso of No. 455
Exhibited at Max Protetch Gallery, New
York, June 1981, Catalogue No. 5, titled:
1959 Carcassonne, France
Collection of the Architectural Archives,
University of Pennsylvania, Catalogue
No. 945.7v, titled: *Travel Sketch,
Carcassonne, France*; Gift of Richard
Saul Wurman

459
VIEW FROM THE BATTLEMENTS,
NO. 2, Carcassonne, France 1959
Pen and ink on paper, 5 1/2 x 8 3/5 in.
(14.3 x 22.2 cm)
Signed lower left: *Lou K '59*
Private collection

460
BATTLEMENT,
Carcassonne, France 1959
Pen and ink on paper, 9 3/5 x 6 1/2 in.
(24.8 x 16.8 cm)
Signed lower right: *Lou K '59 Caracassone*
Private collection

These four ink sketches (Nos. 460–63)
depicting interior views of the

Carcassonne battlements and bastions
have no apparent pencil studies. The first
three were drawn with a quill point and
the last one with a single-weight pen. It is
quite possible that Kahn sketched all of
them upon his return to Philadelphia. In
this drawing the free linework is more
striking than in No. 449. Here, at a much
larger scale, the calligraphic squiggles are

less believable as texturing and shading.
In No. 461 the sharp perspective, with
the vanishing point below the top of the
battlements, provides a clue to the scale
of the space and individual stones.
Sketch No. 463 is almost a duplicate of
No. 462; affected by the pen type, it is
sketched with less freedom and flair.

461
BASTION, Carcassonne, France 1959
Pen and ink on paper, 7 3/5 x 8 1/2 in.
(19.7 x 21.9 cm)
Signed lower right: *Lou K '59 Carcassone*
Exhibited at Max Protetch Gallery, New
York, June 1981, Catalogue No. 10,
titled: *1959 Carcassonne, France*
Collection of Richard Saul Wurman

462
ARCHED BASTION, NO. 1,
Carcassonne, France 1959
Pen and ink on notebook paper,
10 1/10 x 8 1/3 in. (26.0 x 21.3 cm)
Exhibited at Max Protetch Gallery, New
York, June 1981, Catalogue No. 9, titled:
1959 Carcassonne, France
Collection of the Architectural Archives,
University of Pennsylvania, Catalogue
No. 945.3.2, titled: *Travel Sketch,
Carcassonne, France*; Gift of Richard
Saul Wurman

463
ARCHED BASTION, NO. 2,
Carcassonne, France 1959
Pen and ink on paper,
10 1/10 x 8 1/10 in. (26.0 x 20.9 cm)
Collection of Sue Ann Kahn

464
DOWN FROM THE BASTION,
Carcassonne, France 1959
Pencil on notebook paper,
8 3/5 x 6 3/5 in. (22.2 x 17.1 cm)
Collection of the Architectural Archives,
University of Pennsylvania, Catalogue
No. 945.15, titled: *Travel Sketch,
Carcassonne, France*; Gift of Richard
Saul Wurman

This pencil study—simultaneously
showing a level of the bastion and its
stairway to the level below—must have
been of special interest to Kahn. The
implications of spatial continuity and
the perception of two levels at the same
time found their way into much of his
design work.

465
CASTLE INTERIOR,
Carcassonne, France 1959
Pencil on notebook paper,
6 3/5 x 8 3/5 in. (17.1 x 22.2 cm)
Color notations
Collection of the Architectural Archives,
University of Pennsylvania, Catalogue
No. 945.18, titled: *Travel Sketch,
Carcassonne, France*; Gift of Richard
Saul Wurman

466
COURTYARD,
Carcassonne, France 1959
Pencil on notebook paper,
8 3/5 x 6 3/5 in. (22.2 x 17.1 cm)
Collection of the Architectural Archives,
University of Pennsylvania, Catalogue

No. 945.16, titled: *Travel Sketch,
Carcassonne, France*; Gift of Richard
Saul Wurman

The last two pencil studies of the
Carcassonne series depict the confined

spaces of a courtyard and an interior
chamber. Again, as in No. 450, the color
notations indicate Kahn's desire to
generate a pastel or watercolor painting
from this study.

467
VIEW FROM THE RIVER, NO. 1,
St. Cecile Cathedral, Albi, France 1959
Pen and ink on paper, 8 1/2 x 10 1/10 in.
(21.9 x 26.0 cm)
Inscribed and signed lower right:
Lou K '59 Albi
Exhibited at Max Protetch Gallery,
New York, June 1981, Catalogue No. 14,
titled: *1959 St.Cecile Cathedral, Albi,*
France
Collection of Der Scutt

"In the presence of Albi, I felt the belief
in the choice of its architectural
elements, and what exhilaration and
patience were combined to begin it and
work towards its completion. I drew Albi
from the bottom up as though I were
building it. I felt the exhilaration. The
patience it took to build, one didn't need,
for I drew it without bothering about
corrections or correct proportions. I

wanted only to capture the excitement in
the mind of the architect."[1]

The twelve sketches of Albi Cathedral
(Nos. 467–78) are the most concentrated
group of Kahn's drawings depicting an
architectural monument. As is clear from
the above quote, his fascination with this
building goes beyond a mere
appreciation of the building's appearance. Here he discovered the over-
whelming power of architectural forms
generated by simple brick masonry units.
He was captivated by the harmony of
forms—the horizontal and vertical
permutations of majestic cylinders. It was
an important lesson, and Kahn studied
the subject very diligently. His designs
from this time forward were deeply
affected by Albi's massing and powerful
embodiment of the eternal spirit of
architecture — a sensation he also

experienced intensely in Egypt.

The five renditions of the north side of
the cathedral and of the fortified
Archbishop's Palace on the bank of the
river Tarn (Nos. 467–71) demonstrate
Kahn's interest in exploring forms
revealed by the light and as generated by
the basic methods of construction. The
first three sketches (Nos. 467–69) fall into
the first category; No. 472 and, to some
extent, No. 471 into the second. Kahn's
scratchy quill-point technique was quite
suitable for representing the complex
order of the two structures. In the first
three renditions towers and buttresses are
expressed through varied vertical lines
highlighted with shades and shadows.

1. From *Louis I. Kahn: Drawings* (New
York Access Press, Inc./Max Protectch
Gallery, 1981).

468
VIEW FROM THE RIVER, NO. 2,
St. Cecile Cathedral, Albi, France 1959
Pen and ink on paper, 8 3/5 x 9 1/3 in.
(22.2 x 24.1 cm)
Inscribed and signed lower right:
Albi Lou K '59
Private collection

Starting with No. 467, which represents
the complex in a loose but fairly accurate
manner, each progressive rendition
becomes more abstracted. In this sketch
Kahn treats the scene with more
energetic gestures and removes the
conical roof of the fortified palace tower
so it would not interrupt the clear rhythm
of the cathedral's facade.

469
VIEW FROM THE RIVER, NO. 3,
St. Cecile Cathedral, Albi, France 1959
Pen and ink on notebook paper,
9 1/2 x 12 1/3 in. (24.1 x 31.7 cm)
Signed lower right: *Lou K '59*
Exhibited at Max Protetch Gallery,
New York, June 1981, Catalogue No.
12a, titled: *1959 St.Cecile Cathedral,
Albi, France*
Collection of the Architectural Archives,
University of Pennsylvania, Catalogue
No. 945.19.1, titled: *Travel Sketch, St.
Cecile Cathedral, Albi, France*; Gift of
Jack McAllister

470
VIEW FROM THE RIVER, NO. 4,
St. Cecile Cathedral, Albi, France 1959
Pen and ink on notebook paper,
8 1/5 x 10 1/5 in. (21.1 x 26.2 cm)
Exhibited at Max Protetch Gallery,
New York, June 1981, Catalogue No. 12,
titled: *1959 St.Cecile Cathedral,
Albi, France*
Collection of the Williams College
Museum of Art, Williamstown,
Massachusetts. Museum purchase 82.17,
titled: *St. Cecile Cathedral, Albi, France*

In contrast to Nos. 467–69, Kahn's
interest here is in the spatial and formal
essences of the towers and buttresses. He
extracts the generating force of
cylindrical forms: the helix. This is the
realization of the true "form," the
diagram of the spirit of cylindrical space
rising up.

471
VIEW FROM THE RIVER, NO. 5,
St. Cecile Cathedral, Albi, France 1959
Pen and ink on notebook paper,
9 1/3 x 12 3/5 in. (24.1 x 32.4 cm)
Exhibited at Max Protetch Gallery,
New York, June 1981, Catalogue No.
13, titled: *1959 St. Cecile Cathedral,
Albi, France*
Collection of the Architectural Archives,
University of Pennsylvania, Catalogue
No. 945.19, titled: *Travel Sketch, St.
Cecile Cathedral, Albi, France*; Gift of
Richard Saul Wurman

This is the least elaborate of the five
renditions of the cathedral and the
fortified palace. Only a few of the
cylindrical forms are represented with
helicoid lines and the rest are rendered
with an absolute minimum of modeling.
The conical roof on the palace's west
tower reappears without threatening the
integrity of the cathedral in the
background.

472
CHAPTER HOUSE, NO. 1,
St. Cecile Cathedral, Albi, France 1959
Pen and ink on paper, 7 3/5 x 11 7/10 in.
(19.7 x 30.1 cm)
Shown at a traveling exhibition
organized by the Pennsylvania Academy
of the Fine Arts, 1978–1979, Catalogue
No. 84, titled: *Cathedral of St. Cecile,
Albi, France. 1959*
Collection of Sue Ann Kahn

This sketch is devoid of Kahn's usual,
three-dimensional expression of forms,
either through shades and shadows or
through the dynamic linear indications of
spatial and construction characteristics.
Consequently, the building appears two-
dimensional and isolated, reminiscent of
a stage set.

473
CHAPTER HOUSE, NO. 2,
St. Cecile Cathedral, Albi, France 1959
Pen and ink on paper, 12 1/2 x 9 1/3 in.
(32.1 x 24.1 cm)
Inscribed and signed lower right:
Albi Lou K 59
Shown at a traveling exhibition
organized by the Pennsylvania Academy
of the Fine Arts, 1978–1979, Catalogue
No. 85., titled: *Cathedral of St. Cecile,
Albi, France. 1959*
Collection of Sue Ann Kahn

In contrast to No. 472, this sketch shows
Kahn's intense and hasty translation of
the structure's powerful forms. It is
executed in a turbulent manner and
clearly belongs in the realm of notations.
However, it captures the spirit and the
essence of the structure. In that respect, it
is charged with the memory of its
inception and construction.

474
BUTTRESSED TOWER,
St. Cecile Cathedral, Albi, France 1959
Crayon on paper, 10 1/5 x 6 1/2 in.
(26.4 x 16.8 cm)
Present whereabouts unknown

This is Kahn's only known crayon sketch
of Albi Cathedral. Its assured lines
convey the strength of the cylindrical
forms more convincingly than pen-and-
ink renditions. Crayon also allowed
Kahn to rely on extra heavy lines to
communicate the formal relationships
of masses and to depict details through
silhouettes and outlines.

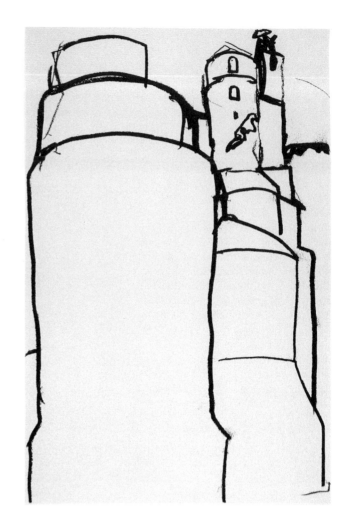

475
BUTTRESSES, St. Cecile Cathedral,
Albi, France 1959
Pen and ink on paper, 9 7/10 x 6 3/5 in.
(25.1 x 17.0 cm)
Inscribed and signed lower right:
Albi Lou K '59
Shown at a traveling exhibition
organized by the Pennsylvania Academy
of the Fine Arts, 1978–1979, Catalogue
No. 86, titled: *Cathedral of St. Cecile,
Albi, France, 1959*
Collection of Robert Venturi

476
CHOIR/EAST END, NO. 1, St. Cecile
Cathedral, Albi, France 1959
Pen and ink on paper, 10 9/10 x 9 1/3 in.
(28.0 x 24.0 cm)
Inscribed and signed lower right:
Albi Lou K '59
Shown at a traveling exhibition
organized by the Pennsylvania Academy
of the Fine Arts, 1978–1979, Catalogue
No. 87, titled: *Cathedral of St. Cecile,
Albi, France, 1959*
Collection of Robert Venturi

This sketch and its almost identical twin
(No. 477) concentrate on the lower part
of the semicircular east end of the
cathedral. In both renditions Kahn relies
almost exclusively on the helicoid
"springs" to frenetically record the spirit
of the cylindrical buttresses—what he
referred to as the "Existence Will." The
speed with which Kahn made these
sketches points to his need to capture on
paper the true nature of the structure
before it concealed its inner secrets.

477
CHOIR/EAST END, NO. 2, St. Cecile
Cathedral, Albi, France 1959
Pen and ink on paper, 10 1/4 x 8 1/10 in.
(26.4 x 21.0 cm)
Inscribed and signed lower right: *Albi 59
Lou K*
Collection of The Museum of Modern
Art, New York; titled: *Sainte Cecile
Cathedral, Albi, France, 1959*. Gift of the
architect

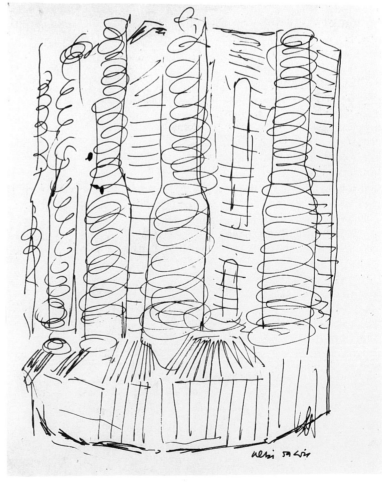

478
VIEW FROM THE EAST, St. Cecil
Cathedral, Albi, France 1959
Pen and ink on paper, 7 1/10 x 9 3/4 in.
(18.4 x 25.1 cm)
Inscribed at bottom center: *Albi 59*
Private collection

This overall view of the cathedral's east
end combines scratchy modeling with
helix lines in a manner very similar to the
view from the north in No. 470. In most
of the sketches of Albi, Kahn isolates
the cathedral from its surroundings,
concentrating on the building as an
object lesson without pictographic
concerns. The tremendous impression
that this cathedral and the Archbishop's
Palace made on Kahn is evident in his
application of powerful cylindrical forms
in his project for the Mikveh Israel
Congregation in Philadelphia and in his
executed buildings for the Indian Institute
of Management in Ahmedabad, India
and the capitol buildings in Dacca,
Bangladesh.

479
NOTRE-DAME-DU-HAUT CHAPEL
INTERIOR, NO. 1, Ronchamp,
France 1959
Pen and ink on notebook paper,
8 1/3 x 10 1/10 in. (21.3 x 26.0 cm)
Exhibited at Max Protetch Gallery, New
York, June 1981, Catalogue No. 2, titled:
1959 Ronchamp, France
Collection of the Architectural Archives,
University of Pennsylvania, Catalogue
No. 945.21, titled: *Travel Sketch,
Ronchamp, France*; Gift of Richard Saul
Wurman

The two sketches of the interior of the
Ronchamp Chapel (Nos. 479 and 480)
are dedicated to Le Corbusier's
glorification of light. Without the use of
obvious shading techniques, Kahn
conveys the play of light on this precious
space by using agitated arrangements of
discontinuous ink lines. It is apparent
from these sketches how the space and
light of Ronchamp touched Kahn's sense
of wonder and the effect it had on his
own designs.

480
NOTRE-DAME-DU-HAUT CHAPEL
INTERIOR, NO. 2, Ronchamp,
France 1959
Pen and ink on notebook paper,
8 1/3 x 10 1/10 in. (21.3 x 26.0 cm)
Inscribed lower right: *Ronchamp 59*
Exhibited at Max Protetch Gallery, New
York, June 1981, Catalogue No. 1, titled:
1959 Ronchamp, France
Collection of the Architectural Archives,
University of Pennsylvania, Catalogue
No. 945.20, titled: *Travel Sketch,
Ronchamp, France*; Gift of Richard
Saul Wurman

That Ronchamp Chapel should constitute
the last of Kahn's artworks in this
catalogue is not unintentional. First,
for chronological reasons it seems
appropriate to place this modern
masterpiece at the end of Kahn's
exploration of medieval monuments
during his 1959 travels. Second, it marks
Kahn's realization of the potential for
exploring the secrets and the spirit of

architecture inside the most renowned
creation of one of modernism's greatest
masters. The reverence Kahn had for Le
Corbusier is encapsulated in his
statement: "When I die I wish to reside in
the city called Le Corbusier."[1]

1. Patricia McLaughlin, " 'How'm I
Doing, Corbusier?' An Interview with
Louis I. Kahn," in *The Pennsylvania
Gazette* 71 (December 1972) 22.

SELECTED BIBLIOGRAPHY

For a complete bibliography on Louis I. Kahn through 1966 see: Brown, Jack Perry. *Louis I. Kahn: A Bibliography.* New York and London: Garland, 1987.

BOOKS

Arnheim, Rudolf. *Art and Visual Perception.* Berkeley: University of California Press, 1954.

Baur, John I. H. *Revolution and Tradition in Modern American Art.* Cambridge, Mass.: Harvard University Press, 1951.

———, ed. *New Art in America.* Greenwich, Conn. and New York: Graphic Society, 1957.

Boesiger, Willy, ed. *Le Corbusier.* New York: Praeger Publishers, 1972.

Brown, Milton W. *American Painting From the Armory Show to the Depression.* Princeton, N.J.: Princeton University Press, 1955.

Bulletin: School of Fine Arts Courses in Architecture, Music and Fine Arts. Announcement, 1922–1923. Philadelphia: The Press of the University of Pennsylvania, 1922–24.

Canaday, John. *Mainstreams of Modern Art.* New York: Holt, Rinehart and Winston, 1962.

Christensen, Erwin O. *A Pictorial History of Western Art.* New York: New American Library, 1964.

Cook, John W. and Heinrich Klotz. *Conversations with Architects.* New York: Frederick A. Praeger, 1973.

Curtis, William J.R. *Le Corbusier: Ideas and Forms.* New York: Rizzoli International Publications, 1986.

Drexler, Arthur, ed. *The Architecture of the Ecole des Beaux Arts.* New York: The Museum of Modern Art, 1977.

Fleming, William. *Arts and Ideas.* New York: Holt, Rinehart and Winston, 1968.

Flexner, James Thomas. *The Pocket History of American Painting.* New York: Washington Square Press, 1950.

Frampton, Kenneth. *Modern Architecture: A Critical History.* New York and Toronto: Oxford University Press, 1980.

Frost, Rosamund. *Contemporary Art: The March of Art from Cézanne Until Now.* New York: Crown Publishers, 1942.

Gardiner, Stephen. *Le Corbusier.* New York: The Viking Press, 1975.

Giedion, Siegfried. *The Eternal Present: The Beginnings of Architecture.* New York: Pantheon Books, 1964.

Giurgola, Romaldo, and Jaimini Mehta. *Louis I. Kahn, Architect.* Boulder, Colo.: Westview Press, 1975.

Greenbough, Horatio. "Relative and Independent Beauty." In Gifford, Don, ed., *The Literature of Architecture, The Evolution of Architectural Theory and Practice in Nineteenth-Century America.* New York: E. P. Dutton, 1966.

Haftmann, Werner. *Painting in the Twentieth Century.* New York: Frederick A. Praeger, 1960.

Heyer, Paul. *Architects on Architecture: New Directions in America.* New York: Walker, 1966.

Hillier, Bevis. *Art Deco.* New York: E. P. Dutton, 1968.

———. *The World of Art Deco.* New York: E. P. Dutton, 1971.

Holman, William G. *The Travel Sketches of Louis I. Kahn.* An exhibition organized by the Pennsylvania Academy of the Fine Arts, 1978–1979. Introduction by Vincent Scully. Washington, D.C.: Museum Press, 1978.

Hunter, Sam. *Modern French Painting.* New York: Dell, 1956.

Janson, H. W. *History of Art*. Englewood Cliffs, N.J.: Prentice Hall, 1970.

Johnson, Nell E., ed. *Light is the Theme: Louis I. Kahn and the Kimbell Art Museum*. Fort Worth, Texas: Kimbell Art Foundation, 1975.

Johnson, Una E. *Golden Years of American Drawings 1905–1956*. New York: The Brooklyn Museum Press, 1957.

Kahn, Louis I. "Silence and Light." In *On the Future of Art*. New York: The Viking Press, 1970.

———. *Architecture: The John William Lawrence Memorial Lecture*. New Orleans: The Tulane University School of Architecture, 1972.

The Louis I. Kahn Archives: Personal Drawings. Vols. 1–7. New York and London: Garland, 1987.

Kepes, Gyorgy, ed. *Education of Vision*. New York: George Braziller, 1965.

Kostoff, Spiro. *A History of Architecture: Settings and Ritual*. New York: Oxford University Press, 1985.

Larking, Oliver W. *Art and Life in America*. New York: Holt, Rinehart and Winston, 1966.

Latour, Alessandra. *Louis I. Kahn: l'uomo, il maestro*. Rome: Edizioni Kappa, 1986.

Le Corbusier. *Toward a New Architecture*. Frederick Etchells, trans. New York and Washington: Praeger Publishers, 1960.

Lesieutre, Alain. *The Spirit and Splendour of Art Deco*. New York: Paddington Press, 1973.

Lobell, John. *Between Silence and Light: Spirit in the Architecture of Louis I. Kahn*. Boulder, Colo.: Shambhala, 1979.

Mellquist, Jerome. *The Emergence of an American Art*. New York: Charles Scribner's Sons, 1942.

Mendelowitz, Danile M. *Drawing*. New York: Holt, Rinehart and Winston, 1967.

Menten, Theodore, ed. *The Art Deco Style*. New York: Dover, 1972.

Moos, Stanislaus von. *Le Corbusier: Elemente Einer Synthese*. Frauenfeld: Verlag Huber, 1968.

Mott, Jacolyn A., and Nancy Fresella-Lee, eds. *The American Paintings in the Pennsylvania Academy of the Fine Arts*. Seattle, Wash.: University of Washington Press, 1989.

Protetch, Max. *Louis I. Kahn—Drawings*. New York: Access Press/Max Protetch Gallery, 1981.

Reed, Herbert. *A Concise History of Modern Painting*. New York and Toronto: Oxford University Press, 1974.

Reich, Sheldon. *John Marin: A Stylistic Analysis and Catalogue Raisonné*. Two vols. Tucson, Ariz.: The University of Arizona Press, 1970.

Ronner, Heinz, and Sharad Jhaveri. *Louis I. Kahn: Complete Work 1935–1974*. Basel and Boston: Birkhauser, 1987.

Rosenberg, Jakob. *On Quality in Art: Criteria of Excellence, Past and Present*. Princeton, N.J.: Princeton University Press, 1967.

Schildt, Göran, ed., and Stuart Wrede, trans. *Sketches: Alvar Aalto*. Cambridge, Mass: The MIT Press, 1985.

Schneider, Pierre, ed. *The World of Manet 1832–1881*. New York: Time-Life Books, 1968.

Scully, Vincent, Jr. *Louis I. Kahn*. New York: George Braziller, 1962.

———. *American Architecture and Urbanism*. New York: Frederick A. Praeger, 1969.

———. *Modern Architecture*. New York: George Braziller, 1971.

Tyng, Alexandra. *Beginnings: Louis I. Kahn's Philosophy of Architecture*. New York: John Wiley & Sons, 1984.

Venturi, Robert. *Complexity and Contradiction in Architecture*. New York: The Museum of Modern Art, 1966.

Weiss, Paul. "Organic Form: Scientific and Aesthetic Aspects." In *The Visual Arts Today*. Middletown, Conn.: Wesleyan University Press, 1960.

Whitfield, Sarah, ed. *The American Tradition: An Exhibition of Nineteenth-Century French Drawings*. Bloomington, Ind.: Indiana University Museum of Art, 1968.

Wilkinson, Norman. *Water-Colour Sketching Out-of-Doors*. New York: Pitman, 1953.

Wright, Gwendolyn, and Janet Parks, eds. *The History of History in American Schools of Architecture 1865–1975*. New York: The Temple Hoyne Buell Center for the Study of American Architecture and Princeton Architectural Press, 1990.

Wurman, Richard Saul. *What Will Be Has Always Been: The Words of Louis I. Kahn*. New York: Access Press and Rizzoli International Publications, 1986.

Wurman, Richard Saul, and Eugene Feldman. *The Notebooks and Drawings of Louis I. Kahn*. Philadelphia: Falcon Press, 1962.

Zucker, Paul, ed. *New Architecture and City Planning*. New York: Philosophical Library, 1944.

PERIODICALS

"Ahmedabad." *Architectural Record* 105 (December 1971):358.

"Art Serves Science: Alfred Newton Richards Medical Research Building, University of Pennsylvania, Philadelphia, PA." *Architectural Record* 128 (August 1960):147–56.

Banham, Reyner. "Louis I. Kahn on Trial: The Buttery-Hatch Aesthetic." *Architectural Review* 131 (March 1962):203–05.

———. "The New Brutalism." *Architectural Review* 118 (December 1955):355–61.

Barker, Virgil. "The Water Colors of John Marin." *Arts* 5 (February 1924): 65–83.

"Behind the Blueprints: Louis Kahn." *Architectural Forum* 93 (September 1950):79.

Benton, Thomas H. "Form and the Subject." *Arts* 5 (June 1924):302–08.

Biberman, Jane. "Portrait of the Architect as a Great Artist." *Inside* 3 (Fall 1982): 28–42.

Boles, Daralica D. "The Legacy of Louis Kahn." *Progressive Architecture* 5 (December 1984):53–55, 74–77.

Burroughs, Alan. "Making History of Impressionism." *Arts* 1 (April 1920):17–24.

Burton, Joseph. "Notes from Volume Zero: Louis Kahn and the Language of God." *Perspecta: The Yale Architectural Journal* 20 (1983): 69–90.

Chang, Ching-Yu, ed. "Louis I. Kahn: Silence and Light." *Architecture and Urbanism* 3 (January 1973).

Collins, Peter. "The Form-Givers." *Perspecta: The Yale Architectural Journal* 7 (1961): 91–96.

Coombs, Robert. "Light and Silence: The Religious Architecture of Louis Kahn." *Architectural Association Quarterly* 13 (October 1981):26–36.

Cret, Paul P. "The Ecole des Beaux Arts: What Its Architectural Training Means." *Architectural Record* 23 (1908):367–71.

————. "The Training of the Designer." *American Architect* 95 (April 1909):116, 128, 131–34, 138–39.

Crowe, Norman A., and Steven W. Hurt. "Visual Notes and the Acquisition of Architectural Knowledge." *Journal of Architectural Education* 39 (Spring 1986):6–16.

Curtis, William J.R. "Authenticity, Abstraction and the Ancient Sense: Le Corbusier's and Louis Kahn's Ideas of Parliament." *Perspecta: The Yale Architectural Journal* 20 (1983): 181–94.

Dean, Andrea O. "A Legacy of Light." *American Institute of Architects Journal* 67 (May 1978):80–89.

"Detail, President's Room, Amos Parrish and Co., N.Y., Lescaze, Architect." *American Architect* 135 (1920):46–47.

Ellis, William, ed. "Forum: The Beaux-Arts Exhibition." *Oppositions* 8 (Spring 1977):160–77.

Field, Hamilton Easter. "Current Art Exhibitions." *Arts* 1 (December 1920): 25–48.

————. "Comments on the Arts." *Arts* 1 (May 1921):32–54.

Frampton, Kenneth. "Louis I. Kahn and the French Connection." *Oppositions* 22 (Fall 1980):21–53.

Graves, Michael. "The Necessity for Drawing: Tangible Speculation." *Architectural Design* 47 (1977):384–93.

————. "Referential Drawings." *Journal of Architectural Education* 32 (September 1978):24–31.

Hewitt, Mark. "Representational Forms and Modes of Conception: An Approach to the History of Architectural Drawing." *Journal of Architectural Education* (Winter 1985):29.

Hitchcock, Henry Russell. "Notes of a Traveller: Wright and Kahn." *Zodiac* 6 (1960):14–21.

Holman, William G. "The Drawings of Louis I. Kahn." *Chelsea* 39 (1980):149–69.

Howe, George. "What is the 'Modern Architecture' Trying to Express?" *American Architect* (1930): 137–38 .

————. "Modernist and Tradionalist: At the 63rd Convention of the A.I.A., Washington, Being a Few Pertinent Points from the Address of George Howe, C. Howard Walker, Ralph T. Walker." *Architectural Forum* 53 (July 1930):49–50.

Hubert, Bruno. "Kahn's Epilogue." *Progressive Architecture* 65 (December 1984):56–57.

Huff, William. "Kahn and Yale." *Journal of Architectural Education* 35 (Spring 1982):22–31.

Hughes, Robert. "Building with Spent Light." *Time* (15 January 1973): 60–65.

Huxtable, Ada Louise. "In Philadelphia, An Architect." *New York Times*, 11 June 1961.

"Interama." *Architectural Record* 141 (March 1967):40–41.

Johnson, Eugene J. "A Drawing of the Cathedral of Albi by Louis I. Kahn." *Gesta* XXV (1986):150–65.

Johnson, Leslie Donald. "Form and Architecture." *Progressive Architecture* 42 (June 1961):168–70.

Johnson, Philip. "Great Reputations in the Making: The Three Architects." *Art in America* 48 (Spring 1960):70–75.

Kahn, Ely Jacques. "The Province of Decoration in Modern Design." *Creative Art* 5 (December 1929):885–86.

Kahn, Louis I. "Architecture is the Thoughtful Making of Space. The Continual Renewal of Architecture Comes from Changing Concepts of Space." *Perspecta: The Yale Architectural Journal* 4

(1947):23.

———. "Class 'A'—III Project—A Shopping Center, Student Work, Beaux-Arts Institute of Design." *American Architect* 125 (1924):366.

———. "Class 'A'—V Project—An Army Post. Student Work, Beaux-Arts Institute of Design." *American Architect* 125 (1924):297.

———. "A Dairy Farm." *Beaux-Arts Institute of Design Bulletin* 25 (March 1949):25.

———. "First Preliminary Competition for 17th Paris Prize, Society of Beaux-Arts Architects. A Monumental Entrance to a Thoroughfare." *American Architect* 125 (1924):210.

———. "Form and Design." *Architectural Design* 31 (April 1961):145–54.

———. "Louis Kahn—Discussion." *Perspecta: The Yale Architectural Journal* 7 (1961):9–28.

———. "On Philosophical Horizons." *American Institute of Architects Journal* 33 (June 1960):99–100.

———. "On the Responsibility of the Architect." *Perspecta: The Yale Architectural Journal* 2 (1953):45–47.

———. "Order and Design." *Perspecta: The Yale Architectural Journal* 3 (1955):59.

———. "Order in Architecture." *Perspecta: The Yale Architectural Journal* 4 (1957):23.

———. "Pencil Drawings." *Architecture* 43 (January 1931):15–17.

———. "Remarks." *Perspecta: The Yale Architectural Journal* 9/10 (1965):303–35.

———. "Second Preliminary Competition for 17th Paris Prize, Society of Beaux-Arts Architects. A United States Veterans Hospital." *American Architect* 125 (1924):446

.———. "Spaces, Order and Architecture." *Royal Architectural Institute of Canada Journal* 34 (October 1957):375–77.

———. "A Statement." *Arts and Architecture* 78 (February 1961):14–15.

———. "'Statements' in Aspen Colo." *Arts and Architecture* 81 (May 1964):18–19.

———. "The Value and Aim in Sketching." *T-Square Club Journal* (May 1930):4, 18–21.

"Louis I. Kahn." *Architecture and Urbanism* (special edition, 1983).

"Louis I. Kahn." *Architecture and Urbanism* (special edition, 1975).

"Louis I. Kahn 1901/1974." *Rassegna* VII (March 1985):4–88.

"Louis I. Kahn: Statements on Architecture." *Zodiac* 17 (1967):54–57.

"Louis Kahn's Death 'Diminishes the Century.'" *Pennsylvania Gazette* 72 (May 1974):78.

"Kahn's Movement Notation." *Design Quarterly* 80 (1971):80.

Lobell, John. "Kahn Viewed as 'Artist in an Age of Methodologists,'" *American Institute of Architects Journal* 67 (July 1978):74, 78.

McCallum, Jan, ed. "Genetrix: Personal Contribution to American Architecture; Louis Kahn." *Architectural Review* 121 (May 1957):34–45.

McCleary, Peter. "The Kimbell Art Museum: Between Building and Architecture." *Design Book Review* 11 (Winter 1987):48–51.

McLaughlin, Patricia. ""How'm I Doing, Corbusier?" An Interview with Louis Kahn." *Pennsylvania Gazette* 71 (December 1972):18–26.

McQuade, Walter. "Architect Louis Kahn and his Strong-Boned Structures." *Architectural Forum* 107 (October 1957):134–43.

"Major Exhibit—Museum of Modern Art." *Art in America* 54 (March 1966):124.

"A Mantel in the Modern Character." *American Architect* 135 (1929):312.

Meyers, Marshall. "Masters of Light: Louis Kahn." *American Institute of Architects Journal* 68 (September 1979):60–62.

"The Mind of Louis Kahn." *Architectural Forum* 137 (July–August 1972):42–89.

Moholy-Nagy, Sibyl. "The Future of the Past." *Perspecta: The Yale Architectural Journal* 7 (1961):65–76.

Molitor, John. "How the Sesqui-Centennial Was Designed." *American Architect* 130 (1926):377–82.

Moore, Dorothy Lefferts. "Exhibitions in New York." *Arts* 15 (March 1929): 173–92.

Norberg-Schulz, Christian. "Kahn, Heidegger and the Language of Architecture." *Oppositions* 18 (Fall 1979):28–47.

Osman, Mary E. "The Travel Sketches of Louis I Kahn." *American Institute of Architects Journal* 67 (May 1978):46–55.

"Palace of Congress in Venice." *Progressive Architecture* 50 (April 1969):42–43.

Pond, Irving K. "Travelling with a Fountain Pen." *American Architect* 130 (1926):435–42, 349–56.

Purves, Alexander. "The Persistence of Formal Patterns." *Perspecta: The Yale Architectural Journal* 19 (1982): 138–63.

Read, Helen Appleton. "Exhibitions in Germany: The Berlin Architectural Show." *Arts* 18 (October 1931):5–17.

Rice, Norman. "Kahn." *Architecture Plus* 2 (May/June 1974):102–07.

"Room, Street and Human Agreement." *American Institute of Architects Journal* 56 (September 1971):33–34

Rowan, Jan C. "Wanting to Be: The Philadelphia School." *Progressive Architecture* 42 (April 1961):130–49.

Rowe, Colin and Robert Slutzky. "Transparency: Literal and Phenomenal." *Perspecta: The Yale Architectural Journal* 8 (1963):45–54.

Sanderson, George A. "Extension: University Art Gallery and Design Center." *Progressive Architecture* 36 (May 1954):88–101, 130–31.

Scully, Vincent, Jr. "Archetype and Order in Recent American Architecture." *Art in America* 42 (December 1954):250–61.

———. "Light, Form, Power." *Architectural Forum* 121 (August 1964):162–70.

———. "The Precisionist Strain in American Architecture." *Art in America* 48 (Summer 1960):46–53.

———. "Wright, International Style, and Kahn." *Arts* (March 1962):67–71, 77.

"Silver Sculpture by Louis I. Kahn." *American Institute of Architects Journal* 8 (February 1970):2.

Solomon, Susan G. "Beginnings." *Progressive Architecture* 65 (December 1984):69–73.

Solon, Leon V. "The Park Avenue Building, New York City." *Architectural Record* 63 (April 1928):287–97.

"The Span of Kahn." *Architectural Review* 928 (June 1974):319–36.

"Spatial Triangulation, City Hall, Philadelphia, Pa." *Progressive Architecture* 36 (June 1945):102.

"Student Architects, Painters, Sculptors Design Together." *Progressive Architecture* 30 (May 1949):14, 16, 18.

"Visionary Architecture and a One-Man Show at the Museum of Modern Art." *Progressive Architecture* 42 (July 1961):48.

Walker, Ralph T. "A New Architecture." *Architectural Record* 48 (January 1928):1–42.

Wilson, Janet. "The Travel Sketches of Louis I. Kahn." *Art News* 77 (September 1978):183.

Ziegler, Carl A. "The Sesqui-Centennial Exposition in Philadelphia." *American Architect* 121 (1922): 382–85.

ILLUSTRATION CREDITS

All photographs, with the exceptions listed below, are the work of Rick Echelmeyer. Numbers refer to plates unless otherwise noted.

Art Institute of Chicago: 408, 409

Ben Blackwell, Photographer: 21

Joel Breger, Photographer: 105, 106

Deutsches Architekturmuseum: 70, 314

Tony Dolinski, Photographer: 31, 41, 96

Jan Hochstim: 9, 12, 16, 23, 40, 45, 54, 58, 62, 68, 71, 76, 78, 80, 86, 88, 97, 107, 108, 146, 149, 151, 165, 176, 178, 179, 182, 185, 196, 205, 226, 242, 248, 260, 265, 270, 271, 331, 341–344, 350–352, 355, 361, 362, 364, 417, 423, 433, 444

Louis I. Kahn Collection, Architectural Archives, University of Pennsylvania: 77, 358, 367, 434, 439, 443, 445, 446, 457, 462, 469, 479, 480

The Museum of Modern Art, New York: 477

Pennsylvania Academy of the Fine Arts: 69, 326

John T. Seyfried, Photographer: 100, 169

Rick Stafford, Photographer: 135, 172, 178, 188, 288, 291

David Ulmer, Photographer: 132, 230

University of Buffalo Photo Service: 448, 449.

Venturi, Scott Brown and Associates, Architects: 475, 476.

Williams College Museum of Art: 470